Cross-currents

Interactions between science and faith

by

Colin A. Russell
Ph.D., D.Sc., C.Chem., F.R.S.C.

GRAND RAPIDS, MICHIGAN
WILLIAM B. EERDMANS PUBLISHING COMPANY

Library of Congress Cataloging in Publication Data

Russell, Colin Archibald.
    Cross-currents : Interactions between science and faith.

    Includes indexes.
    1. Religion and science — History of controversy.
2. Science — History.   I. Title.
BL245.R83   1985   509   85-10199

ISBN 0-8028-0163-3

To Kate and Helena

Acknowledgments

For permission to use the following:

The Open University for material in chapter 2 which has previously appeared in course book A201, *Renaissance and Reformation* Units 15 and 16, 1972, pp.32–35; Methuen and Co. for the extract on pp.57–58 from *England under the Stuarts*, by G. M. Trevelyan, 1938, pp. 53–54; The Victoria Institute for material in chapter 7 which has previously appeared in *Faith and Thought*, 1972–3, *100*, 143; The Bodleian Library, Oxford, for 'The Declaration of Students of the Natural and Physical Sciences' in chapter 8 (MS. ADD. c. 102); The Royal Institution for extracts from Humphry Davy's manuscripts in chapter 9; Andre Deutsch and Alfred A. Knopf, Inc. for the extract in chapter 12 from *Telephone Poles and Other Poems*, by John Updike.

Picture credits: author, 14, 33, 41 (left), 59, 63 (right), 69, 73, 86, 88, 90, 93, 104, 107, 109, 114, 122, 128, 130, 137, 138, 149, 156, 179, 184, 194, 200, 205, 211, 215, 259, 263; Camera Press, 151; Colin Duriez, 63 (left), 170; Evangelical Library, 77; Edward Leigh, Cambridge, 253; Conrad Martens, illustration in *Narrative of the surveying voyages of HMS Adventure and Beagle between the years 1826 and 1936*, Volume II, by Robert FitzRoy (1839): 143; The National Portrait Gallery, London, painting by J. Coluer, 1883: 188; Open University and author: 25, 202, 203; *Reliquiae Diluvianae*, by William Buckland (1823), 15; Science Museum, 102; *A Short History of Astronomy*, by A. Berry (1898) 28, 32, 38, 40, 41(right), 44; Wellcome Institute Library, London, 227, 235.

Contents

Preface

When it was suggested to me by the publishers that I write for them a small book on the history of science I assented fairly cheerfully. Little did I know that four years would elapse before it saw the light of day, and then in a form very different from what I had imagined. The intention had been a modest essay, picking up a few themes from the science-and-religion area and drawing appropriate conclusions. Once I put pen to paper it became immediately obvious that my original chatty concept simply would not do. The themes were too complex, and too important, to be urbanely discussed in a few dozen pages. And so a considerably longer project was inevitable.

Of course I ought to have known. At the Open University I had chaired (for a time), and extensively contributed to, two undergraduate courses dealing with exactly these themes. Several thousand students who have taken these courses have testified to the complexity of the issues of science and belief that they have had to study. I suppose I thought that experience would aid compression. I was woefully wrong, though I have at least the consolation of knowing that the publishers agreed! For their tolerance, flexibility and patience I can express only astonishment and a very real gratitude.

Even within the compass of 265 pages much has had to be left out. But I would stress that this is a book for laymen, not specialists in the history of science, and it is quite long enough already. It will be obvious that psychological and social sciences have been omitted and there is very little on behavioural science.

It is well to stress that this book is written within a Christian perspective. That is not, I hope, synonymous with Christian 'bias'. But such a perspective will obviously determine the whole tenor of the book. It *ought* to mean a greater fairness to views I disagree with, though others must judge of that. The Christian, whatever his faults, is under orders to show partiality to no man and to follow the Lord of truth. Much of what I have written is, I think, agreed by scholars of all kinds whose presuppositions may differ profoundly from mine.

Occasionally one hears the suggestion that a view of science as a product of the 'Christian West' is a distortion of the facts and an evil example of racial prejudice. That is exactly the kind of ill-informed thinking that I hope the book may help to refute. Contributions of Judaism, Islam and even the natural religions are recognized and acknowledged, and no relevant facts are deliberately suppressed. I would simply ask those who attribute ill motives to the mass of historians of science who recognize the crucial role of Christianity in this development, to consider the facts and arguments that follow. However, it is not primarily to them that the book is addressed.

There are very few insights in this book that have not appeared somewhere before. For those who wish to know more, references are given at the ends of the chapters. Titles of papers in academic journals are given if it materially assists understanding. Publishers are named only for post-1900 books. In some citations spelling and/or punctuation have been modernised.

My thanks must go to many people and institutions. The library staff of my own University have been unfailingly kind and efficient in meeting my often outrageous demands. I have also used the libraries of the Royal Society of Chemistry, the Royal Institution, London University and Cambridge University, as well as the Bedfordshire County Library, the Evangelical Library and the British Library. My indebtedness to a multitude of other scholars will be apparent in the footnotes. I am grateful to the members of my own Department, every one of whom has engaged in stimulating discussions on matters highly relevant to my theme. A very deep measure of my gratitude goes to Professor R. Hooykaas of Utrecht. His writings have for long blazed a trail which I have tried to follow, not least his critically important book *Religion and the Rise of Modern Science*. I am even more grateful for his encouragement and friendship. Then I must offer special thanks to Drs Jim Moore, Oliver Barclay and Nick Isbister for trenchant and helpful comments on part or all of the manuscript. In acknowledging this invaluable assistance I have to say that any errors must be laid at my door and that what follows is my responsibility alone.

Several other people have been closely involved in the production of the text. My personal secretary, Mrs Pat Dixon, has transformed my dreadfully messy manuscript into immaculate copy on the word processor. The other secretary in our Department, Mrs Stevie Lansdown, has helped in several other valuable ways. Mr Colin Duriez of IVP has demonstrated diplomatic skills of a high order in combining gentle persuasion with tactful firmness, in seeing this work through the press and dealing with a multiplicity of problems that neither he nor I had encountered before.

To the two youngest members of my family I gladly dedicate this book, knowing that they, in their turn, are already facing some of the questions it raises. I have to thank all the family who have generously accepted my sequestration from ordinary life for far too long, even to including my non-availability for routine chores about the house and garden. Next week I shall paint the garage doors.

COLIN A. RUSSELL

1 Science in history

Say from what simple springs began,
The vast ambitious thoughts of man,
Which range beyond control,
Which seek eternity to trace,
Dive through the infinity of space,
And strain to grasp the whole.

Mark Akenside (1721–1770), *Hymn to Science* (1739)

... they searched in the archives ...

Ezra 6:1

On the northern fringe of Yorkshire's fertile and pleasant Vale of Pickering lies the tiny hamlet of Kirkdale, nestling on the very edge of the formidable North York Moors. The road from Pickering to Helmsley passes it by and few travellers will even be aware of its existence. Yet the church, or 'kirk', from which the dale was named has a unique claim to fame. Its nave is over nine centuries old and above its south doorway is a long stone slab which includes the most complete and perfectly preserved Saxon sundial in the whole country. Not only does a long inscription take us back to the England before the Norman Conquest and, therefore, have a great importance for historians of that remote period; the dial itself testifies to the religious significance of the sun's movement. Otherwise it would hardly have been an appropriate object to memorialize the creation of a new church building from the ruins of an old, and to occupy so conspicuous a place in its fabric. Accurate knowledge of time was needed for commencing the many services as well as for regulating the great annual festivals. Not far from Kirkdale, and three centuries earlier, the Venerable Bede had made careful observations of the Northumbrian tides and of astronomical events, proposed a reform of the church's calendar, and even discussed a primitive atomic theory. A study of nature (which is one of the permanent features of scientific enquiry) and devotion to religion were by no means thought incompatible, and might even be of mutual benefit.

If this seems slightly odd, a still more remarkable sight

awaits us a few hundred yards away, across the swirling Hodge Beck. A couple of narrow openings in a rock-face betray the location of the famous Kirkdale Cave. Discovered

The Saxon sundial at St Gregory's Minster, Kirkdale (c. 1055 AD).

accidentally by workmen in the early nineteenth century, it soon became the focus for national and international attention. Concealed in the far recesses of the cave, and partly embedded in mud, lay a vast profusion of animal bones. The local miners thought at first that these were remains of cattle that had perished in a fairly recent plague. But the Oxford geologist, the Rev. William Buckland, suspected otherwise and hastened to Kirkdale scenting perhaps new and extraordinary discoveries. Nor was he disappointed. The cave of Kirkdale had been a den of hyenas whose bones were now mingled with those of their victims – lions, tigers, elephants and so on. All were long extinct in Britain. This cave, therefore, must be of great antiquity. The presence of mud could mean only one thing: an immense inundation had swept away all representatives of these species in that locality, and only in occasional secluded caves would their bones persist to testify to their existence. And for Buckland, who was already committed to a 'universal deluge', here was indisputable evidence for the catastrophe to which the Bible bore witness: the flood of Noah. He received the Royal Society's Copley Medal and, in 1823, published his *Reliquiae Diluvianae* (*Relics of the Flood*) which used the phenomena of geology to testify to the universal deluge of the book of Genesis. So here again, though in a much more detailed way than in the sundial, a harmonious relationship was established between science and religion.

In fact Buckland's hypothesis is now quite discredited, and glacial action has replaced a universal flood in modern geological explanation. Buckland himself abandoned it in the 1830s, but continued to link geology and theology wherever he could. An amusing account has survived of a visit in 1839 by the British Association to Dudley Caverns, near Birmingham. Buckland and others enthralled the assembled guests with on-the-spot subterranean lectures, demonstrating particularly the kind providence of God in giving to the English such abundance of coal, iron-ore and limestone. Buckland himself sat on a large stone and lectured for over an hour, eventually leading his wondering audience out into the daylight to the singing of 'God save the Queen'. As one German observer remarked, 'the English have a peculiar love of regarding Nature from a theological point of view'.[1]

A cross-section of the cave near Wirksworth, Derbyshire, illustrated in Buckland's Reliquiae Diluvianae *(1823).*

Anecdotes such as these can be multiplied time without number. They stand in strange contrast to the conventional picture of theology and science in open hostility. Yet Galileo *was* imprisoned for defying the Roman Catholic Church over the nature of the solar system, and Darwin *was* savaged (in his absence) by Bishop Wilberforce of Oxford for daring to imply an animal ancestry for man. The impression frequently created today is that of science as almost the polar opposite of Christianity. So what is the relationship between the two? To answer that question we shall need to look closely at science, but to do so within a historical perspective, for it is not a relationship which has stood still over the years.

To mix science and history may sound like a receipe for confusion. History we all know about (or think we do): dates, battles, kings, queens, empires, revolutions, more dates, more battles.... It conjures up memories of musty old book-stores, fragile parchments, immense genealogies and has an unmistakable, if rather charming, olde-worlde image. And it is contentious, with historians disagreeing with one another over what seem to be quite basic matters of fact. By contrast science is about genes, DNA, polymers, plate tectonics, protons and photons, lasers and quasars, black holes and white holes and innumerable other discoveries which have enormous practical significance (at least in principle), which are exceedingly modern and which are usually accorded the status of facts, largely beyond controversy and quite unlike the theoretical reconstructions of the historian.

These impressions of history and of science are of course mere caricatures. But they are sufficiently common to justify the widely held view that trying to blend history and science is like attempting to mix oil and water. It can't be done. They are simply incompatible. In any case, why should anyone want to? Science is about the present and the future; its past (if it has one) is of no relevance to anyone except a few antiquarian eccentrics.

One curious fact in rebuttal of this view lies in a manifesto issued by a distinguished man of science. Thomas Thomson, who lived in the last century, was one of Scotland's most distinguished chemists and founded one of the first chemical research schools in Britain (at Glasgow). His famous textbook *A System of Chemistry* was intended 'to exhibit as complete a view as possible of the present state of chemistry' and to show how this had arisen from much earlier beginnings. Hence by *'blending the history with the science* the facts will be more easily remembered as well as better understood'. In the same vein, a few years earlier, Joseph Priestley had written his *History and Present State of Electricity* and a similar volume on optics. Only in very recent years have overcrowded syllabuses and textbooks tended to ignore the history of science almost completely. (There are signs that this tendency is being reversed, but that is another story.) Meanwhile, university departments dealing with the history of science have sprung up in many Western universities, sometimes in arts faculties, sometimes in science.

A study of the history of science can be justified in many ways, but there is a reason which has a special appeal to those who take seriously biblical Christianity, whether as committed Christians or as its opponents. This is the simple fact that, for most of its history, modern science has been pursued in an ostensibly Christian culture, has acquired presuppositions that derive from biblical theology, and in matters of surprising detail has sometimes displayed the most remarkable conformity with the theological views of its practitioners. William Buckland was a classic example, but only one of many. Historians of science may disagree as to whether such an association has had 'good' or 'bad' consequences for humanity, but very few deny that an important connection has existed. But of course this is not the popular image of the relationship between science and Christianity; this would prefer to think of Christian and scientific world-views as polar opposites and antagonists. And to prove its point it need utter no more than one word: 'evolution'. As we shall see this is to indulge in wild extrapolation. Important though it was, the Darwinian episode was in no sense typical of even Victorian science/religion relations, let alone those in a wider context. So muddied have been the waters by protagonists on all sides that it is almost impossible to disentangle the important issues in an ahistoric manner. Some of the more celebrated 'conflicts' will be encountered later in this book. Before that it will be necessary to examine some of the other ways in which science and Christianity have been related. But first we should clarify one or two terms and identify several different approaches to the history of science in general and to these problems in particular.

Fundamental to any discussion must be the meaning attached to the word 'science'. It is sometimes used simply to 'confer an honorific distinction on something or other'[2] as when we congratulate ourselves on living in an 'age of science' or adopting a 'scientific' approach, or when we denigrate alchemy or astrology as 'pseudo-sciences'. The suggestion is that science must have something rather special and praiseworthy about it. But what? According to T. H. Huxley 'science is nothing but trained and organised common sense'.[3] But this will hardly do. Nagel points out a number of ways in which science differs from 'common sense', arguing that 'the conclusions of science, unlike common sense beliefs, are the products of scientific method', and that this method 'is the persistent critique of arguments, in the light of tried canons for judging the reliability of the procedures by which evidential data are obtained, and for assessing the probative force of the evidence on which conclusions are based'.[4] Ultimately Huxley's and Nagel's definitions differ only in degree, and they have an interesting point in common. Huxley speaks of being 'trained' and Nagel of 'tried canons' for assessing evidence. Hence science cannot be conducted by a solitary being who has never left his desert island. It is a social, as well as an intellectual, activity; other people are needed to 'train' and to 'try'. David Knight puts the matter well when he views science as 'a process of thinking about nature, of talking about nature, and of interrogating and using nature. That is, we shall describe science as an intellectual, a social and a practical activity. It is only if we follow such a broad and comprehensive road that we can do justice to the complexity of science'.[5] We could of course explore this concept in far more detail, but it is sufficient for our present purpose merely to note a few of the distinctive features of science implied in these remarks. For in truth the very notion of science is a time-variable one and the more precisely we define science today the greater the danger that it will be a gross anachronism when applied to an earlier period.

It might not be thought that any clarification of the term 'Christianity' was necessary. However, it is employed nowadays with such profusion (not to say confusion) of meanings that it may be helpful to state how it is used in this book. Broadly, by 'Christianity' is intended the historic faith recorded in the Scriptures of Old and New Testaments and enshrined in the creeds. Its crux is a belief in the person of Jesus Christ as the Son of God, and in his incarnation, death and resurrection. The term would thus include the main branches of the Church, Roman Catholic and Protestant. But it would not encompass those of Unitarian persuasion who deny the deity of Christ, nor those who, while denying atheism, do not accept the possibility of miracles (of which the resurrection was the most important single example).

A sub-class of this group is referred to here as 'biblical Christianity'. This means that body of belief which regards the Scriptures as the ultimate authority in matters of faith. It takes the Bible seriously as, in some sense at least, the Word of God and its doctrines as binding upon Christians. Those who adopt such a position do not, of course, do so merely on hearsay or because they are told to, but on the basis of much evidence, internal and external. There will not be a uniformity of view, however, on many contentious issues. Members of all the major confessional churches may be found in this class, differing as they do on questions of church government, the sacraments, certain ethical questions, and so on. In matters of science (like evolution) they will have many shades of opinion. But what unites them is the conviction that, for all the problems and differences, their ultimate source of data for faith is located in the Scriptures (at least in their original form) and not in tradition. In this they disagree with many, though not all, of their Roman Catholic brethren, but it would be quite unhistoric to identify the group with Protestantism *per se*, if only because some Protestants have rejected not only tradition but also the authority of the Bible.

The approach taken to history of science in the present book is essentially pragmatic, and open to all kinds of evidence. Unlike the old-fashioned Victorian approach to science that was full of 'heroes' and triumphalism, it does not envisage the historic relations between science and religion in terms of conflict. Ironically, in this respect, it differs also from certain modern 'creationist' critiques of science. Indeed, in seeing a continuity between science and religion, it agrees with some Marxist interpretations, sharing with them a holistic view of life and history. We shall, however, disagree in recognizing the complex nature of the human drama, regarding its reduction to the mere status of 'class struggle' as arbitrary and artificial. Within recent history of science this approach has found numerous supporters, most notably Professor R. Hooykaas of Utrecht. Its analysis would acknowledge elements of genuine controversy but would explore them in precise theological terms, would avoid simplistic conflict models and would take fully into account nuances of belief across the ideological spectrum. Scholars in this tradition would accept that much scientific thought is socially conditioned, though that is not at all to deny the 'givenness' of natural phenomena and the uniqueness of science and the possibility of genuinely objective scientific knowledge.

A liberal, pragmatic approach to the history of science is consistent with a high view of biblical Christianity, with its stress on the spiritual dimension of man. It is entirely Christian to recognize, under God, a multiplicity of subsidiary causes for human action and the sheer inability of sinful human nature either to reach perfect understanding or to approach nature in a way that is totally single-minded. The 'rhetoric' of power-hungry individuals, and the reluctance of scientists to admit their false starts and experimental errors, are entirely understandable in these terms. We all share the same weakness, yet again a triumphalist view of science has no place in a theology that teaches us to hope in God, not man – not even scientific man. And the battery of historical data which point to a massive mutual debt between science and Christianity will at least be less surprising to those who are even faintly aware of biblical teaching on creation.

Holders of this view are committed to the God of truth and, therefore, compelled to follow the evidence, wherever it leads. They recognize the force of evidence outside Scripture itself – in the book of nature, for example. In this respect they stand in a long tradition going back at least as far as Calvin and Bacon. It springs from a theism that in its turn derives directly from Scripture, and which recognizes the constant creativity in natural, as well as spiritual, phenomena of a transcendent God. Where they encounter areas of conflict between science and biblical interpretation they simply cannot evade the responsibility of seeking more fundamental explanations than the facile view of Scripture versus science.

Such an approach may well be derived from biblical theology, but in most respects it probably differs not at all from some of the best theologically neutral scholarship currently available. Its distinctive note would be sounded in a more sympathetic appreciation of theological difficulties, in a more realistic understanding of human sinfulness, and in an openness to drastically new ways of understanding the history of science.

In the light of these considerations we can begin to explore the strange and manifold ways in which science has developed over the last four centuries, and, in particular, its interactions with the Christian faith.[6] Nothing quite like the growth of modern science has ever occurred in history, with the possible exception of the rise of Christianity itself.[7] It is not surprising that many metaphors have been called into service to emphasize one aspect or another of 'this thing called science'. It has been compared to a tree (Comte), a temple (Einstein), an adventure (A. S. Russell), a man-devouring monster (Ostwald), an importunate mistress (Newton) and much else besides. It is frequently portrayed as a battle against ignorance, superstition and religion in general.[8] But perhaps the most enduring image is that of a river, found time and time again in the writings of scientists and historians alike.[9] Rivers have much in common with science: small beginnings, capacity for useful work, potential for harm and damage, variable characteristics over a period, and above all the tendency to get bigger, more visible and more powerful. Any working scientist today is all too aware of wading 'through a flood' of periodical publications. Accordingly this book will use as an organizing principle the long and sustained metaphor of science as a river.

This strategy does, of course, have some dangers. It *may* determine what is omitted and what is included. It *may* impart into the account certain hidden assumptions. For instance as rivers never go into reverse and travel uphill it *may* be taken for granted that scientific progress is likewise inevitable and thus, almost surreptitiously, introduce the old note of triumphal, almost imperial, conquest of all other knowledge. In fact these dangers should be very apparent, and it is hoped they have been eliminated by using the picture as a heuristic, explanatory device and nothing more. How far this is true is, of course, for the reader to judge.

So, pursuing the metaphor, we trace the origins of science in two quite distinct areas: the Christian doctrine of nature and, even before that, the rational and mathematical disputations in the world of ancient Greece.

Notes for chapter one

[1] C. C. Gillispie, *Genesis and Geology* (Harper and Row, New York, 1959), p.200.

[2] E. Nagel, *The Structure of Science* (Routledge, 1974), p.2.

[3] T. E. Huxley, *Collected Essays*, iv.

[4] E. Nagel, (ref.2), pp.12–13.

[5] D. M. Knight, *The Nature of Science* (Deutsch, 1976), p.11.

[6] Other wide-ranging accounts include J. Dillenberger, *Protestant Thought and Natural Science*, (Collins, 1961); R. Hooykaas, *Religion and the Rise of Modern Science*, rev. ed. (Scottish Academic Press, Edinburgh, 1973).

[7] So thought Herbert Butterfield (*Origins of Modern Science 1300–1800* (Bell, 1950), p.vii).

[8] See pp.55 and 193f.

[9] Recently Arthur Peacocke has spoken of 'the received wisdom' whereby science is seen as a stream flowing into a wide ocean of yet undiscovered truth (A. R. Peacocke, *Creation and the World of Science* (Oxford University Press, 1979), p.8), and R. Hooykaas has written of the 'powerful river of modern science and technology' (Hooykaas, (ref.6), p.74).

2 Springs on Mount Olympus: science and Greek thought

Thou, Zeus, art praised above all gods;
Many are thy names and thine is the power eternally.
The origin of the world was from thee;
And by law thou rulest over all things.
Unto thee may all flesh speak,
For we are thy offspring.
Therefore will I raise a hymn unto thee
And will ever sing of thy might.
The whole order of the heavens obeys thy word
As it moves round the earth,
Small and great luminaries co-mingled.

Cleanthes (Stoic poet, 2nd century BC)

Greeks look for wisdom.

1 Corinthians 1:22

It is generally agreed that what may be recognized as modern science came into being during the century following the year 1543, when Copernicus proclaimed a sun-centred universe and Harvey discovered the circulation of the blood. 'The scientific revolution' was born after the Middle Ages had given place to the most amazing bursting forth of new life and vitality the West had seen for 1,000 years – the Renaissance. Starting in Italy in the fifteenth century and soon spreading over Europe, it must have seemed then what posterity has called it, a veritable rebirth of culture. Rediscovery of the riches of the classical civilization was accompanied by a profound erosion of mediaeval values, of which the Reformation was merely one aspect.

The Renaissance did not happen overnight, and its causes were deep and complex. To compare it to a giant awakening from ten centuries of slumber, or to a cataclysmic work of new ideas engulfing the world within a few years, is grievously to misunderstand the circumstances and the complexities of the change which, nevertheless, marked a watershed in European thought. It is also far too easy to jump to the conclusion that science was able to emerge when the iron grip of the church was relaxed and the freedom and rationality of the ancient world were restored to the human race. An assessment in these terms is not merely far too simplistic; in important ways it is just wrong. As this chapter will show, science was indebted to Greek thought, and chapter 4 demonstrates that it was also heir to crucial ideas and attitudes enshrined in Christianity.

Greek origins of science

In Athens Socrates taught and Plato learnt and wrote, about 400 years before Christ. This indeed was the cradle of Western philosophy, political and social as well as in the more abstruse realms of metaphysics. Here was perhaps the very finest flowering of Greek thought, surpassing even the achievement of the Ionians and Pythagoreans in earlier days. Following Plato came Aristotle whose ideas about nature dominated human thinking for two millennia. How this happened we must now relate.

In the world of classical Greece the focal point of learning and of scientific activity generally was at Athens. Later, however, Greek ideas began to spread all over the Middle East and the map (see p.25) gives a simplified indication of the main paths of communication of Greek science up to about the fourth century AD.

For our purposes the important place is Alexandria, which became the centre of the intellectual world for several centuries. Founded in 331 BC by Alexander the Great, this city soon became the 'emporium of the inhabited world'. A truly cosmopolitan city, it included Greeks, Jews, Egyptians and many other races. Early in the third century BC one of Alexander's successors bearing the dynastic name of Ptolemy (not to be confused with the astronomer) founded the 'Temple of the Muses' (the origin of our word museum). This became a centre of research, both literary and scientific. It had botanical and zoological gardens and a great library with over 400,000 books (*i.e.* papyrus rolls). The academic activities of Alexandria were modelled closely on the pattern of Aristotle's Lyceum; reverence for Aristotle generally was one of the most characteristic features of the Alexandrian School at the peak of its output. Philosophical discussions were carried on side by side with the pursuit of the ancient crafts of glass-making, metallurgy, dyeing, *etc.* Studies in astronomy were pursued with vigour, and another great Alexandrian Ptolemy (the astronomer) flourished around AD 150.

The days of prosperity at Alexandria were numbered, however, and in about AD 390 the Alexandrian museum was partially destroyed by the Bishop Theophilus. Certainly much of Alexandrian science survived and some of it was to be found during the following century in Syria which for a time became another focal point of scientific activity, particularly in astronomy. In the seventh century a totally new factor emerged with the rise of the religion of Islam. Inaugurated by the prophet Muhammad (born AD 570), it spread like wildfire through the Near East, giving a new unity to the Arab race and overwhelming the centres of Greek culture. The wave of advance swept through Syria from about AD 634, reaching Jerusalem in 636, and overcoming Alexandria five years later. Thus not only did the Arabs become heirs to the city of Jerusalem, sacred to both Jew and Christian, but also (in many ways far more importantly) to the ideas of the cultures they subdued. From now on Greek science went into the custody of the Muslims.

The map shows the overall pattern of the Muslim advance and indicates the extent of their penetration into Western Europe until they were repulsed by Charles Martel at Poitiers in 732. For many centuries after that, however, Moorish culture flourished in Spain, and places like Toledo became one of the few contact-points between Western Europe and the Arabs. Another was Sicily, which in the tenth century offered an alternative bridge between the two worlds; in 1091 it was taken from the Muslims by the Normans and thereafter conditions were exceptionally favourable. Otherwise, the chief contacts between East and West were through the Crusades – clearly not an ideal means of cultural interchange!

Why should these facts be important? The curious thing is that with the Muslim conquest of the Near East and North Africa a good deal of Greek culture became unavailable to the West except through the limited contacts in Spain and Sicily which, because they constituted the only notable exception, acquire a high importance for our story. Thus at Toledo, for example, there was a 'college of translators' where Arabic texts were read out in Spanish by a baptized Jew or Arab and taken down in Latin. In this way a slow but steady trickle of versions of Greek scientific works entered Western Europe. But it is scarcely necessary to state that such a devious process presented its hazards. Apart from anything else there were the

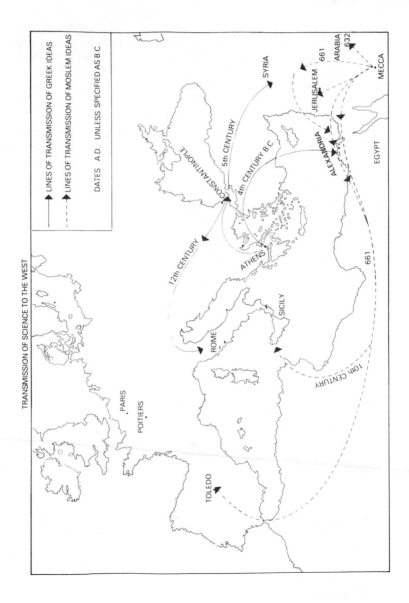

TRANSMISSION OF SCIENCE TO THE WEST

LINES OF TRANSMISSION OF GREEK IDEAS

LINES OF TRANSMISSION OF MOSLEM IDEAS

DATES A.D. UNLESS SPECIFIED AS B.C.

sheer problems of translation; quite commonly a text would be submitted to the following process:

Greek → Syriac → Arabic → Spanish → Latin
(Castilian)

Thus it turned out that the copies of Greek authors that were available in medieval Christendom could be better described (with some exaggeration) as 'perversions' rather than as 'versions'; and to make matters worse even these copies were unavailable to many scholars, who were forced therefore to rely upon the opinions of some commentator.

The great master Aristotle partly managed to escape this fate. As well as translations from the Arabic, his works were available in the original Greek, at least in the thirteenth century. One historian has described him as 'a sort of tragic hero striding through medieval science'.[1] Less fortunate were many of his scientific descendants such as Ptolemy the astronomer, Galen the anatomist, Euclid the mathematician and many others. Thus Ptolemy's great astronomical work the *Almagest* was translated from Arabic into Latin at Toledo in 1175. The medical work of Galen (2nd century) was digested, codified and rigidified by successive Greek and Arab authors, and his doctrine of the four 'humours' constrained medicine until Renaissance men like Vesalius broke its iron grip. The situation was undoubtedly bad, but it would have got very much worse as progressively less reliable versions appeared had it not been for the trickle of Greek manuscripts out of Byzantium from the twelfth century.

The Greek approach to science

Nevertheless something of the Greek approach to nature did survive to guide and direct mediaeval science. Perhaps we should think rather of approaches, in the plural. On one hand was the 'postulations method' of Euclid. Not in the least experimental, it sought to deduce the character of things from axioms that were deemed self-evident; it was used by Archimedes and others, and applied not merely to mathematics (for which it is most obviously suited) but also to optics and astronomy. Not very dissimilar was the 'dialectical method' of Plato which was also deductive. A proposition was chosen and consequences were derived from it, often in a long series of deductions. If the conclusion seemed comfortable to reality the proposition was rendered plausible. One example was the *a priori* assumption of unobservable particles of 'atoms', from which might be deduced the properties of the external world. This, indeed, was the essence of Plato's physics.

In contrast to these theoretical deductive schemes was the 'empirical method' in which observation played a dominant role. Avoiding theoretical particles and long chains of deductive reasoning, it analysed observed phenomena and from the parts it immediately reconstructed other phenomena. It was particularly applied in biology, above all by Aristotle, whose observations of living things can still astonish us by their accuracy and detail.

How, then, did mediaeval science respond to these Greek traditions? Above all, it would seem, in recovering the ideas of theoretical and rational explanation, including science and theology. So far was this true that Dr A. C. Crombie, in a still unsurpassed study of mediaeval science, has commented:

> The basic conception of scientific explanation held by the medieval natural scientists came from the Greeks and was essentially the same as that of modern science.[2]

Thus one of the main sources of scientific thought may be traced right back to the Greeks, travelling circuitously via the Arab world and the Europe of the late Middle Ages. It resulted in new advances in mechanics, optics and astronomy and a more detailed study of the animated world which became arranged in one composite scale of being from the lowest to the highest organisms. By the thirteenth century science was being seen as a potential boon to man, enabling him to gain power over nature. Better instruments became available in astronomy, and chemistry acquired its most valuable tool, the balance.

Even at this time, however, it should not be supposed that the Greek tradition was seen as homogeneous. Alongside the dominant theories of Aristotle were revivals of Platonic teaching, known as neo-Platonism. It was Plato rather than Aristotle who may be said to have inspired the extension of mathematics to all physical science in the thirteenth century. The new mechanics of change and motion reflected very non-Aristotelian concepts of an infinite space and favoured the methodology of Archimedes.

Quite apart from questions of methodology, however, the

legacy of Aristotle was immensely important in shaping the picture of the universe that dominated Western thinking for nearly 2,000 years. Aristotelian cosmology divided the universe into two parts, separated by the sphere of the moon. Aristotelian physics reflected this division. It proceeded from the assumption that there are basically two kinds of motion, natural and unnatural. In that part of the universe beneath the moon's orbit, and obviously including the earth, things tend to move in straight lines. Thus dropped objects fall vertically downwards, while smoke and fire go vertically upwards. The direction of movement was determined by a kind of 'homing instinct', everything going towards its proper place in the universe. Where motion is *not* in a straight line, as in the trajectory of an arrow, that is 'unnatural' and arises from the imposition of other forces. For motion to occur force had to be

Aristotle's world system, showing the celestial spheres carrying the moon, planets, sun and stars around a stationary earth.

applied. Rest was natural, motion unnatural. In the case of the arrow Aristotle envisaged the displaced air somehow coming round to the back of the arrow and thereby continuing to keep it going, while all the time its 'homing instinct' draws it downwards. The resultant is, of course, a curved flight-path.

When motion above the moon's orbit is considered, the natural thing is to move in a circle, not a straight line. Moreover, that high celestial region knows no change apart from change of position. Only the region below the moon experiences decay and other changes associated with corruption and imperfection. Here on earth, and up to the moon, all matter is made of four elements, earth, air, fire and water. Above the moon, however, only one element exists, the 'aether'.

For Aristotle and his heirs the earth was, as it so obviously seems to be, stationary and immovable. Around this ponderous object the heavenly bodies described circular revolutions, carried round on crystalline (though invisible) concentric spheres. Later this simple notion was complicated in all manner of ways, but it remained firmly embedded in popular thought long after it had been shown to be quite incompatible with the phenomena that astronomers actually observed (notably the irregularities of planetary motion and the variable distance from the earth of various heavenly bodies). Modifications by Ptolemy and others left little of the aesthetically pleasing simplicity of the crystalline spheres model, but did retain a central immovable earth and circular movement around it of sun, moon, stars and planets.

Thus, even though Greek influence on science may not seem as monolithic as is often imagined, the very diversity of its effects testifies to its immense significance for the emergence of modern science.

As the Middle Ages came to an end, by the fourteenth century the trickle of more authentic Greek texts from the East was to become a flood. With the new availability of purer and more refined versions of the classics that had not been mediated via the Arabs, it now became possible in the fifteenth century to examine much more reliable copies of the ancient writers.

Associated with this rediscovery of classical texts was the new humanism of fifteenth-century Italy, marking a 'renaissance' or 'rebirth' of the values of the ancient world and a revolt against the constraints upon the human spirit imposed in the Middle Ages. It affected all of life, including education, was associated with a new sense of nationhood and played a major part in initiating the convulsive changes of the Protestant Reformation. But how did it affect science?

There are several schools of thought. The traditional view, much espoused by Victorian writers, suggests it was nothing less than salvation for science, liberating it from the iron grip of theology. One objection to this view is that much mediaeval science had very little to do with theology and that when this was not the case theology was far less inhibiting than Aristotle or even Plato. Moreover, as we shall see, the new science of the seventeenth century was conceived in a theological matrix that was quite as definite as in mediaeval times.

A variation of this view sees Renaissance humanism as *the* vital link between classical and modern science, with the achievements of the twelfth, thirteenth and fourteenth centuries largely ignored. This was apparently how many of the participants in the Scientific Revolution saw themselves, taken in, it would seem, by the humanists' propaganda. However, this not only bypasses the considerable accomplishments of mediaeval science brought to prominence by historical scholarship this century; it also ignores the definite if tenuous continuity between scientific ideas in the Middle Ages and later.

Another approach takes the diametrically opposite view and regards humanism as an *interruption* in the progress of science. This has much to commend it in the light of the continuity known to exist between mediaeval and seventeenth-century science, and is indicated both by the survival of quite distinctively mediaeval ideas in writers like Galileo, and by the volume of mediaeval writings circulating two or three centuries later.

In the light of recent work it seems impossible to deny the indebtedness of the Scientific Revolution to both mediaeval *and* humanist thought (each of which may, of course, be derivative upon Greek culture). This recognizes the distinctive contribution of each. Without doubt humanism fostered the development of mathematical techniques and the tendency to follow Plato in interpreting nature in a mathematical way. In a rather curious way it favoured biological enquiry as attempts were made to identify all the objects mentioned by classical authors. And it certainly promoted a naturalness of artistic representation and a clarity of verbal expression that were to be vital components of the Scientific Revolution.

We shall now look briefly at the ways in which Greek ideas

were associated with developments in two quite separate sciences: astronomy and chemistry.

The absorption of Greek science

In astronomy a dissatisfaction with the mediaeval versions of Ptolemy was inducing astronomers to join the humanist stampede into Italy in the hope of discovering better and purer versions of his masterpiece. Meanwhile others pursued the logical extension of this policy and sought for purer versions of texts by Ptolemy's predecessors, some indeed realizing that a patched-up Ptolemy was not likely to provide any permanent solution to current astronomical dilemmas. This is one way in which it became recognized that Greek thought, particularly on scientific matters, was nothing like as homogeneous as it had been supposed to be; it became possible to talk about early Greeks who clearly lay outside the mainstream of Aristotelian thinking and by Aristotle's own standards would undoubtedly be regarded as deviants. There was even strange talk in Southern Italy of the ancient belief of Philolaus (a fifth-century Pythagorean) that the earth went round a central fire, and that was unorthodox enough.

This was the background to the Copernican revolution. On the one hand there was a down-to-earth, no-nonsense attitude of the more traditional philosophers: a fixed immovable earth with all else going round it. On the other hand we have the serious wrestling of the astronomers with the problem of planets and the development of a system which was getting more and more complicated and less and less reconcilable with the common-sense view, at least as expounded by Aristotle. And behind both of these we have the circulation of strange half-forgotten tales from long ago, which if taken seriously would have done much to undermine the accepted doctrines; finally came the Renaissance, which instead of laying these ghosts actually seemed to reclothe them with flesh and blood. In the year 1473 Nicholas Copernicus was born.[3]

The difficulties encountered by Copernicus and his system will be discussed later (p.41). Here, however, it may be sufficient to stress his enormous debt to the Greeks. In his 'Preface' to *De Revolutionibus* he mentions the Pythagoreans, Hipparchus, Philolaus and Heraclides, all of whom in some way lent support to one aspect or another of his thesis. His objections to his predecessor Ptolemy arose not merely from the latter's inaccurate data (Copernicus made few observations himself) but chiefly from the elaborate system of devices by which planetary motion was explained. These involved orbits whose centres themselves moved in circles round the earth (epicycles), or circular motion about a centre which was different from the earth and which seemed uniform in angular velocity when viewed from another point again (the equant). Copernicus was troubled because the Greek ideals of uniform circular motion were being seriously compromised, and *his* system offered a single planetary scheme for the solar system, whereas Ptolemy needed one for each planet.

Nicholas Copernicus (1473–1543).

Ptolemy's elaborate mechanism was an incarnation of one of the most conspicuous elements of Greek thought: a tendency to see nature in mathematical terms and to seek for mathematical categories of explanation. Yet for Copernicus it was not loyal enough to the Greek heritage. Its departure from the Platonic ideals of uniform circular motion about a centre, and its incompatibility with the Aristotelian scheme of spheres within spheres, alike made it unacceptable to one who had become involved with the ideals of neo-Platonism. Those ideals (which included also mystical reverence for the sun) had been encountered by Copernicus both in Cracow and Bologna.

Renaissance Cracow, Poland, with the university attended by Copernicus.

Thus it was that Sir Herbert Butterfield could say of Copernicus, whose revolutionary ideas mark in many respects the beginning of the modern age of science, that he seems 'a man who still had one foot caught up in Aristotelianism'.

> In general, it is important not to overlook the fact that the teaching of Copernicus is entangled (in a way that was customary with the older type of science) with concepts of value, teleological explanations and forms of what we should call animism. He closes an old epoch much more clearly than he opens any new one.[4]

Copernicus is a good example of the influence of Greek ideas on Renaissance science. But he is only one of many. Another may be found in what eventually became known as 'chemistry'.[5] For centuries the alchemist had been a familiar, if unloved, figure in European cities. His objectives, to say nothing of his methods, had been complex and multifarious. Some of his ilk who sought a quick return by deceiving the gullible though fraudulent 'transmutations' of base metals into gold, often ended up in gaol (if they were lucky), the torture chamber or the executioner's hands. But there were alchemists who deceived not others but themselves, credulous mortals whose earnest efforts to make gold quite unwittingly laid some of the foundations of modern chemical science. Their techniques of separation (above all by distilling) and the substances they discovered and used (such as the mineral acids) kept alive a spirit of enquiry about the material world while also accumulating a great body of empirical knowledge from which chemistry was eventually to emerge. But on what theoretical basis did they proceed?

Untroubled by modern concepts of an element the alchemists held to the age-old four-element theory which affirmed that all matter was made of air, earth, fire and water in different proportions. This idea, attributed to Aristotle, was a characteristically Greek note in Western alchemy. Transmutation was, therefore, a matter of altering the preparation of those elements in (say) copper to make them what they should be for gold. In similar vein Greek medicine had sought to vary the balance between the various 'humours' of the body.

As with astronomy, Greek alchemy was largely mediated to the West via the Arabs, who to this day have left their mark on chemical language with words like 'alchemy' and 'alkali'. But the imprint of Greek thought upon it is unmistakable. Recently this has become even clearer with the recognition that alchemical thought owed much to a large body of Greek literature known as the *Hermetica*. This probably dates from about AD 100 but was widely supposed in the Renaissance to have come from an Egyptian contemporary of Moses, a priest known as Hermes Trismegistus. So rich is this spurious corpus in Greek ideas that it was once inferred that Plato himself had been a disciple of the Egyptian wise men.

For chemistry Hermeticism had a distinctive legacy to which we return later. This was the mystical view of nature as a mother, with metals being generated underground as in a womb. The disciple of Hermes had to emulate her operation as best he could. If an egg required warmth for development of the chick, so did chemical reactions (as we shall call them). Thus the development of furnaces, sand-baths and other heating apparatus grew apace. And a favourite piece of glass-ware, the Vase of Hermes, was ovoid in shape and known familiarly as the 'Philosopher's Egg'. And underlying all the jumbled beliefs about transmutation lay the four elements of Aristotle or variations of them deriving from the sixteenth-century Paracelsus.

To us the limitations of such a science are obvious; the shackles of tradition were hopelessly restrictive. Yet the participants did not see it like that. For them the discovery of better editions of the classics than the Arabic versions commonly available was a liberating experience, just as the fifteenth-century alchemist Lacinius could delight in the supposed agreement among traditional authorities. In the case of Copernicus and many of his predecessors the obvious influence was Greek, rather than biblical, with Platonic idealism uneasily yoked to Aristotle's physics. It was certainly theological, but in a Greek and pre-Christian sense. When, later on, biblical texts were bandied about in opposition to the Copernican system, it was still in a spirit of naive literalism that owed much to Aristotle, something to Aquinas, but nothing at all to Augustine or the sixteenth-century Reformers.

Copernicus and his contemporaries are rather curious bridge figures between the old science and the new. It is hard to disagree with Butterfield's assertion that Copernicus 'closes an old epoch much more clearly than he opens any new one'. Indeed it may be agreed that the discontinuity between mediaeval and modern science had already taken place. Not long before 1400 the great creative period of mediaeval science was over. As Crombie remarks, 'for the next century and a half all that Paris and Oxford produced on astronomy, physics, medicine or logic were dreary epitomes of the earlier writings'.[6] The work of Nicholas of Cusa and Leonardo da Vinci in the fifteenth century were exceptional in several ways and do not dispel the general impression that mediaeval science had, in some senses at least, come to an end.

Notes for chapter two

[1] A. C. Crombie, *Augustine to Galileo* (Peregrine, 1952), vol. ii, p.17.
[2] *Ibid.*, p.118.
[3] On Copernicus see, for an elementary introduction, A. Armitage, *The

World of Copernicus, (S. R. Publishers, 1971); for a more technical account see
T. S. Kuhn, *The Copernican Revolution* (Harvard University Press, 1966).
    [4] H. Butterfield, *The Origins of Modern Science, 1300–1800* (Bell, 1950), p.30.
    [5] On alchemy see M. Eliade, *The Forge and the Crucible,* trans. S. Corin
(Harper and Row, 1971); M. Stillman, *The Story of Alchemy and Early Chemistry*
(Dover, N. Y., 1960); R. P. Multhauf, *The Origins of Chemistry* (Oldbourne, 1966).
    [6] A. C. Crombie, (ref.1), p.121.

3 The Copernican watershed

And now the springs and summers which we see,
Like sons of women after fifty be.
And new philosophy calls all in doubt;
The element of fire is quite put out;
The sun is lost, and th'earth, and no man's wit
Can well direct him where to look for it.
And freely men confess that this world's spent,
When in the planets, and the firmament
They seek so many new; they see that this
Is crumbled out again to his atomies,
'Tis all in pieces, all coherence gone,'
All just supply, and all relation.

John Donne (1571–1631),*The First Anniversarie*, 1611

God made two great lights – the greater
light to govern the day and the lesser light
to govern the night. He also made the
stars. God set them in the expanse of
the sky to give light on the earth, to
govern the day and the night, and to separate
light from darkness. And God saw that it
was good. And there was evening, and there
was morning – the fourth day.

Genesis 1:16–19

Reception of Copernicanism

It is hard for us to imagine the revolutionary nature of
Copernicus' teaching. Quite apart from any religious problems
it might pose (of which more later), the transposition of the old
cosmos by the new required a Herculean mental effort, not so
much to understand it as to believe it. If the earth is not the
stationary hub of the universe, any alternative is both incredible and uncomfortable. It is incredible because it seems
obvious to common sense that we are not moving; we have
none of the impressions to be expected if we are hurtling
through space in a journey round the sun. The standard response, that we have no right to such expectations because all
our familiar surroundings are travelling with us, is in fact

quite a sophisticated idea when first encountered. And it is uncomfortable for reasons we shall examine later.

Perhaps it is not too surprising, then, that many years passed before the ideas of *De Revolutionibus Orbium Coelestium* became common property. Another reason lay in the sheer lack of astronomical evidence. Because the Ptolemaic and the Copernican systems are mathematically equivalent, there was no conceivable observational test that could distinguish between them, at least so far as the solar system was concerned. And in any case Copernicus was no great observer.

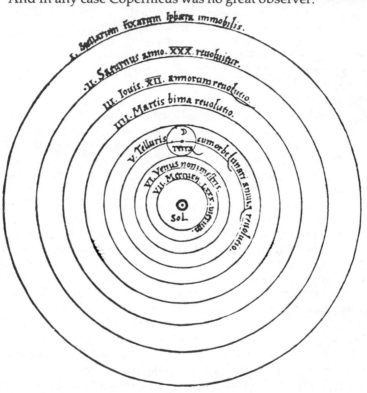

Copernicus' solar system, from the De Revolutionibus.

If, however, one looked at the stars which were supposed by Copernicus to rotate round the sun, then there should be minute differences in their appearance when viewed from different positions in the earth's orbit. It would be rather like the slightly different views of a fairground obtained from a roundabout during its revolution. But, because of the immense distance of the stars from us in comparison with the size of our orbit round the sun, no naked eye observation could remotely hope to tell such differences. Even with the invention of the telescope it took over 200 years before the first observation of stellar parallax was obtained (by F. W. Bessel in 1838).

If it was impossible to refute Ptolemy directly it was much easier to dispose of Aristotle and his crystalline spheres. The astronomers, who did not care for such things, might shrug their shoulders and accept Copernicanism as merely an alternative philosophical scheme to Ptolemy. The common man still thought in Aristotelian terms and his universe was certainly in for some shocks. When they came it was in a series of most remarkable coincidences.

In 1572 an omen appeared in the European skies that proved to be a new star – an exceedingly rare supernova. What was remarkable was not just its brightness (visible even at midday), but the observation made by the Danish astronomer Tycho Brahe that it was in the region of no-parallax, *i.e.*, very far away and far beyond the orbit of the moon. But its location way out in space was in flat contradiction with the teaching of Aristotle and the schoolmen. According to them changes (like new stars) simply did not occur so far from the earth. Nor were matters improved when Tycho discovered a similar remoteness for another celestial novelty, a new comet, five years later. That posed the additional problem of having to make its way through the supposed crystalline spheres to which the planets were attached. Then, when Galileo became the first man to peer at the skies through a telescope (in 1610), he found the planet Jupiter had its own retinue of four attendant moons, the 'perfect' sun had spots on its face, Venus had phases like the moon, and much else that shook ancient cosmology to its foundations. Finally we may record that a meticulous examination of Tycho's matchless observational data by his heir-apparent, Kepler, led the latter to conclude that there was an 8-minute discrepancy between the observed orbit of Jupiter and the best prediction based on circular motion. His proposal that the planet moved in an ellipse not merely paved the way for the Newtonian synthesis. It was the final blow to Aristotelian astronomy.

Of Copernicus himself, little was heard for many years. He was dead within a few days of publication of his book, and he had few other advocates. But two men did play a part in spreading his ideas. Both taught mathematics at the Protestant University of Wittenberg. The younger, Rheticus, had persuaded Copernicus to publish, leaving a local Lutheran pastor Andrew Osiander to see the book through the press (and to add a preface of his own). The older man, Erasmus Reinhold, brought out a new edition of Copernicus' astronomical tables in 1551, thereby giving a further boost to Copernican theory in general.

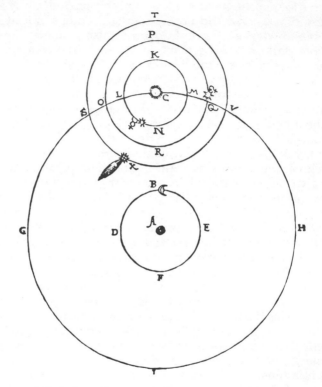

Tycho's world system, showing the comet of 1577.

Curiously, it was in England that Copernicanism first took root to any major extent. Without doubt the Platonic tradition here was stronger than elsewhere in northern Europe, and there seems to have been a greater freedom of thought, though these things are hard to document precisely. In 1556 a Yorkshireman, John Field, published an almanac which alluded to Reinhold, Rheticus and the 'Herculean labours' of Copernicus. In the same year Robert Recorde, physician to Queen Mary and a leading educational reformer, published *The Castle of Knowledge*, a mathematical textbook which discusses whether or

not the earth does move. Twenty years later an Oxford mathematician, Thomas Digges, published an English translation of
part of *De Revolutionibus* with perhaps the first illustration of a
universe with stars distributed through infinite space. Digges,
like many later English Copernicans, had strong Puritan
sympathies.

Two post-Copernican astronomers: Tycho Brahe (1546–1601)
and Johannes Kepler (1571–1630).

Mention should also be made of the Danish astronomer
Tycho Brahe (1546–1601). Not only did his observations of the
supernova (1572) and the new comet (1577) substantially discredit Aristotelian crystalline spheres, but his observations
reached new peaks of accuracy which enabled Kepler, years
later, not only to interpret them but to incorporate the data in
terms of elliptical orbits – a refined version of a solar-centric
universe. Tycho's own alternative cosmology (1588) was
occasioned by lack of stellar parallax and an intuitive conviction
that the earth was too sluggish to move. It may not have helped
Copernicus but it certainly confuted Ptolemy and Aristotle.

Underlying many of the early doubts about Copernicanism
lay not only its apparent conflict with common sense, but also
the opposition of the church. We shall first outline the course
of events and then examine the theological issues involved.

Copernicanism and the church

The fear that his work would be denounced by theologians as well as astronomers had undoubtedly occurred to Copernicus. He took several steps to head off ecclesiastical opposition, the chief of which was to dedicate his book to the Pope (Paul III). Copernicus, himself a canon in the Roman Catholic Church, had been encouraged by Bishop Tiedmann Giese (of Kulm) and Cardinal von Schoenberg, both of whom he mentions in his Preface. His Protestant friend, Osiander, was also apprehensive and in his (anonymous) Preface tried to defuse the situation by pretending that the work was simply an astronomical hypothesis, a calculating device.

In the event anything like a concerted ecclesiastical campaign took 70 years to develop. The earliest opposition, and it was quite sporadic, came from the Protestant camp. The allegation made by A. D. White has been shown to be far too sweeping: 'All branches of the Protestant Church – Lutheran, Calvinist, Anglican – vied with each other in denouncing the Copernican doctrine as contrary to Scripture.'[1] Martin Luther, for example, ignored the question in all his published works, though there is a 27-year-old recollection of a meal-time remark that Joshua told the sun to stand still, not the earth. John Calvin, White tells us in an oft-repeated allegation, took the lead against Copernicanism citing Psalm 93:1 in evidence ('the world is firmly established; it cannot be moved'), and asking 'Who will venture to place the authority of Copernicus above that of the Holy Spirit'? Yet, as Hooykaas[2] and Rosen[3] independently pointed out, Calvin wrote no such thing and did not attack Copernicus in print. It has recently been shown that Calvin did deny a moving earth, but in a sermon and without mentioning Copernicus. His objection was its conflict with common sense, not with Scripture.[4]

However, some opposition to heliocentric views was mounted from the Protestant side, most notably by Melanchthon who quoted the Psalms (19:5 and 119:90) as part of his rearguard defence of an Aristotelian cosmos. Despite this he numbered Copernican admirers amongst his friends.[5] On the whole Protestant opposition was muted and ineffective. The spokesmen were, after all, themselves rebels against ancient authority; and there were strong reasons for declining to treat Scripture as a source of astronomical data (p.46). The atmosphere was, at worst, sultry rather than explosive, with occasional rumblings of distant thunder.

It was otherwise with the Roman Catholic Church. Here the storm-clouds took a whole lifetime to gather, but when the storm did break it was with electrifying force and shattering power. At the focus of all the ecclesiastical wrath was the unfortunate figure of Galileo Galilei.[6] His tragic tale has been rehearsed so often that only the briefest details need to be recorded here. Galileo's famous telescopic observations had been reported in his *Starry Messenger* of 1610 and his *Letters on Sunspots* of 1613. Up to about this time he had enjoyed a good reputation with the authorities, even being ceremoniously received in Rome in 1611. But he had made one or two personal enemies, for reasons that are now quite obscure. In 1614 one of these men, a Father Thomas Caccini, fired at him the first public blast of denunciation.

In a sermon in Florence, Caccini assailed all astronomers including Galileo for opposing Scripture by their new teaching. Did not Joshua command the sun to stand still (Joshua 10:12), so how could Galileo assert that it was motionless at the centre of the universe? It is reported that Caccini echoed biblical words when he said 'Ye man of *Galilee*, why stand ye gazing up into heaven'? (see Acts 1:11).

As it happens this assault on Galileo came to nothing, but in the next few years Galileo's continual advocacy of a moving earth led to growing concern on the part of the authorities. The interventions of a layman in matters of theological principle became increasingly unwelcome. The Congregation of the Index concluded that to teach that the sun was at the centre of the universe 'expressly contradicts the doctrine of Holy Scripture in many passages'. Accordingly a Copernican treatise by a friar named Foscarini was placed on the Index of prohibited books (March, 1616), but *De Revolutionibus* was permitted subject to minor amendments (such as deleting the claim that the system was in accordance with Scripture).

So far Galileo was safe. In May 1616 he was called to Rome to be reminded of the official disapproval of Copernican doctrines, for after all he more than anyone else in Italy had given them support. But he was not required to do more than listen, it seems, and note that the Copernican doctrine 'cannot be defended or used'. For the next seven years there was an uneasy stalemate, with neither side going out of its way to provoke the other. Then, in 1623, the Pope died and hopes began to rise that the situation might be resolved. His successor (Urban VIII) had previously displayed considerable interest in natural philosophy and it must have been with rising optimism that Galileo went for several audiences in the following year.

If so he had underrated the rigidity of establishment think-ing. The situation remained exactly as it had been before. Copernicanism was permitted only as a calculating device, never as a statement about the 'real' universe. Yet in Galileo's mind the conviction had been growing over many years that decisive evidence for the earth's motion might yet be found in one phenomenon: the movement of the tides. The fact that the oceans 'slopped about' the surface of the earth must surely indicate the latter was rotating. But was it safe to publish?

Galileo Galilei (1564–1642), and one of his drawings of the moon.

By 1630 he thought the risk worth taking. So, manuscript in hand, he arrived in Rome that summer with a request for the Imprimatur – official permission to publish. After agreeing to requests to tone down his argument in several ways, and to indicate its tentative nature, Galileo published in 1632 his *Dialogue concerning the two Principal Systems of the World*. It was more accurately a 'trialogue', for it consisted of a four-day debate between two Italian intellectuals (Sagredo and Salviati) and a third man (Simplicio) who was the foil of the piece. His function was to defend the old Aristotelian/Ptolemaic system. He was depicted as the champion of orthodoxy, slow to follow an argument and something of a buffoon. Regrettably (in the light of later events) he was also a thinly-veiled caricature of the Pope himself, representing the papal arguments almost in their original words. Despite the emendations and disclaimers forced upon him, Galileo makes abundantly clear that he is fully committed to a moving earth. Racily written in the ver-nacular, the book was sold out within a few days. Few of its many readers could have failed to perceive the success with which Galileo had scored over the authorities. The laugh was on him, but not for long.

Galileo was immediately summoned to the Inquisition in Rome. On 12 April 1633 he was challenged with a Vatican document purporting to record his interview in 1616. Unlike the certificate which Galileo had prudently obtained at the time, this official minute added that Galileo had agreed not to teach or defend the Copernican doctrine in any way. Clearly he had been in breach of this undertaking, but was it genuine? Despite natural suspicions of forgery, examinations over the last hundred years (including X-ray treatment) suggest its genuineness. The discrepancies were – and are – a mystery. At best we can say they represent different appreciations of the same event. What is clear is that Galileo's actions were in the spirit of the certificate in his possession rather than the document in the Vatican archives.

By this time in his life Galileo was ill, his sight was failing and, at the age of 70, he was in no condition to maintain the fight. Accordingly he temporized and began to admit that all he wrote was out of pride rather than inner conviction. This was not enough for the Pope, still smarting with his own humiliation. Galileo was formally to retract. And so he did, a frail and ageing figure clad in a white penitential shirt compelled untruthfully to deny the conviction of 20 years or more:

> I, Galileo, being in my 70th year, being a prisoner and on my knees, and before your Eminences, having before my eyes the Holy Gospel, which I touch with my hands, abjure, curse, and detest the error and heresy of the movement of the earth.

He was condemned to life imprisonment and his book was placed on the prohibited Index where it remained until 1831. Rumours that on rising from his knees he was heard to utter 'but it [the earth] *does* move' are unsubstantiated and unlikely to be true. His humiliation was total.

Judicious assessment of these events is harder than it seems, if only because of the unsolved historical questions of the two documents. To describe the event as a 'martyrdom' is of course incorrect, as is the allegation of physical torture. Certainly the threat was there, but at Galileo's age it would have been illegal and it was not carried out. Furthermore the Pope did not speak *ex cathedra* so questions of 'infallible pronouncements' do not arise. And it must be conceded that Galileo's tactless lampooning of the Pope was a bad error of judgment.

However, the Church manifestly displayed a monumental insensitivity to the human tragedy involved, though by comparison with some of the Inquisition's activities that was trivial enough, and with hindsight we can readily recognize that they were wrong as well as misguided. The Galileo débâcle, far from ending the debate, crystallized the issues with a new clarity and, within a few years, the Copernican theory of a moving earth was triumphantly pre-eminent.

By 1654 it was claimed that, in England at least, all who knew about astronomy had accepted the Copernican system either as a basis of calculation or as a true statement about the world. Where Roman Catholicism predominated people naturally had to be more cautious. Descartes is often castigated for his ambivalent support for Copernicanism; because he conceived an aether cortex round the earth and moving with it, one could say the earth (relative to the aether) did not move as it travelled round the sun! On the other hand a Calvinist country like Holland soon had prominent and vocal Copernicans like Philip van Lansbergh.

Apart from Galileo's own contribution, the work of Tycho Brahe, Kepler and Newton was so decisive a vindication of the new world-picture that it is hard to see how Ptolemaic or Aristotelian cosmologies could ever survive, save in the darkest corners of obscurantism. Traces did, of course, persist in popular folklore, but otherwise there was a decisive break with the past. For astronomy, for science and for mankind at large Copernicanism was truly a watershed.

Copernicanism and Scripture

The issues underlying the controversies surrounding Copernicanism were much broader than those that were highlighted by the Galileo affair. There one can identify relatively local matters involving personalities and the heightened sensitivities of Vatican officials following the Reformation. Larger questions of freedom and authority, evident enough in 1633, were seen in a broader context as Calvinists and Lutherans, Dutch and English, wrestled with a whole series of problems generated by the Copernican system.

Most obvious of all these problems was the role of Scripture in settling questions of scientific belief. That solutions were reached of a satisfactory kind (at least to the participants) is at once obvious from the wide acquiescence to the Copernican system on all sides. Even the Roman Catholic Church eventually came to terms with it, revoking its anti-Copernican edict in 1757 and removing Galileo's *Dialogue* from the Index in 1831.

What is much more remarkable is that the Protestants, whose whole case for separatism from Rome rested upon the ultimate authority of Scripture, became ready to embrace the concept of a moving earth with a haste that Roman Catholics must have thought astounding. Yet it was a Roman Catholic, Galileo himself, who perhaps gave the most memorable pointer to a way out of the dilemma. It was to recognize a distinction between the kinds of knowledge obtainable from nature and from Scripture. He said (probably echoing one Cardinal Baronicus) that in giving us the Scriptures:

The intention of the Holy Ghost is to teach us how one goes to heaven, not how heaven goes.

He added that the divine author of Scripture had no purpose to teach us physical facts about the universe, since that would be 'irrelevant to the highest goal, that is to our salvation'.[7]

It must be admitted that Galileo did not hold that no physical truths were deducible from Scripture. His point was that such derivation is difficult and no-one should be condemned as a heretic for getting it wrong. By an ingenious argument he even concludes that the 'sun, stand still' passage in Joshua was more susceptible to a Copernican than a Ptolemaic interpretation. And when he quotes the Douai version of Proverbs 8:26 ('He had not yet made the earth, the rivers, and the hinges of the terrestrial orb') he argues that 'hinges would seem to be ascribed in vain to the earth unless it needed them to turn upon'.

Galileo, it may seem, did not take his views to their logical conclusion. He could not deny that Scripture could ever be used to lead to a technical understanding of nature. That step was, however, taken by several leading writers on the Protestant side. Kepler offers a good example. In 1609 he addressed the question that arose when sense impressions are at variance with 'the true nature of things', as when the sun seems to be moving across the sky. He argues that Scripture, being addressed to both 'scientific and ignorant men', would most naturally speak with 'the senses that are human'. By way of illustration he quotes Psalm 19 and Joshua 10. He continues:

> If anyone alleges on the basis of Psalm 24 ('The earth is founded upon the seas')...that the earth is floating on the waters, may it not be rightly said to him that he ought to set free the Holy Spirit and should not drag Him into the schools of physics to make a fool of Him?

Strong words, but that is how Kepler saw the danger of 'biblical' science. When Ecclesiastes declares (1:4) 'the earth remains for ever' it is 'no new principle of physics', but rather 'a question of ethical instruction' warning us of our own frailty and impermanence, even in comparison with the stability of the earth.

Kepler is more expansive about Psalm 104 which some men think is 'wholly concerned with physics'. At some length he asserts that it is instead a hymn to God the Creator disclosed from the deep mysteries of the universe.[8]

One other example must suffice: John Wilkins, the Puritan who became Bishop of Chester as well as brother-in-law to Oliver Cromwell. He urges us to 'exempt Scripture from philosophical controversies'. On the basis of Job's confessed ignorance (Job 42:3) he reckons that the 'holy men' of Scripture had no 'special inspiration' into the 'humane arts', but acquired their knowledge 'by instruction and study, and other ordinary means', like the rest of us. He asks:

> Why then may we not think that those primitive saints who were the pen-men of Scripture, and eminent above all others in their time for holiness and knowledge, might yet be utterly ignorant of many philosophical truths which are commonly known these days? 'Tis probable that the Holy Ghost did inform them only with the knowledge of those things whereof they were to be the pen-men, and that they were not better skilled in points of philosophy than others.[9]

In similar vein he speaks of stars falling from heaven as being meteors, not literal stars (Mark 13:25; Revelation 6:13). He disagrees with earlier expositors who implied that, as the moon was said in Scripture to be 'a great light', it was bigger than the stars (Basil), or denied spherical heavens because they are compared to a tent (Chrysostom).

This kind of approach was widely shared among Protestants in the seventeenth century. Yet it was not new, and it certainly does not represent a rearguard action in the face of scientific progress. Professor R. Hooykaas has decisively shown the importance of the principle of 'accommodation' voiced clearly by John Calvin in the previous century.[10] While wholly accepting Scripture to be in a full sense the Word of God, Calvin urged that the Holy Spirit accommodated himself to the conventional usages of the day when speaking of the natural world. 'Moses spoke in a popular way ... One should not look there for astronomy and other abstruse sciences; it is a book for laymen'. Far from diminishing the importance of Scripture this accentuates it by stressing the universality of its appeal to learned and unlearned alike. Calvin was under no pressure from science to think like this; to do so was a logical conclusion from his own Reformation insights which were themselves derived from the totality of Scripture. They may also, in some measure, be detected in the writings of Augustine and other early Church Fathers.

Copernicanism and the plight of man

If Copernicus was eventually to cause considerable upheavals in his own Church and to challenge traditional views of Scripture, it has been argued that he was to have an even more profound effect as the implication of his doctrine became clear for the human race as a whole. If he were even partly right, he had exposed a whole range of human problems which, however unpalatable, simply had to be faced. All of them were basically *theological* problems, but of a kind so different from matters of biblical interpretation just discussed as to render the latter insignificant by comparison. Indeed one reason for the survival of a geocentric view of the universe for any length of time, may have been that by taking refuge in the traditional view these alarming new difficulties could be avoided.

Before dogmatic statements are made about such things, however, one needs to be fully aware of the dangers of hindsight. Because *we* can perceive certain implications of Copernicanism, it does not follow that this was historically the case at any other time than our own. With that caution in mind we can identify three inter-related problems.

First there was the question of *the centrality of man*. One recent author has described man as 'demoted spectator':

Man was demoted from the center of the universe to a

spinning, peripheral planet.... The new cosmology...
threatened the whole Aristotelian scheme of purpose and
meaning in which man's spatial location was correlated
with his status in the cosmic hierarchy.[11]

It is an attractive hypothesis. But in fact the literature of the
day offers little to support it, and it is not hard to see why. At
the very inception of his theory Copernicus had gone out of
his way to stress that, in a universe as vast as ours appears to
be, the displacement of the earth is trivial in comparison with
its immense distance from the fixed stars. If the earth was
already an insignificant speck in the cosmos a merely technical
and minor displacement was scarcely likely to be too upsetting.

Despite the lack of evidence to corroborate the first part of
Barbour's statement above, it cannot be denied that the second
part identifies an extremely important aspect of the whole
Copernican transformation. This was to undermine the correlation between physical position and actual status, a correlation
which was thoroughly Aristotelian. If anything, Aristotle's
insistence on the imperfection of all below the lunar sphere,
was less flattering and comforting to man than the Copernican
system. But it was certainly not a biblical concept, for nowhere
in Scripture is the earth accorded a superior position in the
cosmos, or is·position portrayed as indicative of value or
worth. Quite the opposite is true.

The values of this world are contrasted again and again with
spiritual worth. Supremely, Christ came not to the political
'centre' of the world (Rome), its intellectual 'centre' (Athens) or
even the religious 'centre' of his own people (Jerusalem). So
Christians might well have welcomed the demystifying effect
of Copernicanism for just that kind of reason. Yet, as Hooykaas
points out, there is little written evidence that they did.[12] It
may help to explain the ready acceptance of Copernicanism,
but we shall have to wait and see what further historical
evidence emerges.

All the evidence so far available suggests that the new
cosmology was not seen as a demotion of man. The facts of the
incarnation and the priceless worth of each individual human
being in the sight of God continued to be taught by all branches
of the church.

The only reason why we should be surprised would be a
failure to grasp the distinction between a *world-picture* and a
world-view. The former is a physical model of the universe:
the latter is an assessment of meaning and significance. A

world-view is about ultimate causes, values and essential nature. For Copernicus the world-picture was no longer man-centred, but the world-view was just as man-centred as ever (although that was not to allege that the world existed only for man's benefit): 'God so loved *the world...*' (John 3:16). The fact that these two positions could be held simultaneously is a measure of the extent to which Aristotelianism was on the wane and a truly biblical theology resurgent.

A second problem brought to light by Copernicus was *the loneliness of man.* The universe had now to be extended so greatly (to explain the lack of observed stellar parallax) that it was virtually infinite. Man's home, if it ever had been cosy, was now a speck in the nightmare loneliness of infinite space. How could there be a God 'up there' who even noticed him, still less cared? As Alan Richardson has pointed out:

> The rise of modern science...robbed him [man] of his comfortable sense of being at home at the centre of the universe; instead of the crystal spheres and the bright heavens above them, it revealed the terrifying infinity of the cosmic waste land. Frightened and alone in a vast, silent void, man has been left to comfort himself as best he may....'[13]

He quoted Thomas Hood's disllusionment and recollection that ''Tis little joy to know I'm further off from heaven than when I was a boy'.

Yet, again, we must be careful not to read back into history the *angst* of our own age. We do in fact discover occasional hints of disquiet, as when Thomas Digges said that, if it really was beyond the fixed stars, the throne of God was a fearfully great distance away. That most sensitive of men, Blaise Pascal, confessed that 'the eternal silence of these infinite spaces terrifies me'. But this is not the dominant note to be sounded in the seventeenth century, and in any case notions of an infinite universe had been canvassed in earlier times (*e.g.* by Nicholas of Cusa). As before, the correlation between a physical condition (isolation) and a spiritual one (abandonment) is by no means a logical necessity.

Finally there arose with new urgency another old-established problem: the question of *the uniqueness of man.* Speculations on this subject had been quelled by the church on numerous occasions, by Thomas Aquinas for instance. But if the earth was no longer the unique object it had been supposed, it now became much more reasonable to enquire whether worlds other than ours might be inhabited. It is sometimes represented that for asserting that this might be the case Giordano Bruno was burnt at the stake in 1600. In fact his death at the hands of the Inquisition was occasioned by a comprehensive indictment of which plurality of worlds (and an infinite universe) constituted a minority of the charges. What is remarkable is the number of writers who openly speculated on the plurality of worlds in the next few decades, Kepler and Wilkins among the most prominent.

Again it is possible with hindsight to wonder why this should have been so. There were no references in Scripture to other worlds, but that objection was readily disposed of by Wilkins and others. In matters that are not fundamental to its purpose negative evidence cannot be deduced from the Bible. A more serious objection could be this: if other worlds were inhabited by man-like creatures, had they, too, fallen and had there been an infinity of crucifixions to rescue them also? But that again reflects more modern beliefs about the uniformity of law and matter throughout the universe. According to Gassendi, any inhabitants of the moon and planets would differ greatly from us, while the astronomer Huygens compared humanity to 'a company of mean fellows living in a little corner of the world', suggesting elsewhere life might be different. Speculations about plurality have continued to our own day. One feature common to most of the seventeenth-century writers was an insistence on God's ability to create life anywhere and that the universe existed for God's glory rather than man's benefit.[14] This subtle shift in emphasis is sufficient to account for the early popularity of the speculations. It is a modest, if significant, indicator of the ascendancy of biblical values over those of Aristotle. While insisting on the dignity and worth of man, it denied the pre-Christian Aristotelian association of position and status as well as a cosmos bifurcated by the sphere of the moon. And it allowed humanity to face without fear or favour all the scriptural assertions about itself as well as the flood of new data from scientific observation and experiment.

Notes for chapter three

[1] A. D. White, *A History of the Warfare of Science with Theology in Christendom* (Arco, 1955), vol. i, p.126.

[2] R. Hooykaas, *J. World Hist.*, 1956, *3*, 136.

[3] E. Rosen, *J. Hist. Ideas*, 1960, *21*, 431.

[4] R. Hooykaas, *Religion and the Rise of Modern Science*, rev. ed. (Scottish Academic Press, Edinburgh, 1973), p.154.

[5] *Ibid.*, p.122.

[6] On Galileo see G. de Santillana, *The Crime of Galileo* (Heinemann, 1961); J. J. Langford, *Galileo, Science and the Church* (Michigan University Press, 1971).

[7] Stillman Drake (trans.) *Discoveries and opinions of Galileo* (Doubleday, N. Y., 1957), especially Galileo's 'Letter to the Grand Duchess Christina' of 1615 concerning the use of biblical quotations in matters of science (pp.145–216).

[8] J. Kepler, *Astronomia Nova* (1609), trans. C. A. Russell, in D. C. Goodman (ed.), *Science and Religious Belief, 1600–1900, A Selection of Primary Sources* (John Wright/Open University Press, 1973), pp.21–25.

[9] J. Wilkins, *A Discourse Concerning a New Planet*, (1640), in D. C. Goodman, (ref. 8), pp.85–98.

[10] R. Hooykaas, (ref. 4), pp.114 *et seq.* and see also C. J. Rheticus' *Treatise on Holy Scripture and the Motion of the Earth*, (North Holland Publishing Co., Amsterdam, 1984).

[11] I. G. Barbour, *Issues in Science and Religion* (SCM Press, 1968), p.33. One may compare the evaluation by Freud of the blows inflicted on the 'naive self-love' of man by Copernicus, Darwin and himself.

[12] R. Hooykaas, 'The impact of the Copernican Transformation', Unit 2 of O.U. Course AMST283 'Science and Belief: from Copernicus to Darwin' (Open University Press, Milton Keynes, 1974), p.69.

[13] A. Richardson, *The Bible in the Age of Science* (SCM Press, 1964), p.164.

[14] On the plurality of worlds issue, see, *e.g.*, R. Hooykaas, 'The impact of the Copernican Transformation', pp.81–85, and (for the 19th-century debate) J. H. Brooke, *Ann. Sci.*, 1977, *34*, 221.

4 Converging streams: science and biblical ideology

The spacious firmament on high,
With all the blue ethereal sky,
And spangled Heavens, a shining frame,
Their great Original proclaim:
Th'unwearied Sun, from day to day,
Does his Creator's power display;
And publishes to every land
The work of an almighty hand.

Soon as the evening shades prevail,
The Moon takes up the wond'rous tale;
And nightly, to the list'ning Earth
Repeats the story of her birth:
Whilst all the stars that round her burn,
And all the planets in their turn,
Confirm the tidings as they roll,
And spread the truth from pole to pole.

What though, in solemn silence, all
Move round the dark terrestrial ball?
What though no real voice, nor sound
Amid their radiant orbs be found?
In reason's ear they all rejoice,
And utter forth a glorious voice;
For ever singing as they shine:
'The hand that made us is divine.'

Joseph Addison (1672–1719), from *The Spectator*, 1712

You alone are the LORD. You made the
heavens, even the highest heavens, and all
their starry host, the earth and all
that is on it, the seas and all that
is in them. You give life to everything,
and the multitudes of heaven worship you.

Nehemiah 9:6

A common view of Renaissance science a century ago emphasized only its Greek origins. The Scientific Revolution was seen as the triumph of Greek thoughts emerging from the

vanishing mists of mediaeval theology. Rationality had con-
quered superstition and science won its first round against
religion.

Few scholars accept that view today. To assert, as we shall
do, that Judaeo-Christian roots were also important is not to
dispute the Greek heritage, but is to deny its monopoly.
Indeed it can be cogently argued that the older view is not
merely a half-truth, but actually misleading to a high degree.
The thesis of this chapter is that science arose in the West, not
when Christian theology was submerged by Greek rationalism,
but rather when Greek and other 'pagan' ideas of nature were
shown to be inadequate in the new climate of biblical awareness brought about at the Reformation. In conformity with
this view is the dominant role in the new science played by
Protestant countries like Britain, the Netherlands and
Germany, as opposed to traditionally Roman Catholic ones
like Italy, Spain and France. Caution is needed in such matters,
for did not Italy have its Leonardo and its Galileo, and in due
course France its Descartes and the great Académie des
Sciences? However, it is interesting to note Francis Bacon's
observation that 'when it pleased God to call the Church of
Rome to account... at one and the same time it was ordained
by the Divine Providence that there should attend withal a
renovation and new spring of all other knowledges'.[1]

Such an invocation of Providence became common in later
science, as we shall see. It was, for Bacon, an entirely natural
interpretation of a series of apparently fortuitous happenings
in diverse fields which forced themselves on people's attention,
though they were quite incompatible with traditional science.
We can briefly mention only a few. It had been widely asserted
that the tropical regions and the southern hemisphere were
uninhabitable, yet voyages of exploration in the fifteenth
century had returned with tales which suggested the exact
opposite. As William Watts later observed (1633), 'The
thoughts of the philosophers have been contradicted by the
unexpected observations of the navigators'. Then came the
discoveries associated with Tycho Brahe, Galileo and Kepler
(see p.39).

In all these accidental discoveries it is as though men were
for the first time being forced to recognize the implications of
empirical data as opposed to reasoning from traditions, however ancient or revered. Whether they would have done so on
their own may be doubted. What now seems clear beyond
contradiction is that a rediscovery of certain doctrines of

biblical Christianity led to a qualitatively new perception of nature, that was now large enough to encompass these new discoveries and to make possible the Scientific Revolution.

The important word here is 'rediscovery'. As is not uncommonly the case in history of science, ideas can lie unexploited for years – even centuries – before their potential is realized. Then something happens, often in the world that is external to science, and the potential becomes actual. R. G. Collingwood has written of the church's historic faith:

> The presuppositions that go to make up this 'Catholic faith', preserved for many centuries by the religious institutions of Christendom, have as a matter of historical fact been the main or fundamental presuppositions of natural science ever since.[2]

Until the Reformation there had been something like a slow seepage of these ideas into the emerging scientific culture. Now, and quite suddenly, this turned into a flood.

In fact several strands of Christian ideology may be discerned in the emergence of the new science. They were bound together at many points, rather like the separate strands in a DNA helix. At the risk of being somewhat arbitrary we shall separate them and discuss them one by one.

Removing the myth from nature

Perhaps the most dramatic way of distinguishing between attitudes before and after the Scientific Revolution is to say that, instead of being thought of as an *organism*, the universe was now imagined as a *mechanism*. Everything, it seems, was from now on to be regarded in terms of jostling atoms moving in blind obedience to mathematical laws. All of nature, with the possible exception of humanity, was ultimately to be explained along these lines, at least in principle. Of course there was an immense way to go before this became a reality, but the hope was there. The whole 'mechanical philosophy' has been most famously summed up by Robert Boyle, who saw the universe itself as one vast interlocking mechanism 'like a rare clock, such as may be that at Strasbourg'. For him chemistry was explicable simply in terms of particles or atoms. Thus acids owed their sharp taste to tiny spikes on the atoms themselves. In a somewhat similar way Descartes considered the material universe in strictly mechanical terms: the planets were swept around by a system of vortices; the heart ejected blood as a boiling kettle gives off steam, and so on. He regarded man as a duality, with the soul (located in the pineal gland) controlling the machine-like body. He once compared the human body to an elaborately contrived system of fountains in an aristocrat's garden. Controlling everything was the 'fountaineer' (the soul); water-pumps represented muscles and tendons, water-pipes the nerves, reservoirs the ventricles of the brain and so on. The elaborate systems of pressure-pads causing unwelcome visitors to be sprayed with water or threatened by a movable 'Neptune' corresponded to external stimuli on the organs of sensation. Descartes' 'ghost-in-a-machine' was to trouble philosophers and theologians alike in years to come. In the seventeenth century it was the quintessence of a mechanical philosophy and a universe bereft of myth.

Putting it like that may give the impression of rampant materialism with precious little Christian content or room for God. Even the Greeks had Aristotle's 'Prime Mover' and Plato's 'Demiurge'. This conception of nature sounds more like that of the Greek atomists who have often been accused of atheism. Yet in fact such impressions are false. We shall see why in a moment. Another misconception that needs dispelling is that all this occured at once. What actually happened was a gradual transition, even in England where it was perhaps most notice-able, but the tide began strongly to turn about 1650. However, even Newton at the end of the century was not wholly com-mitted to a mechanical explanation of everything material.

This is how the historian G. M. Trevelyan colourfully depicted English life just before the 'mechanical philosophers' took over:

> The idea of regular law guiding the universe was unfamiliar to the contemporaries of Francis Bacon. The fields around town and hamlet were filled, as soon as the day-labourers had left them, by goblins and will-o'-the-wisps; and the woods, as soon as the forester had closed the door of his hut, became the haunt of fairies; the ghosts could be heard gibbering all night under the yew-tree of the churchyard; the witch, a well-known figure in the village, was in the pay of lovers whose mistresses were hard to win, and of gentlemen-farmers whose cattle had sickened. If a criminal was detected and punished, the astonishing event was set

down as God's revenge against murder; if a dry summer threatened the harvest, the parson was expected to draw down rain by prayer. The charms that ward off disease, the stars of birth that rule fortune, the comet that foretold the wars in Germany, the mystic laws that govern the fall of the dice, were the common interest of ordinary men and women. In a soil that imagination had so prepared, poetry and Puritanism were likely to flourish loftily among lofty men, basely among the base. The better kind of men were full of ardour, fancy and reverence. The ignoble were superstitious, ignorant and coarse. The world was still a mystery, of which the wonder was not dispelled in foolish minds by a daily stream of facts and cheap explanations.[3]

This may be a trifle over-romanticized, and not all would accept Trevelyan's view that 'high triumphs of the imagination' (as the work of Shakespeare) were made possible precisely because science was excluded from ordinary life. But it is wholly correct in identifying popular beliefs in non-material agencies, and occult influences on ordinary life. Nor was this just a fancy of the ignorant. To a greater or lesser extent the notion of the universe as an organic whole, linked together in this non-mechanical way, was endemic in all mediaeval and Renaissance thinking. This is the 'myth' whose dispelling led to or accompanied the Scientific Revolution. Before we can understand the devastating effect upon it of biblical theology we need to elaborate some of its characteristics in a little more detail.

First, there is this question of non-material forces, 'influences', 'sympathies' and so on. These were 'the secret powers of Nature' whose operation could only be understood (if at all) in a very vague way. Otherwise, of course, they would not be secret. They lay behind the whole of sympathetic magic, for example. They were represented by the effects on human life of movements by the heavenly bodies. Alchemical changes were understood in complex allegorical terms and may have had a deep if incomprehensible spiritual significance. When the Elizabethan doctor Robert Fludd wished to heal a wound, he applied the ointment not to the patient but to the weapon which hurt him. Examples could be multiplied almost without end.

This organismic universe was more than an assemblage of dead matter jerked into motion by occult forces. From the earliest civilization there was a deep-seated belief that nature itself was alive. Aristotelian thought is founded on this idea. Thus the planets and stars move in their courses because that is their most fitting place and they have their own life and even health. Stones fall downwards to earth because they have a kind of homing instinct. And 'Nature abhors a vacuum'. Robert Fludd proclaimed that 'Nature is the noblest daughter of the Creator' who 'reveals her essence and virtue to none but the sons of God'.[4] Even Islamic writers testify to a 'World Soul'[5] in which they follow in the footsteps of Plato. For the Greeks, on whom so much later thinking depended, the whole cosmos was vibrantly alive with the energies of the gods. 'Nature' should have a captial N.

The notion of an organic universe did not, in itself, offend Christian susceptibilities, derived from Scripture. After all what to us is inanimate nature is sometimes exhorted to 'praise the Lord' (as in Psalm 148), though this can equally well be understood rhetorically.[6] Very different, however, was the challenge to Christian thought presented by an extension of the organismic view to virtually one of pantheism.

As far as records go back, the tendency to deify nature has been one of the most characteristic features of human thinking. In ancient Egypt the cult of sun-worship, centred on Heliopolis, was readily understandable where 'in a country essentially rainless, the daily circuit of the sun is of blazing importance'.[7] Since that period 5,000 years ago, man's worship has been offered to almost every part of nature, whether moon, stars, trees, animals or almost anything else. Above all it has been directed to 'Mother Earth'.

Salt mine at Wieliczka, Poland.

Given the notion of earth as a female being, it is not hard to see how people would imagine that it is the womb of nature. In the 'bowels of the earth' (telling phrase!) minerals are born and great mysteries of procreation enacted. Indeed, it makes good empirical sense, up to a point. Dig over your flower-bed and remove the stones; within a few weeks more will have appeared. There are still people who believe stones grow in the earth. Then again, the temperature rises as one descends into the earth and everyone knows that warmth is necessary for germination. Thus alchemists of many periods and places have sought to emulate 'Mother Earth' with their furnaces and sand-baths, so hoping to generate gold. Their frequent failures do not seem to have deflected them from their belief.

From this attribute it was but a step to regard nature as a *divine* organism. According to Robert Fludd, 'This noble and most pure Virgin is decked with such divine light that some have wondered whether this splendid Nature, this Psyche, minister of life to all creatures, is herself god or whether god himself is she.'[8] Or as a modern commentator on alchemy has observed, 'For the primitive miner, as for the Western alchemists, Nature is a hierophany. It is not only "alive" it is also "divine", it has, at least, a divine dimension.'[9] Nor was this at all a new phenomenon. Amongst the Greeks the Stoics identified nature with Zeus, while even the so-called atomists deified nature nearly as much as their predecessors. In the neo-Platonic revival of the Renaissance much of this nature worship was focused on the sun, regarded as a symbol if not an embodiment of Deity. It may be detected in Copernicus' famous lines:

> In the midst of all dwells the Sun. For who could set this luminary in another or better place in this most glorious temple, than whence he can at one and the same time lighten the whole.... And so, as if seated upon a royal throne, the Sun rules the family of the planets as they circle around him.

What is really remarkable about these beliefs, even making allowance for rhetorical and allegorical uses of language, is that they were rampant in an avowedly Christian era. That they are entirely 'natural', and that they are suffused through almost all pre-Christian religions, must be undeniable. Yet two features of a pantheistic view of nature stand out with stark simplicity:

1. They are hard to reconcile with any conception of science and are likely to militate against scientific enquiry; investigation and manipulation of nature would amount to blasphemy.

2. They run counter to views of nature embodied in the Bible.

This second point requires some elaboration. A biblical theology of nature is complex in some respects, but underlying it is one dominant theme: the world around us did not happen by chance but was created and is upheld by one transcendent God. Right through the Old Testament psalmists, prophets and other writers proclaim the sovereignty of God over his creation and denounce those who worship works of nature or (worse still) works of man. While the prophets thunder against idolatry of all kinds and lash those who worship 'the Queen of Heaven' (Jeremiah 7:18) they also exhort Israel to remember 'the LORD, who has made all things, who alone stretched out the heavens, who spread out the earth' (Isaiah 44:24), to whom this earth is but a 'footstool' (Isaiah 66:1; Matthew 5:35). This same God controls the weather (Psalms 29:3–10; 89:8–10; 135:7) and 'natural' disasters (Deuteronomy 28:20–25, 27, 38–40; Psalms 105:26–36; 107:33–34). And he it is, not the fertility gods of the land, who is to be thanked and adored when the harvest spills over in fabulous abundance (Deuteronomy 26:11; Psalm 65:9–13). The great sea-monster that terrified the Canaanite peoples is seen by Job as the greatest of God's creatures (Job 41) and by the Psalmist as simply one of his playthings (Psalm 104). The Genesis creation narratives merely set the tone for the later unanimous testimony of Scripture that creation is God's handiwork, and his alone. There is perhaps even unconscious humour in Genesis 1:16 when that great object of worship in the ancient world, the sun, is introduced. Like a football team relegated from First to Fourth Division at one catastrophic stroke, he appears merely on the fourth 'day' of creation. But 'In the beginning, God' (Genesis 1:1).

It is admittedly only in recent times that we have come to realize the magnitude of the chasm between an almost universal nature religion and the faith of Israel in one transcendent God. It was not realized much before this century how deeply was the cult of the Baal gods implicated in nature-worship. Nor was the contrast between biblical and (say) Babylonian creation stories so vividly understood, despite considerable points of similarity. Yet even in mediaeval times and earlier it was abundantly clear to any who troubled to examine the biblical text that to view nature as divine was unjustified and sinful and that, as the apostle Paul observed, to worship and serve the creature rather than the Creator is actually to exchange the truth of God for a lie (Romans 1:25).

Rediscovery of this belief did not have to wait till the seventeenth century. Some of the early Christian 'Fathers' who wrote in the first four centuries AD viewed nature as an organism, but even Eusebius (who called nature 'universal mother') insists that 'she' is subject entirely to God's commands and cannot act spontaneously. But these men did not fail to warn against Pantheism, as when Tatian asserted that 'God is spirit not pervading matter, but the maker of matter'.[10] Words such as these fell on deaf ears in the following centuries and, as we have seen, the organismic universe survived until the end of the Middle Ages, and beyond. Its ultimate demise has still to come, but it went into steep decline as the biblical concepts of nature re-emerged with the rise of the mechanical philosophy.

Professor R. Hooykaas, of Amsterdam and Utrecht, has demonstrated the intimate connection between the new science and what he calls the 'de-deification' of nature. He points out how the French physician Basso undermined the concept of nature as a kind of Viceroy to God, because 'He who is present everywhere, works all things immediately'.[11] Even more directly Robert Boyle condemned the Aristotelians who, denying the universe was created by God, 'were obliged to acknowledge a provident and powerful being that maintained and governed the universe which they called nature'. As he observes, they sometimes put nature on a level with God, and at other times simply confuse the two.[12] He commended mechanical philosophy for its *clarity* (no more obscure principles and intelligences at work) and its *extensiveness* (covering chemistry as well as physics). Taking care to distance himself from the old Greek doctrine of Epicurus, that the world was brought into being by chance encounters between atoms, Boyle observed:

Thus the universe being once framed by God and the laws of motion settled and all upheld by his perpetual concourse and general providence; the same philosophy teaches, that the phenomena of the world are physically produced by the mechanical properties of the parts of matter, and that they operate upon one another according to mechanical laws.

'Tis of this kind of corpuscular philosophy, that I speak.[13]

Isaac Newton himself put it like this half a century later:

> All these things being considered, it seems probable to me, that God in the Beginning form'd Matter in solid, massy, hard, impenetrable, moveable Particles... The Changes of corporeal Things are to be placed only in the various Separations and new Associations and Motions of these permanent Particles.[14]

Francis Bacon (1561–1626), Lord High Chancellor of England from 1618, and Robert Boyle (1627–1691).

At this stage in the argument it is important to recognize that the mechanization of nature had social as well as theological dimensions. Carolyn Merchant, in her well-named book *The Death of Nature*, has agreed with other writers that in the seventeenth century, plagued with social unrest, the machine was a unifying model for both science and society. She rightly affirms that 'while social and historical conditions did not determine the specific content of the mechanical philosophy or form an impetus to construct a philosophy in direct response to social circumstances, they helped to make plausible some presuppositions about nature and to invalidate others'.[15] Thus William Harvey, who discovered the circulation of the blood, dedicated his book to Charles I, comparing the heart in the body to the king in his realm. After Charles' execution, the analogy was prudently dropped.

The laws of nature

Thus nature has been demythologized, deprived of its mystique as well as its capital 'N', and reduced (or elevated, according to one's viewpoint) to the level of a machine of unimaginable complexity. Whether applied to a human body (Descartes), to the phenomena of chemistry (Boyle) or, as we shall see (ch.5) to the whole universe of Newtonian physics, the elimination of myth has changed for ever not only how we think about science but also the ways we do it. Alongside this process went another, inseparable from it: a growing recognition that this 'mechanical' universe does not behave capriciously but according to certain regular principles. These are the laws of nature which in their modern form as scientific laws did not emerge clearly until the seventeenth century.

It had, of course, been known for centuries that nature behaved in a regular way. In the thirteenth century Roger Bacon had spoken of laws of reflection and refraction while seeking to reduce optics to a mathematical form. But it was not until the seventeenth century that 'laws of nature' were widely spoken of in their modern sense, separable from moral and other kinds of law and possessing predictive power. In that sense the phrase was used by both Boyle and Newton. Boyle, later on in the passage just quoted, contrasted two ways of understanding the projection of an image by a concave mirror: one was by witchcraft and the other by 'optical and mathematical laws'. And Newton continually rejected 'occult qualities' as explanations of gravitational phenomena, preferring 'general laws of nature', such as the laws of motion which he had discovered.

In the first major attempt to trace the history of this concept, Zilsel[16] argues strongly that it emerged directly from biblical doctrines. He cites many passages from the Old Testament which illustrate that the divine lawgiver is the central idea of Judaism and that nature is included in his rule. Thus Job 28:26 reads 'he [God] made a *decree* for the rain and a *path* for the thunderstorm', and Proverbs 8:29 'he gave the sea its *boundary* so that the waters would not overstep his *command*'. The italicized words are all the same in Hebrew (*choq*), and in the

Latin translation of the Bible (the Vulgate) appear as *lex* (= law).

The Old Testament writers were not, of course, chiefly concerned with nature as such – the word does not even appear. But they were committed to God's sovereignty over *everything*, particularly in the light of their own marvellous experience of liberation and deliverance. As Alan Richardson put it so well, 'If God is known as the Lord of nature, this is because he has already been encountered as the Lord of history.'[17]

All this stands in remarkable contrast to other prevailing beliefs in antiquity. Zilsel points to the relative paucity of references to natural law in the ancient world. But those that may be found show a fundamental difference from the biblical concept – a point which Zilsel did not make but which became the focal point of another important paper in this subject.[18] The author, F. Oakley, argues that 'natural law' may be *immanent* (*i.e.* inherent within matter itself) or else *imposed* upon matter by God. The former concept may certainly be detected in Stoic and other pagan writings. The latter is, however, quite distinctively Judaeo-Christian. His argument is that it is this which underlay the rise of modern science. It may be found in some of the early Christian writers, such as Origen who held that laws regulating changes in matter were established by God. But later the Greek idea of immanent law became dominant.

In fact both these approaches can be detected in mediaeval science and theology. It is remarkable how, in the thirteenth century, Thomas Aquinas combined the biblical idea of God as lawgiver with Platonic and Aristotelian notions of a natural law immanent in the universe. But in 1277, three years after Aquinas died, there came a powerful re-assertion of the freedom and sovereignty of God which undermined the notion of laws somehow embedded in nature and capable of even limiting the power of God. Prompted by the Pope, the Bishop of Paris, Etienne Tempier, issued a decree condemning the thesis that God could not make a void (an empty space), that he could not allow any form of planetary motion other than circular, and so on. From this point developed a stream of *voluntarist* theology which admitted no limitations on God's absolute power and which regarded natural law as tantamount to divine command.

In England, William of Ockham (*c.* 1285–1349) codified these ideas in what became known as *nominalism*. He argued that God has established a framework of natural laws which nominally hold but may be temporarily abrogated – as in the case of miracles. In the fourteenth century John Buridan and Nicholas Oresme maintained the emphasis on God's creative freedom. Amongst the Reformers of the following century Zwingli spoke of the world brought by God under 'law and order' and Melanchthon of the 'perpetual laws' by which the universe works. And their Jesuit contemporary Suarez frequently refers to the laws which God has imposed upon nature.

Thus it came about that the mechanical philosophers of the seventeenth century had a rich heritage on which to draw. They had no hesitation in doing so. Descartes could specifically refer to 'laws which God has put into nature', and Boyle could write of 'laws of motion prescribed by the author of things'. More pointedly still, Newton asserted that, so absolute was God's freedom, that he could even 'vary the laws of nature' at his will.

It remains to ask why the notion of a scientific law burst forth with such power in the seventeenth century, when the doctrine of a sovereign, transcendent God had been applied to natural law for so long. Perhaps it is best understood in terms of other cognate ideas that were surfacing at the same time and which, therefore, made the theological doctrine seem so much more relevant; they might include the mechanistic view of nature and some of the other themes explored later in this chapter. But perhaps we should also take into account the new products available from instrument-makers and other skilled artisans (like the telescope and microscope). Zilsel writes of Descartes:

> Like Galileo, he took over the basic idea of physical regularities and quantitative rules of operation from the superior artisans of his period. And from the Bible he took the idea of God's legislation. By combining both he created the modern concept of natural law.[19]

He goes further in socio-political explanation, arguing that the concept of a lawgiver whose laws extend over nature itself sprang from a comparison of nature and state. With the passing of fedualism and the establishment of powerful centralized monarchies on the Continent it was rational to think of God as an absolute monarch over nature. That this socio-political explanation on its own is inadequate has been pointed out by that great contemporary historian of Chinese science, Joseph

Needham, who observed that, although China had an even longer period of 'imperial absolutism', in that country we hardly meet at all with the idea of the laws of nature. Clearly, as Zilsel so persuasively argues, 'the law metaphor originates in the Bible'.

Whatever be the precise connection between mediaeval Christianity and the rise of science, there can be no doubt as to the immense importance of biblical categories of thought for the emergence of scientific laws. A. N. Whitehead has observed in a famous passage that this modern concept of science 'must have come from the medieval insistence on the rationality of God, conceived as with the personal energy of Jehovah and with the rationality of a Greek philosopher.... Faith in the possibility of science...is an unconscious derivative from medieval theology'.[20] Others have more simply said that men looked for scientific laws only when they had recognized a lawgiver. In so far as this belief implies a uniformity of law throughout the universe the French philosopher of science, Pierre Duhem, has an interesting comment. As we have seen, the discovery by Tycho Brahe of a new star beyond the moon's orbit (1572) and of a comet (1577) in the same region of supposed unchangeableness was followed by Galileo's recognition of sunspots and solar prominences (1610). The Aristotelian notion of a fundamental distinction between sub-lunar and supra-lunar spheres was thereby discredited, but Duhem claims the unification of the universe with one set of laws was a direct result of Christian theology. Mascall wryly notes that this may be going too far, but we can fully agree that it ought to have been![21] The durability of Aristotelianism should not be underestimated.

The experimental method

Thus far we have seen how the removal of myth from the natural world and the concept of scientific laws were fully consistent with biblical doctrine, and were historically dependent upon it. But recognition of a machine-like universe, operating according to laws impressed upon it, does not constitute science, not even the science of the seventeenth century. There is the question of how this universe should be approached. It is perhaps in the answer to this question that we can begin to see why science as we know it did not arrive until after the Reformation.

First, we need to appreciate the contrast between two modes of attack. Fundamentally they are *reason* and *experience*. On one hand we deduce things about nature from certain agreed principles. On the other we make experiments or observations and allow these to have a determining role in our conclusions. Of course this is a very rough and ready distinction and can be refined almost endlessly. But it is adequate for our present purpose.

The well-known caricature of the Greek philosopher attempting to prove from first principles the number of teeth in a horse, when he could just as well have examined the animal in the field outside, has sufficient truth to underscore the essentially deductive character of Greek 'science' which, like mathematics, was an activity of the mind rather than a matter of observation. Like most such generalizations, that goes too far. Plato was not the only Greek philosopher, and Aristotle made biological observations of the most astonishing acuteness. Yet for nearly two millennia the Greek legacy of science was one in which experiment played little part, and 'reason', in the shape of ancient and mediaeval philosophy, was triumphant. To imagine, even after Aquinas, that this was all the fault of dogmatic Christian thelogy would be to fall into the errors of the naive positivist historians from the last century (of whom more anon). But whatever the cause the effect was clear. As the Puritan John Wilkins wrote in 1640:

> Because in those times all Sciences were taught only in a rude and imperfect manner, therefore 'tis likely that they also had but a dark and confused apprehension of things, and were liable to the common errors.[22]

What had happened at this time was the rise of *experimental* science on a considerable scale, based on the principle of *rational empiricism*. Of course experiments had been conducted in the Middle Ages and many notable observations date back to Aristotle and even beyond. But the principle of relying *chiefly* on experiment is quite definitely post-mediaeval, and its emergence is indissolubly linked to the growing conviction that nature is the creation of an all-powerful God acting of his own free will. The universe is thus *contingent* (or dependent) upon God's will and is not a *necessary* (or inevitable) object which he did not choose to bring into being. Acceptance of this premise leads at once to a specific view of how science may progress.

It was put classically in a paper by M. B. Foster ('Creation, Doctrine and Modern Science') as long ago as 1934, arguing that the contingent can be known only by experience or experiment. He says:

> The reliance upon the sense for evidence, not merely for illustration, is what constitutes the empirical character peculiar to modern natural science...Modern natural science could begin only when the modern presuppositions about nature displaced the Greek (this was, of course, a gradual process, but its crisis occurred at the date of the Reformation); but this displacement itself was possible only when the Christian conception of God had displaced the Pagan, as the object (not merely of unreasoning belief, but) of systematic understanding.[23]

We can put this in other words: if God is somehow limited by nature, or if nature is otherwise self-sufficient, it can be understood only by reason from certain infallible first principles. But if nature is brought into being by a voluntary act of God, we cannot have any first principles (except what he may have given us) and we must resort to experiment and testing.

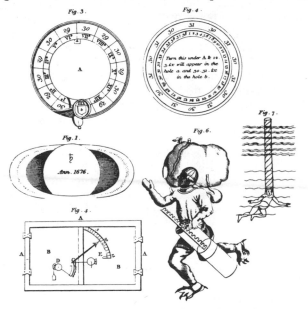

The early Royal Society: some observations, experiments and fantasies.

The biblical text consistently exhorts man to do just that. It is a continuous recital of God's saving acts in history, and attention is constantly drawn to events past and present. The Israelites are invited to contemplate the data of their history, as indeed is the Christian church (*e.g.* in 1 Corinthians 15). As for nature itself the Old Testament shows a familiarity with the use of a plumbline to test for verticality (Isaiah 28:17; Amos 7:7–8; *etc.*) and of metal assaying by fire (Proverbs 17:3; Ezekiel 22:17–22; Zechariah 13:9, *etc.*). At the very least it is unlikely that those experimental operations were disapproved of since both are used as symbols of divine activity. The fire-assay metaphor is continued in the New Testament (*e.g.* 1 Corinthians 3:13; 1 Peter 1:7).

Use of 'testing' as a symbol of *human* activity can also be found in both Old and New Testaments. The Christian is urged to 'prove all things' (1 Thessalonians 5:21), especially those that are good (Romans 12:2; Ephesians 5:10, *etc.*), and the Greek verb means 'to assay'. While it is true that unbelieving 'tests' of God are reproved (Exodus 17:2; Matthew 4:7), the repentant Jewish people are invited even to put God to the test (Malachi 3:10), and the 'experimental method' in religion is encapsulated in the timeless invitation to 'Taste and see that the Lord is good' (Psalm 34:8).

That these attitudes should be carried over into science is perhaps only natural in view of the steady accumulation of new data that cried out for recognition. William Watts' remark in 1633 that 'The thoughts of the philosophers have been contradicted by the unexpected observations of the navigators' might well have included the astronomers as well. But there were other things happening at the same time that also conspired to favour the experimental method, not least the rise of Calvinist theology.

R. Hooykaas has disclosed the relevance of Calvinism for the experimental method which certainly tended to flourish in Calvinist countries like Holland. One of its most distinctive features, shared to some degree with all the Reformed traditions, was its emphasis on the priesthood of all believers and encouragement of lay criticism of clerically propagated doctrines. As Hooykaas observes:

A return to the sources was urged: to the Book of Scripture in one case, to the book of nature (older even than the ancients) in the other.[24]

This notion of the two books found its clearest expression in Francis Bacon's *The Advancement of Learning* of 1605: he urged that no-one should maintain that a man can search too far, or be too well studied in the book of God's Word or in the book of God's works; divinity or philosophy; but rather let men endeavour an endless progress or proficience in both.[25]

In that spirit Nathanael Carpenter could exclaim in 1622, 'I am free, I am bound to nobody's word except to those inspired by God.' And whatever he may, or may not, have done in actual experiment, it was Bacon who most forcibly urged the inductive method and a willingness to face the facts 'like a little child'. And it was he who invoked aid from the alchemists 'who call upon men to sell their books, and to build furnaces; quitting and forsaking Minerva and the Muses as barren virgins, and relying upon Vulcan'.[26]

Ironically it was that most mechanistic of philosophers, Descartes, who failed to perceive the priority of experience over reason, and on the grounds that the human mind was so constructed as to recognize 'clear and distinct' truths about nature. Yet the actual conformity between experience and his mechanical models was often quite poor. His vortex theory violated Kepler's Laws, for example, and his heart/kettle analogy was incompatible with Harvey's detailed observations, which clearly established (1628) that the heart acts as a *pump* to effect a circulation of the blood. When Descartes claimed that 'starting from sensible effects and sensible parts of bodies I have tried to investigate the insensible causes and particles underlying them', he was implying the old distinction between appearance and reality. Thus if our experience appeared to contradict his own rules of dynamics (which it generally does), 'we should be obliged to trust more in our reason than in our senses'. For this he was severely taken to task by Pascal, Boyle, Newton and others. Descartes apart, however, experience and experiment were the keynotes of the new science.

Controlling the earth

By the early seventeenth century it was quite possible for intelligent people in Western Europe to have abandoned the belief in an organismic universe, and to have embraced instead the concept of one vast, interlocking mechanism governed by well-defined laws which were now open to investigation by

the process of experiment. But why should any one bother?
This question of motivation resolved itself into one (or both)
of two intentions:

(a) For the glory of God.
(b) For the benefit of man.

Each was intimately related to biblical ideas circulating with a
new vigour and freshness. They were summed up by Bacon's
assertion that knowledge should be 'for the glory of the Creator
and the relief of man's estate'. While the former intention was
more concerned with *understanding* the world, the latter included also the ambition of *controlling* it. To that strategy we
now turn.

To use the experimental method to understand then sub-
jugate nature required first of all the conquest of certain
prejudices. One of these was that such a task might be an act of
impiety. Said Bacon, 'many have not only considered it to be
impossible but also as something impious to try to efface the
bounds nature seems to put to her works.' This follows at once
from any pantheistic or semi-divine view of nature. But that
was already being rejected in the mechanization of the world
picture. More inhibiting, perhaps, might be the legacy of
contempt towards manual activities that was so noticeable in the
slave-owning society of ancient Greece. This persisted in
some measure through the Middle Ages, when it was possible
to dismiss an opponent as 'a mechanic and not a philosopher'.[27]

It is now many years since R. H. Tawney so clearly identified
the role of Puritanism in the growth of the Protestant work
ethic. He prefixed one chapter with Tyndale's translation of
Genesis 39:2:

And the Lorde was with Joseph, and he was a luckie felowe.[28]

The Puritans' willingness to become involved with manual
work (including the manipulation of nature) sprang as much
from the conviction that God (the Lord of nature) was with
them, as from a detailed knowledge of many biblical passages
which command labour (Genesis 2:5; Deuteronomy 5:13),
honour craftsmen with specific skills (Exodus 35:35), and
include amongst them Paul (Acts 18:3) and even Jesus (Mark
6:3).

In that spirit Bacon remarked that 'It is reserved only for
God and angels to be lookers-on'. His Puritan contemporary

John Bunyan commented that 'the soul of religion is the practical part'. With some vehemence Robert Boyle complained that:

> In about two thousand years since Aristotle's time the adorers of his physics, at least by virtue of his peculiar principles, seem to have done little more than wrangle.

Such indifference to the practicalities of life permits naturalists 'to be very careless and lazy'.[29] There were now very positive reasons for nothing less than an onslaught upon nature, given the erosion of these attitudes that had hindered its conquest for so long. These were, in Bacon's memorable phrase, associated with 'the relief of man's estate'.

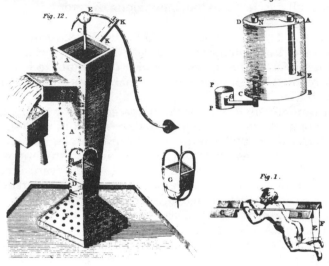

The early Royal Society: putting nature to use.

A recognition that this was even possible may well have come through the real or imagined value of chemical medicines developed by Paracelsus and others in the sixteenth century and by a new co-operation between scholars and craftsmen in the Netherlands especially.[30] It was fuelled by the millenarian vision of Bacon and others that accorded so well with the political ideas of Puritanism. As science progressed, so Utopia would be seen just round the corner, even in the sense that a right control of nature would reverse the effects of the fall. That view of Bacon's may hardly have been scriptural but it

was, as one historian has recently written, 'completely in keeping with the dominant Calvinist tradition in England'.[31]
Bacon wrote:

Man by the Fall fell at the same time from his state of innocency and from his dominion over created things. Both these losses can even in this life be partially repaired; the former by religion and faith, the latter by arts and sciences.[32]

This is a clear reference to Genesis 1:26:

Then God said, 'Let us make man in our image, in our likeness, and let them rule over the fish of the sea and the birds of the air, over the livestock, over all the earth, and over all the creatures that move along the ground.'

These words, and similar ones in Psalm 8:6–8, furnished for Bacon and his contemporaries a clear mandate for controlling nature, in fact for the active promotion of scientific technology. Nature must be 'commanded', and that means understanding and obeying it.

In similar vein Robert Boyle compared the impending conquest of nature to the conquest of Canaan (Numbers 14), and the detractors of that enterprise to the unbelieving Israelites.[33] So convinced was Boyle of God's benevolent intentions towards man that he conceded that God would even 'alter by miracles the course of nature, for the instruction or relief of man', as in the oft-quoted deliverance of the three friends from the raging furnace in Daniel 3.[34]

Although a few scholars have seen the theology of Bacon and others as mere rhetoric to justify their commitment to natural philosophy, this is a minority opinion and does not in any case explain why such rhetoric should be thought effective. Charles Webster asserts that 'theology must be accepted as a factor directly relevant to scientific concepts'[35] and on the more specific point of controlling nature R. Hooykaas writes the following:

The biblical conception of nature liberated man from the naturalistic bonds of Greek religiosity and philosophy and gave a religious sanction to the development of technology, that is, to the dominion of nature by human art.[36]

To the glory of God

Given a multitude of biblical references to the heavens declaring the glory of God (Psalms 8:1–2; 19:1–6; 50:6, *etc.*) and majestic passages like the last three chapters of the book of Job, it may seem strange that in the seventeenth century man had to be exhorted to study nature for the glory of God. Yet this is to look through modern spectacles, for there were in truth two very good historical reasons why they had been reluctant to do so. In a curious way they were polar opposites, yet their effect was similar.

The first of these reasons was a lingering belief that matter was somehow evil. This was specially associated with the third-century sect of the Manichees, whose compound of Persian, Gnostic and Christian religions led to a debasement of matter to such an extent that the soul should avoid as much contact with it as possible. Although the sect (which rejected all the Old Testament) was denounced vigorously, it took some centuries to die. More important, some aspects of its belief survived into the Middle Ages and had been associated with the more extreme forms of monasticism. It was, of course, perfectly possible to cite scriptural texts which appeared to support such views; from the curse entailed on the earth by Adam's sin (Genesis 3:17–18) to the apostle Paul's vision of a creation 'groaning as in the pains of childbirth' (Romans 8:22) it is possible to identify biblical evidence that nature has been affected by the fall. And there are other references to the visible world being in some sense enthralled to the devil (Job 1; Luke 13:16; Ephesians 2:2; Colossians 1:13; Revelation 2:9; 3:9, *etc.*). But biblical evidence includes the complementary assertions that Satan's power is limited (Job 1; Luke 10: 18, *etc.*) and that nature subsists not through Satanic power but through the agency of Christ himself (Colossians 1:15–17). And nowhere in the Bible is the study of nature proscribed. On the contrary, as we have seen, it is given definite if limited encouragement.

Nevertheless Manichean views had lingered long enough for Bacon to open his *Advancement of Learning* (1605) with an assault on 'the zeal and jealousy of Divines' which led some to suppose that science has in it 'something of the serpent'. This might not necessarily imply the full Manichean doctrine of an evil nature, but it could reflect a low order of priority. In patristic times Gregory complained that a study of nature did not lead to 'realities themselves', while Clement regarded it as merely a first stage on the religious pilgrimage (despite which patristic enthusiasm for nature was considerable).[37]

He cites numerous Scriptures, particularly in Ecclesiastes (*e.g.* 1:8, 18; 3:11), in contradiction of this negative attitude to nature. He adds that 'no parcel of the world is denied to man's inquiry and invention', arguing from Proverbs 20:27. For a modern writer to imply that what Bacon was attacking was 'the theological view of nature and man' is misleading, to say the least.[38]

Once the inhibiting effects of the 'forbidden nature' concept had been overcome, science could begin to implement the scriptural injunction with confidence and joy. As Calvin had said:

> Being placed in this most delightful theatre let us not decline to take a pious delight in the clear and manifest works of God.[39]

The second, and opposite, influence of Manicheism was the belief in 'divinity' of nature. As we have seen, this was rapidly receding at the end of the Middle Ages, but again sufficient remained for Bacon to take notice. Clearly a divine nature was as inappropriate an object of manipulation as an evil one. He was at pains to stress that the works of God in nature show his power and wisdom 'but not his image', adding 'Therein the heathen opinion differeth from the sacred truth; for they supposed the world to be the image of God.... But the Scriptures never vouchsafe to attribute to the world that honour, as to be the image of God, but only the *work of his hands*.'[40] Only man is the image of God, and that image is defaced. A study of nature was thus undertaken to glorify God in the greatness of his work.

That, in essence, was the declared objective of many a follower of Francis Bacon and many a scientific enquirer who embraced the ideals of Puritanism. Examples almost without number could be quoted. For them study of nature was an act of worship. Even Kepler, outside the English tradition, spoke of 'thinking God's thoughts after him' as he contemplated the starry heavens. Whereas Bacon had claimed that 'natural theology' 'sufficeth to convince atheism' this was not his first thrust. But after the troubled years of the Civil War, and the proliferation of many alarming sects and groups which were atheistic in intent if not declaration, natural theology was to acquire a new and clearer role. It was to be the spearhead of a concentrated attack on those who by word and deed would deny the very existence of God.

But that is the subject for another chapter.

'The starry heavens'; studying astronomy to the glory of God and with the help of Newton.

Notes for chapter four

[1] F. Bacon, *The Advancement of Learning* (1605) in T. Markby (ed.), *The Two Books of Francis Bacon* (1856), p.42.

[2] R. G. Collingwood, *An Essay on Metaphysics* (Oxford University Press, 1940), p.127.

[3] G. M. Trevelyan, *England under the Stuarts,* 17th ed. (Metheun, 1938), pp.53–54.

[4] R. Fludd, *Tractatus Theologo-Philosophicus* (1617) cited in J. Goodwin, *Robert Fludd* (Shambala, Boulder, 1979), p.15

[5] Seyyed Hossein Nasr, *Islamic Science: an Illustrated Study* (World of Islam Festival Publishing Co. Ltd., 1976), pp.51 and 71.

[6] Interestingly the most extreme example of this in regular Christian use is the ancient hymn called the *Benedicite.* It does not appear in the Hebrew Old Testament, but only in the Greek version which (significantly) originated in Alexandria.

[7] H. Frankfort *et al., Before Philosophy* (Pelican, 1951), p.43.

[8] R. Fludd, (ref. 4), p.15.

[9] M. Eliade, *The Forge and the Crucible* (Harper and Row, N.Y., 1971), p.171.

[10] D. S. Wallace-Hadrill, *The Greek Patristic View of Nature* (Manchester University Press, 1968), p.128. See also D. C. Lindberg, 'Science and the early Christian Church', *Isis,* 1983, 74, 509–530.

[11] R. Hooykaas, *Religion and the Rise of Modern Science,* rev. ed. (Scottish Academic Press, Edinburgh, 1973), pp.16–17.

[12] R. Boyle, *A Disquisition about the Final Causes of Natural Things* (1688), p.36.

[13] R. Boyle, *The Excellency and Grounds of the Mechanical Hypothesis,* (1674), abridged by P. Shaw, *Collected Works* (1725), vol. ii, p.187.

[14] I. Newton, *Opticks* (1730), Query 31.

[15] C. Merchant, *The Death of Nature* (Wildwood House, 1982), pp.195–196.

[16] E. Zilsel, 'The genesis of the concept of physical law', *Phys. Rev.,* 1942, 51, 245–279.

[17] A. Richardson, *The Bible in the Age of Science* (SCM Press, 1964), pp.138–139.

[18] F. Oakley, 'Christian theology and the Newtonian science: rise of the concept of the laws of nature', *Church History,* 1961, 30, 433–457.

[19] Zilsel, (ref. 16), p.269.

[20] A. N. Whitehead, *Science and the Modern World* (Cambridge University Press, 1926), p.17.

[21] E. L. Mascall, *Christian Theology and Natural Science* (Longmans, 1956), p.15.

[22] J. Wilkins, *A Discourse concerning a new Planet* in D. C. Goodman (ed.), *Science and Religious Belief, 1600-1900, A Selection of Primary Sources* (John Wright/Open University Press, 1973), p.91.

[23] M. B. Foster, 'The Christian doctrine of creation and the rise of modern science', *Mind,* 1934, 43, 446–468, reprinted in C. A. Russell (ed.), *Science and Religious Belief, A Selection of Recent Historical Studies* (Hodder and Stoughton, 1973), pp.294–315 (311–312).

[24] R. Hooykaas, (ref. 11), p.112.

[25] F. Bacon, (ref. 1), p.8.

[26] *Ibid.,* p.64.

[27] On Bacon's advocacy of 'the power of art' see R. Hooykaas, (ref. 11), pp.62–74.

[28] R. H. Tawney, *Religion and the Rise of Capitalism* (Pelican, 1948), p.197.

[29] R. Boyle, *Considerations and Experiments touching the Origin of Qualities and Forms,* in *Collected Works* (1772), vol. iii, p.75.

[30] R. Hooykaas, (ref. 11), pp.88–91.

[31] C. Webster, *The Great Instauration: Science, Medicine and Reform 1626–1660* (Duckworth, 1975), p.329.

[32] F. Bacon, *Novum Organum* (1620), Book ii, aphorism 52.

[33] R. Boyle, *Some Considerations touching the Usefulness of Experimental Natural Philosophy,* in *Collected Works* (1772), vol. iii, p.424.

[34] R. Boyle, *Ibid.,* in *Collected Works* (1772), vol. ii, p.17.

[35] C. Webster, (ref. 30), pp.493–494.

[36] R. Hooykaas, (ref. 11), p.67.

[37] D. S. Wallace-Hadrill, *The Greek Patristic View of Nature,* pp.5, 7–8

[38] B. Willey, *The Seventeenth Century Background* (Pelican, 1972), p.37.

[39] J. Calvin, *Institutes,* cited in C. E. A. Turner, 'The Puritans and science', *Christian Graduate*, 1953, 6, 68.

[40] F. Bacon, (ref. 1), p.86.

5 Deepening waters: the Scientific Revolution

Why need I name thy Boyle, whose pious search,
Amid the dark recesses of his works,
The great Creator sought? And why thy Locke,
Who made the whole internal world his own?
Let Newton, pure intelligence, whom God
To mortals lent to trace his boundless works
From laws sublimely simple, speak thy fame
In all philosophy.

James Thomson (1700–48), *The Seasons: Summer*

He [Christ] is the image of the invisible God, the firstborn over
all creation. For by him all things were created: things in heaven
and on earth, visible and invisible, whether thrones or powers or
rulers or authorities; all things were created by him and for him.
He is before all things, and in him all things hold together.

Colossians 1:15–17

The new philosophers in seventeenth-century England

In the light of strong similarities between biblical and scientific
ideologies (outlined in the previous chapter), one might take
for granted the Christian roots of the Scientific Revolution.
That, however, would be dangerous, because it could lead to
quite unjustified historical deductions merely on the basis of
associations of ideas which in the end turn out to be entirely
coincidental. In the early days of radio, for example, there was
a re-emergence of 'spiritualism'. Both might be said to involve
(or claim) communication over long distances! Yet no-one has
yet proposed that one influenced the other. What is needed in
such cases is a detailed examination of individual attitudes.
Do those similar ideas jostle with each other in one cranium?
Better still, are there groups of people united in both sets of
belief? If so how large, influential and representative are they?
We are in the realm of quantitative, or at least semi-
quantitative, research. It is called 'prosopography' by the
initiated and 'history by numbers' by the sceptics. When
applied to the early pioneers of mechanical philosophy it

yields results of more than ordinary interest.

Concentrating for the present on England, we can hardly underestimate the early importance of the Royal Society, founded in 1662. Its origins are complex and still not perfectly clear in some details. According to its first 'official' historian Thomas Sprat, its prehistory dates from the late 1640s and can be located in a group of gentlemen seeking rational discourse away from the turmoil of political unrest and basing their activities on Oxford. They included John Wallis (Savilian Professor of Geometry from 1649), John Wilkins (Warden of Wadham College from 1648) and Jonathan Goddard (Warden of Merton College from 1651). In 1654 their company was strengthened by Robert Boyle, later to be dubbed 'the father of chemistry'. There were several loose associations of like-minded men. Some were centred on Wadham College, which boasted a small chemistry laboratory in addition to a telescope used by Christopher Wren and Wilkins' botanical garden. Others met for a short while in the rooms of William Letty, soon to become Professor of Anatomy.

Counter-claims have been advanced for London. Since 1598 Gresham College in Bishopsgate had been a centre of experimental philosophy where medicine, astronomy and geometry were taught and the science pertaining to the act of navigation was specially cultivated. By the 1630s its fortunes were declining, but it received fresh impetus when another informal group of mechanical philosophers began to meet on its premises. At first they included Wallis and Wilkins, and they continued to meet (not necessarily at Gresham College) after these and others had moved to Oxford. Then there was Boyle's famous 'Invisible College'. This was a group of associates of Robert Boyle who had no fixed meeting-place (hence their 'invisibility'), but may have been centred on London-based Irish Protestant friends of his sister Katherine (Lady Ranelagh). Yet another London group was associated with that ardent Baconian Samuel Hartlib.

When members of the Oxford group began to trickle back to London from 1658 informal meetings in the capital became the focus for various proposals for a more organized institution. The upshot was the adoption of a formal constitution at a Gresham College meeting late in 1660, and the award of its first Royal Charter by Charles II in 1662. The Royal Society had been born. Although it later lapsed into somnolence for very many years, in those heady days it was, as it is today, a centre of excellence and a focus for all that was best in English science. So who were its members? What did they have in common?

Many attempts have been made to answer this question. Most recently attention has been concentrated on the professional and educational backgrounds.[1] But for fifty years or more great interest has been attached to the religious allegiances. First, and most obviously, all early members of the Royal Society were Protestants. This is not surprising in view of the social and political conditions. What some people still find remarkable is that many of them were also Puritans; they are surprised that the tight-lipped, joyless exponents of an iron religious creed could ever unbend to consider such frivolities as scientific experiments, let alone have the wit to understand them. Yet that is only because 'Puritan' and 'puritanical' are given a totally unhistorical meaning today. The early Puritans, like Bunyan, did take their faith seriously, but they laughed and made music and love like anyone else, and they, more than their contemporaries, delighted in the world of nature.

Attempts to give a rigorous definition of 'Puritan' have often foundered for the simple reason that the term changed meaning over the years. From about 1560 to 1640 it was applied to members of the state church who sought to bring *all* its practice into line with Scripture and to abandon practices sanctioned by tradition alone. From 1640 to 1660 it tended to mean those like Baptists and Quakers who were outside the Church of England and maintained a radical biblical theology. From 1660 onwards it has greater imprecision, but is often applied to people like Independents and Presbyterians who were excluded from the Church of England and became 'nonconformists' or 'dissenters'. This confusion is a minefield for the unwary, and detailed studies often yield conflicting results merely because of this linguistic chaos. But few would deny that in some senses at least Puritanism was highly important for the early Royal Society.

One of the earliest attempts to discuss the role of Puritans in science was in 1935 when Dorothy Stimson examined the membership of the early Royal Society. Of the original members in 1663 she concluded that 42 out of 68 (62%) for whom such information was available had strong Puritan leanings. 'That experimental science spread as rapidly as it did in seventeenth century England seems to me to be in part at least because the moderate Puritans encouraged it.'[2]

Shortly after this R. F. Jones[3] cited many seventeenth-century writers who commented on the connection between science and religious reform, indicating a strong contemporary consciousness of 'the part which the Puritans played in furthering the values of science'. Then in 1938 the American sociologist R. K. Merton produced an epochal work, *Science, Technology and Society in Seventeenth Century England*, whose findings included that Puritan attitudes, at the very least, 'did much to encourage' the infant Royal Society.[4]

In spite of much criticism the essence of Merton's thesis has survived. Much depends on the precise definition of 'Puritan' and it is of interest to note that the people in 1663 to whom Merton applies this name were by that time Anglicans and might, therefore, be better styled 'ex-Puritans'. Counting heads in this way can indeed be a perilous exercise for, as Charles Webster points out, the procedures and definitions adopted largely determine the conclusion. It is, in Christopher Hill's words, an 'unreal dispute'. However, whether one considers the founding members of the Royal Society or those who played an active scientific role, the general conclusion is inescapable: they were men to whom the traditional Puritan values meant a great deal.

In more recent times this view has been amplified and expanded by Hill,[5] Webster[6] and Hooykaas.[7] True, there have been protests. T. K. Rabb, for instance, has denied that science, education and political change resulted from Puritan influence, but that all four were the product of radical thinking generally, occasioned by the political turmoil of the times, marked by the English Revolution, the Commonwealth and the eventual Restoration.[8] Yet even this does not deny the conformity that existed between Puritan and scientific thought, whatever the precise causal relationship between them, and that this conformity was appreciated by leading English men of science.

Other writers, notably B. Shapiro, have stressed the importance for science at this time of the more middle-of-the-road Latitudinarians.[9] These were Anglicans who espoused Calvinist theology but were less radical than the Puritans in their demands for reform. They include men like Grindal, Whitgift and Abbot. The fact of the matter is that during this tempestuous period of English history political allegiances shifted so rapidly and ecclesiastical divisions so altered that labelling individuals with precision is an almost impossible task. But again we need not despair. Underlying the bewildering variety of parties associated with science was a common core of biblical allegiance common to Puritanism, to the wider Calvinism and indeed to Protestantism as a whole. Of the resonance between that allegiance and the growth of science there can be no possible doubt.

Let us look at a few individuals. Francis Bacon occupies a central position in the early period. To be sure he had a Puritan mother, but according to Rabb he rejected her Puritanism. This may be justified by her own sad reflections on his spiritual state, by his own choice of a tutor at Cambridge (Whitgift), by his circle of friends and above all by his personal behaviour. R. Hooykaas observed 'though no Puritan himself, he had been educated in the spirit of Elizabethan Puritanism'.[10] And those values he was never to lose nor did he seem to want to do so. Christopher Hill has urged the centrality of Calvinist views in Bacon's thought, while Charles Webster has asserted that 'Bacon's philosophy seemed to be providentially designed for the needs of the Puritan Revolution'.[11]

Robert Boyle is another key figure to whom the term 'Puritan' has been denied, presumably because of his Royalist sympathies.[12] Yet, again to quote Hooykaas, he was 'a "Puritan at heart" if ever there was one'. Not only do his writings exude a spirit of biblical devotion and piety, they also harmonize exactly with the writings of others who more obviously bore the name Puritan. That 'God intended the world should serve man, not only as a palace to live in, and to gaze on but for a school of instruction' could have been the view of almost any Puritan writer at that time.

As a youth he had begun to question the formal Anglicanism in which he had been reared. His family motto 'God's proficence is mine inheritance' seemed too good to be true, but he was unable to dismiss as coincidence several remarkable deliverances from serious accident he had experienced. However, by his early teens he was searching for something more than an undemanding and comfortable faith in a God who merely hovered in the wings. The notion that God might have taken part in the drama of history in the person of Christ was fascinating, but was it true? One hot summer, while staying in Geneva, he found his answer. A violent thunderstorm awakened the sleeping youth to more than ordinary fear. Terrified that the judgment day was at hand he resolved, in his panic, to spend whatever might be left of his life in dedication to the service of God. He wrote 'Christ who long had lain asleep in his conscience (as he once did in the ship) must now as then be wakened by a storm'. It was the beginning of a pilgrimage which led quite quickly to a fully committed faith in Christ and in his redemption and forgiving grace. Though afterwards ashamed that fear should have been the spur, he never forgot his encounter during the storm at Geneva.

Boyle immersed himself in biblical theology. Writing an *Essay on the Scriptures* he urged their study in the original languages, to which end he learnt (in addition to Greek which he knew already) Hebrew and even Chaldee and Syriac. As he said, 'the truths [in the Bible] are so precious and important that the purchase must at least deserve the price.' In the spirit of that evaluation he later became closely associated with movements to make the Bible available to the Indians of North America as well as his fellow-countrymen in Ireland.[13] In missionary fervour he was indistinguishable from the Puritans who were behind that enterprise. Although supporting the restored monarchy and offered a peerage by Charles II, he declined the honour. He also refused the Lord Chancellor's pressing invitation that he should accept ordination, mainly because he lacked 'an inward motion to it by the Holy Ghost'. In this and in much else he was a Puritan in all but name. So it was in his science. On one hand he saw no conflict with faith: 'the seeming contradictions betwixt Divinity and true philosophy will be but few, the real ones none at all.' And on the other there was a positive duty to arrive at a knowledge of God's attributes, through 'the contemplation of his works and the study of his word'. Even after death these two enterprises were to remain united, in the Boyle Lectures which he endowed, using science to justify the ways of God to men.

In concentrating on Boyle we have been able to take advantage of the extensive literature he has left, scientific and religious. Most famous of all is his *Sceptical Chymist,* a truly seminal work in the history of chemistry. He wrote on the theory of colours, the 'spring' of the air (with Boyle's Law on gaseous pressures), respiration, gems, porosity and all manner of curious topics, such as a reflection 'upon his manner of giving meat to his dog'. Never reluctant to seize his pen, he poured forth tracts and memoirs on divine love, on the style of Scripture, on swearing and on the excellence of theology. Uniting his religious and scientific needs he wrote an important essay on *Final Causes* and also *The Christian Virtuoso* and much else. So we can speak with considerable confidence of Boyle's synthesis of science and faith. With him and many lesser figures in mind it is hard to disagree with the verdict of Charles Webster:

There is ample evidence to suggest that the entire Puritan movement was conspicuous in its cultivation of the sciences, that its members became vigorous proponents of a variety of new approaches to natural philosophy, and that...their scientific beliefs were framed with conscious reference to their religious views.[14]

We must now see where it was all to lead. Attention must be focused on another figure, greater than Boyle and perhaps than any other man in the world of science for two centuries.

Carving a new channel: the Newtonian universe

Isaac Newton was born in 1642 at Woolsthorpe Manor, near Grantham in Lincolnshire. His childhood, if rather unsettled, was otherwise unremarkable. After attending Grantham Grammar School he entered Trinity College, Cambridge where he eventually became a Fellow and, in 1669, Professor of Mathematics. His subsequent career gives little hint of the towering achievement of his Cambridge years. In 1696 he became Warden (later Master) of the Mint, was elected President of the Royal Society in 1703, received a knighthood in 1705 and died in 1727.[15]

Woolsthorpe, Newton's birthplace.

The date and circumstances of Newton's birth gave him a sense of personal destiny and divine mission that he was never to lose. He was born prematurely, a sickly child with poor prospects of survival. Like Isaac, his biblical namesake, he had experienced an almost miraculous deliverance. And like Jesus he never knew an earthly father, for his own had died three months before. He was, after all, born on Christmas Day and he had no qualms in making such comparisons. Much has been written to suggest that Newton's father-deprivation drove him with consuming zeal to seek his heavenly Father and to establish with him a special kind of relationship. Be that as it may, Newton was also well aware that the year of his birth was that of Galileo's death. On his shoulders, in a sense, fell the mantle of Galileo, the man who had first used the telescope to validate the Copernican theory and whose studies of falling bodies had constituted a foundation stone for classical mechanics. On that base Newton was later to erect his own epoch-making laws of motion. Underlying all these apparently fanciful ideas of divine mission lay a profound conviction that could be expressed in one word characteristic of Newton, his age and the central problem of science: Providence.

Newton's career at Cambridge, still quite undistinguished to even a close observer, was suddenly interrupted in 1665. News of the rapidly spreading Plague drove many from towns and cities to the safer countryside, and Newton returned to Woolsthorpe for nearly two years. There this tense and introverted scholar was able to unwind, and at last his genius began to be evident. Writing many years later he described events like this:

In the beginning of the year 1665 I found the Method of approximating series and the rule for reducing any dignity of any Binomial into such a series. The same year in May I found the Method of Tangents of Gregory and Slusius, and in November had the direct Method of Fluxions, and the next year in January had the Theory of Colours and in May following I had entrance into the inverse method of Fluxions. And the same year I began to think of gravity extending to the orb of the Moon and (having found out how to estimate the force with which a globe revolving within a sphere presses the surface of the sphere) from Kepler's rule of the periodical times of the Planets being in sesquialterate proportion of their distances from the centre of their Orbs, I deduced that the forces which keep the

Planets in their orbs must [be] reciprocally as the squares of their distances from the centres about which they revolve; and thereby compared the force requisite to keep the Moon in her Orb with the force of the gravity at the surface of the earth, and found them answer pretty nearly. All this was in the two Plague years of 1665–1666. For in those days I was in the prime of my age for invention and minded Mathematics and Philosophy more than at any time since.[16]

Even allowing for some exaggeration it is clear that in rustic seclusion Newton had discovered: the binomial theorem, the differential and integral calculus and the composite nature of white light. Surpassing all of these titanic achievements was one which, even more than they, altered the course of human history: the law of gravitation. Whether or not it was suggested by apples falling in the orchard, it was Newton who discovered that gravitational acceleration between two objects is inversely proportional to the square of the distance between them. Perhaps it is worth briefly explaining what Newton did.

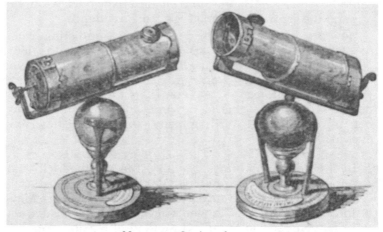

Newton's reflecting telescope.

First it must be stressed that the documentary evidence available suggests that, in this matter, Newton's memory was playing him tricks. It seems that even though he had certainly worked on the problem at Woolsthorpe it was finally settled many years later in 1680/1. Back in the 1660s he had no clear definition of mass and his ideas of force and inertia were still half-formed. As his latest biographer has put it:

Newton had caught sight of the dynamics that would crown and complete Galileo's kinematics; he had scarcely begun to examine its depths.... Some idea floated at the border of his consciousness, not yet fully formulated, not perfectly focused, but solid enough not to disappear. He was a young man. He had time to think on it as matters of great moment require.[17]

Suffice it to say that he had already begun to speculate whether the same force which brings down a falling apple might not also restrain the moon in its orbit and that an inverse square law of attraction might not be correct. When, many years later, Robert Hooke plied him with questions about planetary motion they included the query as to the shape of an orbit governed by the inverse square law. Several others, including Halley and Christopher Wren, had accepted the inverse square law but had been unable to confirm it. After much protracted calculation Newton came up with the answer in 1680: it was an *ellipse*. This, rather than a circle, had been the orbital shape demonstrated by Kepler in 1609, and it was also on the basis of Kepler's third law (that the cubes of the mean radii of planetary orbits vary with the squares of their periodic times) that Newton came to his triumphant conclusions.

The simple formula for gravitational attraction (a) between two masses (m_1 and m_2) separated by a distance r is:

$$a = \frac{m_1\, m_2}{r^2}$$

This formula, and Newton's associated three laws of motion, have been the foundation of celestial mechanics until subsumed in the even larger synthesis of Einstein. Even in the late seventeenth century it was clear that Newton had produced a system of no ordinary importance.

In the first place Newton's recognition of gravitational attraction between masses swept aside all the swirling vortices of matter by which Descartes had explained planetary motion. Newton's universe was no less *mechanical* than his, but more awesomely simple and a great deal emptier (save only for the all-pervasive weightless fluid called 'the aether' that was said to fill every nook and cranny of space). However, Descartes would surely have rejoiced to see the complete elimination of cosmic intelligences and other mystical paraphernalia that may have been the last lingering remnants of an organismic universe. Only the mysterious force of gravity acting over immense distances was left to remind people of the myriad occult forces which once were thought to control all things.

The fact that Newton demonstrated that the same laws hold for celestial and terrestrial phenomena, did not merely heap further scorn on the old Aristotelian division of the universe by the sphere of the moon, it also constituted a potent justification for the scientific credo in the idea of natural laws, and, moreover, on a universal scale. Boyle's comparison of the universe with a great clock was now seen, not as a fanciful literary flourish, but as a symbol of terrible appropriateness. If indeed the universe functioned entirely according to pre-determined laws, if in principle all physical events were entirely predictable, whatever was the role of God?

Sir Isaac Newton (1642–1726).

It happens that Newton thought he had an answer. His theology of nature was a complicated affair and varied to some extent with time. What does seem to have dawned gradually upon him was a conviction that, left to itself, the universe would somehow run down and needed therefore a 'replenish-ment of motion' which only God could supply. One might suppose that this implied the clockmaker was needed from time to time to rewind his instrument. The agency God could use to keep his 'cyclical cosmos' going might be those occa-sional if spectacular visitors to the earth's neighbourhood, the comets. By 1706 he believed that observed irregularities in planetary motion clearly indicated a 'running-down' of the machine and the necessity for divine intervention.

This conclusion led his great continental rival Leibniz to complain that such a universe implied an imperfect Creator, a second-rate clockmaker, incapable of making a machine that could run for ever. It was a very mean notion of the wisdom and power of God, who was thereby in effect reduced to the role of cosmic plumber, tinkering with a worn out machine.

To invoke the Deity to explain the otherwise inexplicable is a classic case of 'God-in-the-gaps'. But it is unfair to level this charge at Newton, for his God was so much more than that. However, as events turned out, this aspect of Newton's theology did rather backfire. In the course of the eighteenth century refined observation did in fact disclose that planetary orbits were not as irregular as Newton had feared, and his own gravitational law was sufficient to account for all the observed phenomena. At the end of the century the French astronomer Laplace demonstrated this with Gallic elegance in his *Système du Monde* (1796). The anecdote is often repeated that, when he presented a copy to Napoleon, the general asked about the place of God in his scheme; he is said to have replied, 'Sire, I have no need of that hypothesis.'

It is relevant to point out (a) that the story lacks documen-tation and is probably apocryphal, (b) that the alleged reply has nothing to do with theism but only with science, or (c) that in any case Laplace was a practising Roman Catholic. What is important is that by this time it was not necessary to invoke the Deity in physical theories and that theological explanations in science had been further discredited. The universe was more like a machine than ever.

However upsetting such conclusions might have been to simple-minded believers who heard them, they were in fact much more disturbing in science itself. This followed from one simple fact which we have already observed. The com-munity of science was, on the whole, deeply committed to a Christian ideology. This was obviously true of Puritan science in England. But it was no less the case with others whose theology was less radical and perhaps less precise. Much good work on electricity was performed in France during the seventeenth century, and almost all the practitioners were Roman Catholics. They, like those of Calvinist persuasion, were aware of the problem, though their anxiety was less because, presumably, their Newtonianism was held with less conviction. But everyone knew that trouble lay ahead.

Dangerous currents: nature and God

The dilemma posed by the success of the mechanical philosophy was, therefore, about the relation of God to his universe. How could it be apparently self-sufficient and yet under his control? Of the various solutions proposed none was *merely* a response to the challenge of mechanical philosophy, but each was given special point by the scientific issues, and arguments from science were fiercely employed on both sides of the disputes. Broadly speaking, five positions can be identified. They can be summarized as a series of propositions.

1. *Pantheism: God does not exist except as 'nature'*

This of course is the most radical solution of all. For practical purposes it was indistinguishable from atheism, which in the late seventeenth century was not just a quick way out. In England it was nourished by the burgeoning of free-thinking sects who, like their more orthodox counterparts, flourished during the Commonwealth. By 1690 it was sufficiently widespread to be deemed a threat to society (often because of a real or imagined connection between atheism and anarchy). So at least we may infer from the number of books and tracts published against it. In relative terms, however, its adherents must have formed a tiny minority. Men of science, so far as they noticed them, spoke with one voice against their beliefs. For that reason, or for others, they failed and atheism was never more than a disreputable curiosity in eighteenth-century England.

In France things were different. The *philosophe* movement arose early in the eighteenth century as a literary phenomenon. Its members followed in the steps of Fontenelle, Secretary of the Académie des Sciences, who combined a sceptical world-view and an intimacy with science. His successors developed a materialist philosophy which, as Butterfield observes, 'was encouraged by the obstructive attitude of the Roman Catholic clergy in France, who helped to strengthen the impression that the Church was the enemy of scientific discovery, and, indeed, of anything new'.[18] Although Descartes and his scientific heirs would have repudiated such views, they became endemic in the writings of d'Holbach, Diderot and other contributors to the great exposition of all knowledge, the *Encyclopédie*. If ever an era was grotesquely misnamed that was it: the 'Enlightenment'.

Title page of Cuvier's copy of Buffon's L'Histoire Naturelle *(1749).*

2. Deism: God created the universe and now leaves it to itself

This is deism. Like atheism it has its roots in the turbulent gatherings of Commonwealth days, and indeed in the materialist philosophy of Thomas Hobbes. It does not deny the existence of God and does not equate him with nature. Instead it limits his role to an initial act of creation.

In 1696 an ex-Presbyterian minister, John Toland, published the first major deist manifesto *Christianity not mysterious*. Thirty-four years later Matthew Tindal produced 'the Deist's Bible', *Christianity as old as creation*. During that period deism emerged as a powerful element in English life. It had two noteworthy features. First, it exalted reason above revelation and in so doing it downgraded to such an extent the biblical teaching about Christ that it was, for all practical purposes, unitarian. In this respect it resembled two much earlier heresies. Arianism dates back to the Alexandrian priest Arius in the fourth century who denied Christ's eternal Godhead and sinlessness. Socinianism was a sixteenth-century variant, though not disputing Christ's human perfection.

Secondly, it offered a solution to the 'interventionist' dilemma. A God who intervened in history neither in the incarnation nor in the day-to-day affairs of the world, would leave no traces of irregularity in a universe that worked according to its own laws. Presumably these laws were impressed upon matter at the moment of its creation:

> Yea, the first morning of Creation wrote
> What the last Dawn of Reckoning shall read.

As we might say, the universe was 'programmed' to work the way it does at the very beginning. The clockmaker invented the clock, wound it up and walked away.

Deism also became a prime target for clerical abuse. Unlike atheism, it managed to acquire an aura of respectability nevertheless, and it may be found in literature right up to today. Where it founders, then as now, is in its total incompatibility with almost the whole of biblical theology. The notion of an absentee Clockmaker is aeons away from an understanding of the God who leads his people, controls their destiny and answers their prayers. It is light-years removed from the God who becomes incarnate in Jesus.

3. *Semi-deism: God intervenes in the world on rare occasions*

This is a 'God-in-the-gaps' approach. God's interventions are only recognized when all other explanations fail. Newton, as we have seen, lent credence to this view with his invocation of

God when the laws of mechanics appeared to break down. It was taken up by numerous of his followers, such as Samuel Clarke, who urged 'an extraordinary interposition either of God himself... or at least of some intelligent agent far superior to man' (1705).[19]

A variant of this view had been widely held before science focused the question so sharply. This related to miracles, both in biblical times and later. Boyle did not believe God was bound to the orderly arrangements that he normally made. Thus he has 'vouchsafed to alter by miracles the course of nature, for the instruction or relief of man',[20] as in the survival of the three men in the fiery furnace of the book of Daniel. Nor did Boyle *suppose* that miracles ceased after the New Testament times; he saw them at work in the very evangelization of the New World in which he himself was active.

When applied to scientific problems the 'occasional intervention' model has been referred to by Hooykaas as 'semi-deism', and has persisted until our own day. He has located it in several later writers, particularly some geologists of the nineteenth century, such as William Buckland. In refutation of the position he cites the Victorian clergyman Charles Kingsley, who claimed that miracles are 'not arbitrary infractions but the highest development of that will of God whose lowest manifestations we call the Laws of Nature, though really they are no Laws of Nature, but merely customs of God'.[21] That, however, was two centuries after Newton's enforced isolation in Woolsthorpe. His great rival, Leibniz, put the matter even more succinctly:

> Sir Isaac Newton, and his followers, have also a very odd opinion concerning the work of God. According to their doctrine, God Almighty wants to wind up his watch from time to time: otherwise it would cease to move. He had not, it seems, sufficient foresight to make it a perpetual motion.[22]

Before we follow the logic of that position we should pause to note a rather interesting alternative view.

4. Human instrumentalism: God controls nature through humanity

The place of man in nature is a matter of perennial interest. In relation to the problem of Providence in a mechanistic universe it arises once more and in a curious way. A characteristically Puritan emphasis had been on man's position as viceroy to

God. If the world was really constructed in a deterministic fashion, was man the means whereby God constantly modified and adjusted the causal chains of events? Whether man's own actions were determined, and freewill was an illusion, did not seem crucial issues at this stage. In either event mankind could be God's agent for manipulating the material universe. The Calvinistic emphasis on divine sovereignty in predestination is, at very least, consistent with this view of man's instrumental role in the universe.

It is of course true that men cannot work miracles. There is still room for God to act directly. But in an otherwise deterministic universe man's every action will have cosmic consequences. As Francis Thomson wrote generations later:

> Thou canst not stir a flower
> Without troubling of a star.

Traces of this view are hard to identify precisely, probably because it must have seemed the least interesting aspect of 'the glory, jest, and riddle of the world' (as Alexander Pope described man). However, in an exposition on the Lord's Prayer, Samuel Clarke concluded that the phrase 'Thy kingdom' can mean 'a kingdom of glory' in the future, and a 'kingdom of grace', where God exerts dominion over the wills and actions of free agents.[23] Apart from the last phrase this was entirely consistent with contemporary Puritan prayers for the spreading of the kingdom of God by preaching and by mission.[24]

5. Radical Christian theism: God is the immediate as well as the ultimate cause of all phenomena in nature

The view of a radical theism that *all* natural phenomena depend on God was not at all new in the seventeenth century. It had been discussed by Church Fathers and was thoroughly in keeping with the whole biblical world-view. It seems at times to be present in the writings of Boyle, Clarke and others, but is overshadowed by the prevalent notion of a rule of law which does, indeed, make God redundant *as a scientific hypothesis*. To appreciate its full impact one needs to take a step back from the practice of science with all its day-to-day demands, and at the same time adopt a new openness to the overall teaching of Scripture. It is interesting that one of the clearest formulations of the view came from John Wesley who, though greatly interested in contemporary science and well-disposed towards it, had saturated himself in biblical doctrines. His views were widely shared as the eighteenth century developed and have been prominent ever since amongst those who still make the Bible their basis of faith.

Wesley was writing about a typical 'natural' disaster, an earthquake at Lisbon.

> If by affirming, 'all this is purely natural', you mean, it is not providential, or that God has nothing to do with it, this is not true, that is, supposing the bible to be true. For supposing this, you may discant ever so long on the natural causes of murrain, winds, thunder, lightning, and yet you are altogether wide of the mark, you prove nothing at all, unless you can prove, that God never works in or by natural causes. But this you cannot prove, nay none can doubt of his so working, who allows the Scripture to be of God. For this asserts in the clearest and strongest terms that *all things* (in nature) *serve him:* that (by or without a train of natural causes) he 'sendeth his rain on the earth', that he 'bringeth the winds out of his treasures', and 'maketh a way for the lightning and the thunder:' in general, that 'fire and hail, snow and vapour, wind and storm, fulfil his word.' Therefore, allowing there are natural causes of all these, they are still under the direction of the Lord of nature. Nay, what is nature itself but the art of God? Or God's method of acting in the material world? True philosophy therefore ascribes all to God.[25]

When modern insurance companies no longer attribute thunder storm strikes to an 'Act of God', they are not necessarily demonstrating atheism. They could be acting within the spirit of a radical Christian theism in which, not the occasional 'disaster', but *everything* is, in truth, an Act of God.

Notes for chapter five

[1] E.g. M. Hunter, *The Royal Society and its Fellows 1660–1700: The Morphology of an early Scientific Institution* (British Society for the History of Science, Chalfont St Giles, 1982).

[2] D. Stimson, 'Puritanism and the new philosophy in seventeenth century England', *Bull. Inst. Hist. Med.*, 1935, 3, 321–334 (334).

[3] R. F. Jones, *Ancients and Moderns* (St Louis, 1936).

[4] R. K. Merton, *Science, Technology and Society in Seventeenth Century*

98   *Cross-currents*

England (Harper and Row, 1970) (originally a long article in *Osiris*, 1938, 4, 360–632).

[5] C. Hill, *Intellectual Origins of the English Revolution*, rev. ed. (Oxford University Press, 1980).

[6] C. Webster, *The Great Instauration: Science, Medicine and Reform 1626–1660* (Duckworth, 1975).

[7] R. Hooykaas, *Religion and the Rise of Modern Science*, rev. ed. (Scottish Academic Press, Edinburgh, 1973).

[8] T. K. Rabb, 'Puritanism and the rise of experimental science in England', *J. World Hist.*, 1962, 7, 46, and later writings.

[9] B. J. Shapiro, 'Latitudinarianism and science in seventeenth century England', *Past & Present*, 1968, no.40.

[10] R. Hooykaas, (ref. 7), p.139.

[11] C. Webster, (ref. 6), p.514.

[12] On Boyle see R. Pilkington, *Robert Boyle, Father of Chemistry* (Murray, 1959); and R. E. W. Maddison, *The Life of the Honourable Robert Boyle* (Taylor and Francis, 1969).

[13] R. E. W. Maddison, 'Robert Boyle and the Irish Bible', *Bull. John Rylands Lib., Manchester*, 1958, 41, 81–101.

[14] C. Webster, (ref. 6), p.503.

[15] The latest (and best) biography of Isaac Newton is R. S. Westfall, *Never at Rest* (Cambridge University Press, 1980).

[16] This oft-quoted statement from a manuscript note about fifty years after the event is cited by R. W. Westfall, (ref. 15), p.143.

[17] R. S. Westfall, (ref. 15), pp.153 and 155.

[18] H. Butterfield, *Origins of Modern Science 1300–1800* (Bell, 1950), p.150.

[19] S. Clarke, 'A discourse concerning the unchangeable obligations of natural religion and the truth and certainty of the Christian revelation' (1705) in R. Watson (ed.), *A Collection of Theological Tracts* (1785), vol. iv, p.248.

[20] R. Boyle, *Some Considerations touching the Usefulness of Experimental Natural Philosophy* in *Collected Works* (1772), vol. ii, p.17.

[21] Letter to Sir William Cope, written on the eve of the 'arch-miracle' of Christmas, 1858; in *Charles Kingsley: his Letters and Memories of his Life* (3rd ed., 1877), vol. ii, p.67.

[22] H. G. Alexander (ed.), *The Leibniz-Clarke Correspondence* (N.Y., 1956), p.11.

[23] S. Clarke, *An Exposition of the Church Catechism* (1799), pp.249–250.

[24] I. H. Murray, *The Puritan Hope* (Banner of Truth Trust, 1975), pp.99–103.

[25] *The Works of the Reverend John Wesley* (1812), vol. xi, p.403.

6 Harnessing the river: making use of science

Thy voice produc'd the seas and spheres
Bid the waves roar and the planets shine;
But nothing like thyself appears,
Through all these spacious works of thine.

Isaac Watts (1674–1748), *Horae Lyricae* (1709)

For since the creation of the world God's invisible qualities –
his eternal power and divine nature – have been clearly seen,
being understood from what has been made, so that men are
without any excuse.

Romans 1:20

Practical uses of science: Nonconformists and technology

In St Patrick's Cathedral, Dublin, is a remarkable monument.
Erected in 1631, it perpetuates the memory of the first Earl of
Cork, father of Robert Boyle and of thirteen other children, all
of whom are depicted in its massive stonework. Despite its
solemn function it really is quite a cheerful affair, contrasting
strongly with the sombre memorial to the Cathedral's most
famous Dean, Jonathan Swift (1667–1745). Curiously, the Royal
Society in which Boyle played a prominent part evoked little
sympathy with 'the gloomy dean', who lost no opportunity to
pillory it in his immortal *Gulliver's Travels* (1726).

Gulliver is visiting the island world of Laputa (which
descends from the sky in the manner of a British Airways TV
commercial). Strangest among its many unusual features is
the 'academy' – a thinly veiled caricature of the Royal Society
or of Bacon's 'New Atlantis'. Here, he meets a man engaged
for eight years 'upon a project for extracting sunbeams out of
cucumbers', another seeking 'to calcine ice into gunpowder'
and yet another who had been for 'thirty years employing his

thoughts for the improvement of human life':

> He had two large rooms full of wonderful curiosities, and
> fifty men at work. Some were condensing air into a dry
> tangible substance, by extracting the nitre, and letting the
> aqueous or fluid particles percolate; others softening marble
> for pillows and pin-cushions; others petrifying the hoofs of a
> living horse, to preserve them from foundering. The artist
> himself was at that time busy upon two great designs; the
> first to sow land with chaff, wherein he affirmed the true
> seminal virtue to be contained, as he demonstrated by
> several experiments which I was not skilful enough to com-
> prehend. The other was, by a certain composition of gums,
> minerals, and vegetables, outwardly applied, to prevent
> the growth of wool upon two young lambs; and he hoped,
> in a reasonable time, to propagate the breed of naked sheep
> all over the kingdom.[1]

Whatever it was about the Royal Society that drew Swift's
venom, it is quite clear that he was perfectly aware of their
claim that science could be used to benefit mankind. At least
from Bacon onwards this had been an insistent note that could
hardly have been missed. So was it true?

Regretfully one has to confess that it was not. Science made
little difference to the lot of ordinary humanity until about
1850. Certainly exceptions can be traced, but the high Baconian
hopes, by and large, were doomed to be largely unfulfilled for
two centuries or more. Of course this does not deny that the
intention was there, though as fulfilment became increasingly
elusive one can readily understand why the utilitarian claims
for science became muted as time went on. People's motives
for doing science have usually been complex and there were
plenty of other reasons – particularly Christian reasons – for
pursuing it apart from material advantage.

However, there were some occasions where science, like a
rapidly flowing river, could be turned to good use in an
obvious and practical sense. Botany offers the most compelling
examples. The oldest natural history society in the world was
founded in London in 1689 and concerned itself with rural
expeditions to collect herbs useful for medicine, as had the
even older Society of Apothecaries. A wealthy merchant, Peter
Collinson, established a botanical garden and by the 1740s was
developing methods of cultivation for use in the American
colonies. His friend John Fothergill made a name for himself

not only in the epidemiology of diphtheria but also in the scientific study of rare plants from overseas. The application of botanical knowledge for the cultivation of plants in the New World was assiduously pursued by John Bartram who, in 1765, became Botanizer Royal for America.

These few examples are all from England, and all three individuals named were also members of the Society of Friends, or Quakers. They illustrate a connection that has often been pointed out between the application of science and Quakerism, a movement founded by George Fox (1624–91) and marked for many decades by simplicity of life, courageous independence, devotion to the Scriptures, strong social conscience and great solidarity amongst its members. It has been urged that the Quaker independence of thought and insistence on the unity of life 'produced the ideal mental attitude for the scientist'.[2] In education they, like other Dissenters, were excluded from Oxford and Cambridge, and in the Dissenting Academies their children were exposed to science teaching to a greater extent than anywhere else in England throughout the eighteenth century. Most famous of all their protégés was John Dalton (1766–1844), founder of the chemical atomic theory.

However, there are many reasons against concluding too rapidly that the application of science was notably favoured by a Christian ethic – a Quaker one in this case. The first is the trivial but obvious fact that Friends did not have a monopoly in exploiting scientific discoveries. Nicholas Culpeper's *Herbal* of 1653 had helped to establish modern pharmacology, while William Withering was one of England's leading botanists who, in his classic *Account of the Foxglove* (1785), described the immensely important medical uses of digitalis. But they were Anglicans. Then, of course, the Quaker community was virtually confined to England and America until the nineteenth century, so its relevance can easily be exaggerated. More important still is a further consideration. Admittedly the Quaker contribution to the Industrial Revolution and the growth of British industry was spectacular. In fact little of this contribution was directly founded on science.

Consider the famous Quaker clockmakers, such as the Bedfordshire-born Thomas Tompion whose clocks played an important role in the Royal Observatory (1676) and who became a close associate of early Fellows of the Royal Society. His was clearly a case of meticulous craftsmanship being turned to good use in science, rather than vice versa. His cylinder escapement (patented in 1695) and his almost frictionless clock mechanism owed little to scientific insight and everything to precise workmanship. Or again, the immense services of Abraham Darby to the iron industry seem to have originated in an almost accidental manner. In about 1707 this Quaker brassfounder discovered that charcoal could be replaced by coke in the smelting of iron. His iron-making business at Coalbrookdale was carried on by other members of the dynasty. The first iron bridge in the world (1777) still stands at what is, in truth, the cradle of the Industrial Revolution. Yet in all the prodigious expansion of the iron industry, with many other important innovations of Quaker provenance, there is hardly any evidence that the promoters saw themselves as applying science. What *is* characteristic of the Quaker enterprises, however, is an acute business sense which revealed itself not only in technology but in banking (Lloyds), chocolate-making (Rowntree, Fry, Cadbury), biscuit-making (Huntley and Palmer), pharmacy (Allen and Hanbury) and so on. In the nineteenth century Quakers became prominent in industries that *were* becoming science-based, such as soap-making (Crosfield), tanning (Richardson) and mining and assaying (Pattinson). And they were famed for their humane treatment of their work-force. But in so far as their characteristic ethic promoted the application of science, it did so in exactly the same way as for other kinds of knowledge and skills.

Coalbrookdale: cradle of the Industrial Revolution.

It is difficult to establish a precise connection between the Quaker ethic and the application of science; it is rather easier to do so for Nonconformity in general. Even here, however, the complex relation between science and technology indicates considerable caution.

Setting aside for a moment the important question as to how far eighteenth-century technology was science-based, we can easily perceive a significant Nonconformist contribution. To quantify this is much more difficult. In 1964 E. E. Hager attempted to identify the religious persuasions of leading industrial entrepreneurs in 1770. He concluded:

> The most striking contribution to the number of entrepreneurs...is that of the English Nonconformists. In contrast to their 7 per cent of the population of England and Wales, they contributed 41 per cent of the English and Welsh entrepreneurs whose religion is known, while the Anglicans, who constituted almost all of the remaining population, contributed only 58 per cent. The Nonconformists contributed about nine times as many entrepreneurs, relative to their total number in the population, as did the Anglicans.[3]

Since then he has been criticized on the basis of his selection, on some of his identifications, on the figure of 7 per cent for the Nonconformist population of England and Wales, and on the propriety of lumping together as 'Nonconformists' such a diversity of persuasions as Quaker, Baptist, Unitarian and so on. Yet when all this is said the great importance of Nonconformists will clearly remain, even if exact figures may be hard to obtain. Other studies have led to a similar conclusion.

Returning to the questionable role of science in the early Industrial Revolution, we should beware of over-simplifications. In Tawney's famous Lecture on the subject in 1884, science was totally ignored. Other writers have concurred with the apocryphal schoolboy's essay which began, 'About 1760 a wave of gadgets swept over England'! Others again have 'explained' the Industrial Revolution in purely economic terms. Most are now agreed that the contribution of science was, at best, patchy. Thus it is no longer possible to describe the invention of the steam engine as part of the scientific enterprise. Heroic tales of James Watt and his kettle, with a following exercise in Baconian induction, simply do not fit the facts. Indeed here as elsewhere science was indebted to technology, instead of the other way round, for out of practical experience with the steam engine was born that most arcane of modern sciences, thermodynamics. The Victorians had their reasons for propagating the myth, as we shall see, but myth it was.

However, as the eighteenth century drew towards its end science and technology grew closer together.[4] In France the extreme shortages of raw materials during the Revolutionary Wars brought Government pressure to bear on chemists to find alternative means for making saltpetre, soda and other desirable commodities. In 1774 an intensive programme of recognizably scientific research led the Swedish chemist C. W. Scheele to discover a new gas that was, by its bleaching action, within three decades to transform the European textile industry: chlorine.

In America, Benjamin Franklin applied electrical science to practical problems and invented the lightning conductor; Benjamin Rush, Professor of Chemistry at Philadelphia when only 23, learnt how to apply his subject to overcome the shortages occasioned by the War of Independence. Both signed the Declaration of Independence in 1776.

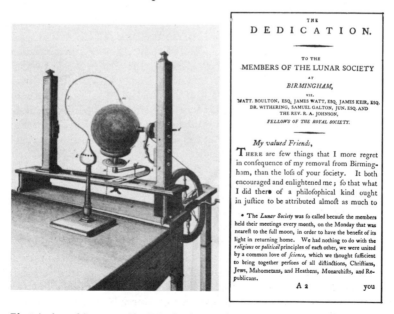

Electrical machine as used by Priestley for generating static electricity; a scientific pamphlet by Priestley (1793) and dedicated to members of the Lunar Society.

Meanwhile in England such knowledge of atmospheric electricity as the Royal Society had been able to acquire was being put to perfunctory use in the installation of lightning conductors on a few high buildings. Most notably a belief in the practical utility of science may be found enshrined in an extraordinary society in the Birmingham area from about 1750. This was the Lunar Society (so-called from its practice of meeting on the nearest Monday to the new moon). Its fourteen members included Erasmus Darwin (botanist, physician and grandfather of Charles), Matthew Boulton and James Watt (founders of the great engineering firm bearing their names), James Keir (manufacturing chemist), Josiah Wedgwood (of pottery fame), William Withering and Joseph Priestley (who discovered oxygen and invented soda-water). Their consuming interest was the application of science to industry or medicine. As one writer has said, they were 'a brilliant microcosm of that scattered community of provincial manufacturers and professional men who found England a rural society with an agricultural economy and left it urban and industrial... These men were the harbingers of the Industrial Revolution'.[5] This was an informal grouping, with no printed records, but we do know a good deal about the members. Two characteristics are immediately obvious. Although politics and religion were banned, in their discussions there was considerable commitment to political radicalism and a tendency towards Nonconformist Christianity. Most supported the American Revolution and (in its early stages) the French Revolution also. And there were several prominent non-Anglicans in their midst, most notably the Unitarian minister Joseph Priestley, whose political and religious radicalism led to the burning of his house and chapel by a 'Church and King' riot in 1791.

At the end of the century more formal institutions appeared with the application of science high on their agendas. In the Literary and Philosophical Societies of Manchester (1781) and Newcastle (1793) the same mixture of radicalism and dissent was visible from the first. Unitarians played a specially prominent part in the foundation of each, the Manchester Society meeting at first in a back room of Cross Street Chapel. Between all these institutions there was much intercourse and some overlapping membership.

It is hardly possible to overlook the continuity of Nonconformist influence on the growth of technology. As science assumed a more conspicuous role that influence continued to

be exerted, but inevitably one must ask whether its continuance owed anything at all to science or was merely a legacy of
past concerns with technology. And if we are dealing with
three variables (Nonconformity, science and technology), what
causal relations exist between them? The historical data point
clearly to a congruence, but are much less decisive in suggesting which favoured what.

If we take three variables (N, S and T) and assume only that
they are causally connected in some way, there are twelve
ways in which this could happen (the arrow means a causal
connection):

N—→S—→ T   N—→ T—→S

S —→T—→N   S —→N—→T

T—→S—→N   T—→N—→S

sequential

independent

Some of these seem unlikely, but historical analysis must be
open to any of them. At present it seems *likely* that those with
an asterisk will be most important, but much more research is
needed before we can be sure. Fortunately one thing is
abundantly clear. Between science, technology and English
Nonconformity in the eighteenth and nineteenth centuries
there has been a high degree of *congruity*. Had that not been
the case one could not have stimulated any other. That fact
alone is of abiding importance. It may become clearer by
considering just two of the variables (S and T) in the Industrial
Revolution.

Professor A. R. Hall has distinguished two possible
approaches to the science/technology relation. One, which he
calls 'realist', looks for 'precise examples of a technical
innovation's being derived consciously from pre-existent

Priestley's house sacked in the 'Church and King' riots of 1791.

theoretical knowledge of a non-trivial character' (*i.e.* science as often understood). The other 'nominalist' approach 'seeks to apply, in one formulation or another, the word *scientific* either to the process of technical change in the eighteenth century or at least to the mental habits of those who affected these changes'.[6] Much recent scholarship now favours the latter view. Scientific theories did not generate technical invention but were able to explain or rationalize it after the event. Above all it was a question of 'mental habits' or attitudes, an openness to new light, a sense of adventure, and a determination to wrestle with nature and control it.

If eighteenth-century science, or some of it, is looked at in that way, we can begin to see the relevance of Nonconformity. As Tawney wrote long ago of the outburst of industrial activity after 1760:

> Among the numerous forces which had gone to form it, some not inconsiderable part may reasonably be ascribed to the emphasis on the life of business enterprise as the appropriate field for Christian endeavour, and on the qualities needed for success in it, which was characteristic of Puritanism.[7]

To account for the specific harnessing of science for material benefit the same explanation may be offered. For the principal heirs of Puritanism were the Nonconformists, at least in England. Under the Wesleys, and perhaps more especially under Whitefield, the evangelical revivals were attended by a renewal of much distinctively Puritan theology. This, as we have seen, had already shown itself conducive to a scientific world-view. Moreover, to be a Nonconformist usually meant a deliberate opting-out of the Established Church, suggesting a certain independence of mind as well as moral courage. Both attributes are indispensable in the practice and application of science.

Of all the Nonconformist sects to be closely associated with technology at the end of the century, it is interesting that Unitarianism is the most prominent. With its relaxed (some would say 'loose') attitude to doctrine and its denial of the full deity of Christ, it is hard to see that this sect could claim to embody the essence of Puritanism. Yet its close links with science cannot be denied. How can this be squared with a 'Puritan' stimulus for science?

Perhaps we should not take too seriously our modern, rigid classifications. When a man, or a community, sheds some old-established beliefs (albeit crucial ones), values that went with them are not automatically jettisoned at once. In other words a general Puritan ethic may survive even the erosion of vital doctrines – if only for a time. Whether this consideration is very relevant to the Unitarian case is somewhat doubtful, as 'rational Dissenters' (as they were sometimes called) were largely unaffected by the Methodist revival. Of much greater importance is the fact that in the acquisition of wealth, the Unitarians were less inhibited than other groups of Dissenters. On this question Wesley asked his followers, 'How then is it possible for a rich man to grow richer, without denying the Lord that bought him?'[8] Baptists and Presbyterians were regularly warned against covetousness and the dangers of riches. Even the Quaker ironmaster Richard Reynolds confessed, 'I am at all times enabled to consider the things of this life in that degree of subordination and inferiority to the concerns of the next.'[9] But it has been argued that such attitudes to money-making by the application of science or in any other way are not commonly to be found amongst Unitarians at this time.[10]

If there is any truth in the argument above, it follows that no simple relation existed between the harnessing of science for

Priestley was often caricatured. This cartoon combines chemistry, politics and theology.

practical ends and the specific involvement of Nonconformists in that enterprise. But one other thing is clear. Science is best performed and applied in a spirit of rational, free enquiry, and historically this is derived directly from values enshrined in the Bible. The one thing that is true of *all* Dissenters is their rejection of formalized, ecclesiastical authority. Where, on a wider scale, this authority is seen to be limited, science may well flourish. At the other extreme, as in Spain and Italy, technology languished for far longer than in non-Catholic countries.

Ideological uses of science: natural theology

Looking back at the spectacular progress of science in the seventeenth century, we may well wonder at the curious manner in which it was applied. At first, as we have seen, this was hardly in a practical way at all. Its first large-scale applications were indirect and in the world of ideas. Science could be used to persuade or cajole men into certain desirable social attitudes. A good example is offered by the 'official' historian of the early Royal Society, Thomas Sprat. Writing at a time when political and religious differences had fragmented English society, he thought that discussions on affairs of state or 'spiritual controversies' would merely rub salt into the wounds of society and make matters worse. So he offered his own sovereign remedy:

> The most effective remedy to be used is, first to assemble about some calm, and indifferent things, especially Experiments. In them there can be no cause of mutual Exasperations: In them they may agree, or dissent without faction or fierceness and so from indulging each other's company, they may rise to a bearing of each other's opinions.[11]

Science, in other words, is a great reconciler. Such a claim for an ideological use of science will elicit a variety of responses. One may well blink in disbelief at the astonishing naivety embodied in so preposterous a proposal. If the ills of a world rent by division and strife were so easily curable, surely science would have demonstrated this over and over again? In fact it has done nothing of the kind, having apparently no more a reconciling function than (say) music, golf or any other kind of social activity. Sprat, however, was unable to share in our historical hindsight stretching over nearly three centuries; for him experimental science was still a novelty and his optimistic creed could not be falsified by later experience. In any case *The History of the Royal Society* was so sustained a piece of propaganda, intended to counter the hostility of people like Swift, that it was an obvious ploy to portray the Society's activities as conducive to the peace of the realm. That, however, has not inhibited some historians from repeating Sprat's platitudes as though they represented a determined strategy on the part of many who practised or taught at that period or even later.

There is another aspect of Sprat's apologia more revealing than his skill as a propagandist. It is the notion that peace on earth can be obtained, not through obedience to the gospel of Christ, but through the conduct of scientific experiments. Of course it is unfair to Sprat to suggest that he denied the reconciling force of the Christian faith, but in practice he does give this impression. We can only conclude that he, an Anglican and future bishop, regarded biblical studies as chiefly divisive, for had they not led to the rise of Nonconformity and the proliferation of dissenting sects? If that were true an additional, even an alternative, stabilizing influence was required. In this way he could defend not only science but also the Established Church.

Not all, however, were as convinced as Sprat that science was under threat. With the multiplication of extremist sects of all kinds, and increasing tendencies to atheism as well, it was now clearer than ever before that mainstream Protestant Christianity was in some danger. So there arose a phenomenon that was neither new nor peculiarly English in origin but became almost a national characteristic for two or more centuries. This was the sustained used of science to justify the claims of Christianity, a form of *natural theology*: 'from Nature up to Nature's God'.

1. *The rise of natural theology*

Natural theology in its broadest sense had existed since at least the Middle Ages. Elements of it may be traced back to the Greeks. It was at first concerned to demonstrate the existence of God from logic, the universal sense of moral values, the existence of the world, and so forth. In its narrower sense it argues for a Designer from the design and purpose in the world specially disclosed by science. This was the distinctive mark of natural theology from the seventeenth century onwards. It then became a consciously held, concerted attempt to use science not for *technological* but for *teleological* purposes (*e.g.* to argue for design). We must now see how it arose.

Once again we find a crucially important figure was Robert Boyle. He it was who gave such popularity to the famous analogy between the universe and a clock (see p.56). Unlike Descartes, who denied that the purposes of God ('final causes') could be discerned in nature, Boyle regarded it as 'a duty' to seek for them, and the opposite of presumption. This became a cornerstone of his strategy as he probed the world of living creatures for signs of 'the great Creator's wisdom' and paraded them in triumph against the hosts of atheism and unbelief. More remarkable still was the biological work of John Ray (1628–1705), described with some justification as 'the father of natural history'. A Fellow of Trinity College, Cambridge, he resigned from Anglican Orders after the Act of Conformity of

1661, thereafter devoting his time to a study of the plant and animal kingdoms. His book of 1691, *The Wisdom of God in the Works of Creation*, reflected not only his immense erudition but also his deep Christian commitment. This was the book, according to C. E. Raven, 'which more than any other determined the character of the interpretation of nature till Darwin's time'.[12] These are Ray's remarks about the camel:

> That such an animal as this, so patient of long thirst, should be bred in such droughty and parched countries, where it is of such eminent use for travelling over those dry and sandy deserts, where no water is to be had sometimes in two or three days' journey, no candid and considerable person but must needs acknowledge to be an effect of Providence and Design.[13]

The promotion of natural theology by Boyle was not only assured during his lifetime; it was guaranteed by a codicil to his will. This document (July 1691) established a Boyle Lectureship 'for proving the Christian religion against notorious infidels, viz. atheists, theists [deists], pagans, Jews, Mahometans, not descending lower to any controversies that are among Christians themselves'. Boyle was just in time. Five months later he died, and the restless society of post-Restoration England was an ideal audience for Lectures which, whatever their original intent, might offer some pointers to stability, unchanging truth and eternal certainty. A new and powerful tool lay ready to hand, the massive and austere synthesis of natural knowledge achieved by Isaac Newton. The Boyle Lectures were to become the first popular expositions of Newtonianism. It has also been argued that they helped to underpin the social ideology of the Established Church at that time (a debatable point, briefly considered later, p.123). What is much more significant is that beyond doubt they ratified and strengthened the programme for Christian apologetics espoused by their founder.

The first Boyle Lecture was delivered by Richard Bentley: 'A confutation of atheism from the origin and frame of the world.' Bentley (1662–1742) was then the ambitious young chaplain to the Bishop of Worcester; eventually he became Master of Trinity College, Cambridge. A classical scholar, he corresponded at length with Newton himself for information on scientific and philosophical issues. In his first reply Newton confided:

When I wrote my treatise about our system [*Principia*] I had an eye upon such principles as might work with considering men for the belief of a Deity and nothing can rejoice me more than to find it useful for that purpose.[14]

In that spirit Bentley urged 'that universal gravitation, a thing certainly existent in nature, is above all mechanism and material causes, and proceeds from a higher principle, a Divine energy and impression' and that 'the present frame of sun and fixed stars could not possibly subsist without the Providence of that almighty Deity "who spake the word and they were made"'.[15]

A Boyle Lecture by John Williams, Bishop of Chichester, emphasized the regularity of law in nature and also God's occasional suspension of such law as in the inspiration of the biblical authors. His insistence on the importance and veracity of Scripture demonstrates that not all Boyle Lecturers wished to underplay the role of revelation. Some indeed hovered on the very fringes of heresy, as William Whiston (whose Lecture sought to show that fulfilment of biblical prophecies was made credible by Newton's natural philosophy). He was dismissed from his Cambridge Chair of Mathematics on a charge of Arianism. Samuel Clarke, who lectured in 1704 and 1705, appears to have held similar views, though with greater discretion. He it was who later defended Newton's world-view in correspondence with Leibniz (see p.91).

Of the other Boyle Lecturers little need be said, with the one exception of William Derham (1657–1735). His *Physico-Theology* attempted a comprehensive search for signs of purposive design in nature, concluding 'that the works of God are so visible to all the world, and withal such manifest indications of the being and attributes of the infinite Creator, that they plainly argue the vileness and perverseness of the atheist, and leave him inexcusable.'[16] Especially was he struck by the suitability of 'the terraqueous globe' for the habitation of man.

The Boyle Lectures were enormously successful, judging by the number of times they were reprinted and the tributes to them by men of letters through the century. Naturally they were imitated and the flood of similar books included such unlikely titles as *Water Theology*, and even *Insect Theology*. This kind of literature reached its climax in the *Natural Theology* of William Paley (1743–1805), first appearing in 1802 and still being studied in the twentieth century. The tradition was continued beyond Paley with the famous Bridgewater Treatises, 'On the power, wisdom and goodness of God, as manifested in the creation.' They were endowed by a bequest from Francis Egerton, eighth Earl of Bridgewater (1756–1829). Contributors included Thomas Chalmers (Scottish theologian), William Whewell (philosopher, scientist and Master of Trinity College, Cambridge), Sir Charles Bell (surgeon and anatomist), William Buckland and William Prout (chemist).[17] Darwin notwithstanding, natural theology is by no means dead even in our own time.

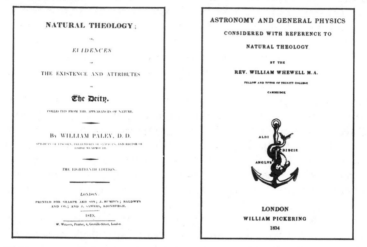

Title pages from William Paley's Evidences, *and one of the Bridgewater Treatises.*

2. The basis of natural theology

Throughout the eighteenth century science was frequently used in this way to support the Christian faith. Its basis lay in a decisive shift in the balance of importance accorded to *revelation* and *reason*, with a swing towards the latter.[18] Natural theology was a typical feature of the new age that was dawning, the so-called Enlightenment. Its most distinctive mark was a conviction that man could now discover more about the world by the rational pursuit of scientific enquiry than by listening to the advocates of revealed religion. After all, it seemed, the interpreters of Scripture had more than once been confounded by empirical knowledge. And if this were true of nature, might it not also be true of everything else, including God?

The polarization between 'revelation' and 'reason' is often misunderstood. It was not a contrast between what we might

call 'rationality' and 'irrationality'. In other words it was not
about an attitude of mind. Rather it was concerned with the
sources of knowledge, with the raw data from which our
understanding of the world must be constructed. Was knowledge of this kind to be obtained from empirical enquiries
('reason') or from the Bible ('revelation')? In either case all the
resources of rational thought would need to be applied to
whichever data-base was selected. After all, the philosopher
John Locke wrote of *The Reasonableness of Christianity* (1695)
and asserted that '*Revelation* is natural *reason* enlarged by a
new set of discoveries communicated by God immediately,
which *reason* vouches the truth of, by the testimony and
proofs it gives that they come from God.'[19]

This idea that 'revelation is natural reason enlarged' suggests
that the Bible gives a kind of close-up enlargement of things we
could also perceive in quite other ways. Possibly, as Calvin
suggested, our reason is distorted by sin, so the Scriptures
give not only a magnified but also a corrected picture, rather
like certain kinds of spectacles. In any event the two pictures
are clearly different, and in the eighteenth century their relative
importance changed dramatically. If science had now shown
natural things to be so much more accessible to reason, could
this not also be true of divine things? Could there in fact be a
whole theology derived from science itself? Such a *natural
theology* was not new, as we have seen, but in the eighteenth
century it burst forth with almost explosive energy and, for a
time, surpassed revealed theology in prominence. It represented, far more than the rhetoric of a Sprat, a major ideological
application of science.

Given that natural theology depended so much on the
capacity of unaided human reason, how far was it dependent
upon revelation? In fact, very little, though the extent of its
independence varied with individuals. There were those, for
instance, who gave it such autonomy that they were free to
launch the bitterest attacks on the Christianity of the Bible.
These were the deists, emphatic on a once-for-all creation by a
now remote Deity whose imprint could nevertheless be clearly
perceived in nature. Tindal thought true Christianity was
merely 'a republication of the religion of nature', while Voltaire
believed what now passes for the gospel was 'nothing more
than the perversion of natural religion'.

Others, however, accepted the independence of natural from
revealed religion but hoped that one would lead to the other. In
practice this often meant that revelation was crowded out, as in

Wilkins' *Of the Principles and Duties of Natural Religion*, where it was relegated to the final chapter and then in an emasculated form. Another bishop, Joseph Butler, actually said that natural religion was 'the foundation and principal part of Christianity'. Not surprisingly this downgrading of revelation led to a grotesque distortion of biblical doctrine.

It must be stressed that there is nothing inherently incompatible between natural and biblical theology. Numerous references in the New Testament, especially, assign a definite if limited role to evidences for God to be found in the external world.

The apostle Paul argued with the Greeks on the basis of their own experience, even citing their own literature and drawing deductions from it (Acts 17:22–29); he even adds the now direct revelation of God in Christ (vv.30–32). Elsewhere he proclaims that for everyone God's 'eternal power and divine nature have been clearly seen, being understood from what has been made', so those who ignore such evidence are 'without any excuse' and worthy of the wrath of God (see Romans 1:18–23). Yet with equal plainness he has just acknowledged his debt to the gospel, 'For in the gospel a righteousness from God is *revealed*' (v.17). Richard Bentley placed at the head of his sermon[15] Paul's reminder to the Lycaonians that God has not left himself without witness in the natural world (Acts 14:17). Scripture itself, therefore, testifies to a limited role for natural theology, but makes it subservient to the truth which God has revealed through prophets, apostles and above all through Jesus Christ.

3. The critique of natural theology

The use of science to justify the Christian faith, and the extensive employment of the argument from design, did not escape criticism as the century passed. Natural theology was assailed on grounds of philosophy and logic, of theology and (eventually) of science itself. We shall look briefly at the first two assaults now and at the last one in the following chapters.

First, there were *philosophical* objections. These were canvassed in considerable detail by David Hume in his posthumous *Dialogues concerning Natural Religion* (1779). The arguments were complex and, it has to be said, cut little ice at the time. Later they have been taken far more seriously. It is quite impossible to do them justice here, but we can notice one or two important aspects that became apparent to many of

Hume's contemporaries.

Most obvious of all was the danger of circular argument. For example, it was common to deduce the Unity of God from the universality of scientific law. Said William Whiston in his *Astronomical Principles of Religion* (1717): 'The universe appears thereby to be evidently one universe, governed by one law of gravity through the whole'; consequently we may infer one God as its Creator, a belief 'now for ever established by that more certain knowledge we have of the universe'.[20] Yet it does appear that the universality of physical law was a presupposition made by Newton as a corollary to his own theological convictions!

Another instance of apparent circularity appears in the approach to the inexplicable in nature. Given that a Designer could be inferred from clear signs of 'design' in nature, what of those natural phenomena which appeared to have no purpose at all? One has to think only of the enormous prodigality and apparent waste in the natural world – the huge proportion of ungerminating seeds, unfertilized eggs, or of stars which cannot even be counted.

To this dilemma there were two approaches. One was merely to plead ignorance and take refuge in the inscrutability of divine wisdom. Thus Derham concludes his reply to objectors with the words of Paul, 'Nay but, O man, who art thou that repliest against God?' (Romans 9:20, AV). Such a response is perfectly acceptable provided one has first accepted that God exists and has created the universe. But that is precisely what Derham (and many others) set out to prove.

The other approach in the face of apparent purposelessness in nature was to explore the facts in greater detail to see if this were actually the case. Such a challenge would – and did – generate a great deal of extra research activity and evinces yet another theological motive for 'doing science'.

One could not find a better example of this than John Ray, especially when confronted with the problem of multitudes of seemingly useless and unpleasant creatures like insects. Confidently Ray would proclaim that 'because so many creatures live upon ants and their eggs, Providence hath so ordered it that they should be the most numerous of any Tribe of Insects that we know'. He could also find reasons for the production of 'noxious insects': they were food to other creatures, they could yield medicines for humanity, and they could even be a scourge in the hand of God for the wicked.[21] One might wonder whether any puzzling phenomenon in nature would leave him speechless. In fact it would not, for the simple reason that he was not concerned to derive a doctrine of God from mechanical philosophy. What he was trying to do was to show that a prior belief in a beneficent Designer was entirely consistent with nature as we see it, though not necessarily in a purely Newtonian sense. As a biologist of the first rank he was more aware than most of the difficulties of a purely mechanical explanation of living things and he did not tie himself to such categories. Considerations of function and teleology are, however, dominant even when applied to such 'a poor and contemptible quadruped' as a mole. Relating her sense of sound, shortness of limb and breadth of forefeet to her sub-terranean habits he asks, 'What more palpable argument of Providence than she?'[22] What indeed, provided always that *on other grounds* such conviction could be held with confidence?

Yet Ray was guilty of far less circularity of argument than this might suggest. He was saying in effect: here are many phenomena of nature where design is so clear that a Designer is surely implied; there are others where design emerges on deeper inspection; and if there are some for which this has not yet appeared to be the case, let us suspend judgment mean-while. He does *not* argue from a few limited examples, but ranges over an immense area of natural history. And in this respect he is surely being true to the spirit that has come to characterize science. If anomalies occur, explore them, try to explain them, and (if you fail) do not overturn the whole theoretical framework until they are seen to be of compelling importance. Keep them in view by all means, but also keep them in proportion.

If circularity was more obvious in arguments about uni-versality of scientific law or about the inexplicable in nature, it was most dangerous in questions of value and morality. These concerned evidence not for the wisdom of God but for his goodness. Given the apparent suffering in nature, how could one infer a benevolent God? Again the answer could reside in our ignorance, as Derham protested. It was also possible to argue that pain and suffering in the insect world, for example, was an illusion.

Paley was even able to affirm, 'It is a happy world after all,'[23] but his intellectual contortions to minimize human pain stretched credulity to its limits. Voltaire, in *Candide*, argued caustically that the earthquake in Lisbon undermined this whole approach.[24] Basil Willey has trenchantly summarized this whole aspect of natural theology as 'cosmic Toryism':

whatever is, is best.[25]

All these objections, and more, found their way into the onslaught on natural theology initiated by Hume. At the root of his objection lay the insistence that we cannot logically infer a Creator for our world, since we have no experience of the creation of any other. Beneath this lay his notion of causality. We cannot say one event caused another unless there have been instances of the two occurring together. Even then we cannot infer a physical necessity uniting the two events. Hume's objections deserve far more space than we have for them. But one thing must be added. The very logic which so relentlessly attacked the argument from design was also in danger of undermining the whole scientific enterprise. Dr John Brooke has written:

> If there really were no physical ties between causes and effects, if, as has sometimes been said, there were no grooves in the universe, if, as Hume himself said, all events in nature were 'loose and separate', then what guarantee had the scientist that his laws of nature were binding? It is a stern reminder of the close harmony of science and belief among the physico-theologians that, in order to impugn the rationality of their natural theology, Hume had to impeach the rationality of their science.[26]

A sceptic in matters religious, Hume was also a sceptic in matters scientific.

If the natural theology of the eighteenth century could be questioned on the grounds of its own internal logic, it was also vulnerable to attack from the supporters of biblical theology. The reasons could hardly be more obvious. Despite its sanction by Scripture, the actual practice of natural theology was accompanied by a downgrade of revelation to such an extent that Christianity became reduced to the arid precepts of Deism. Alan Richardson has graphically put it thus, if with some measure of rhetorical overstatement:

> Neither in Butler nor in his contemporaries is there any awareness at all that the heart of Biblical religion is the proclamation of the saving acts of God in history, or that Christianity began as the proclamation of an historical event and not as the republication of the religion of nature.[27]

The God of Deism does not interfere in nature; still less would he break into human history. The incarnation being incredible in such a system, Trinitarian theology was rendered super-fluous and the road to Unitarianism made open. By the same token, a non-intervening absentee God would not work miracles, so the resurrection was denied by those who followed this road to its very end. A natural theology intended as pre-evangelism might turn out to undermine the very basis of evangelism itself by denying the evangel.

To a modern Christian this all seems to have been so dis-tressingly unnecessary. Yet recent pronouncements by David Jenkins, Don Cupitt and others simply emphasize how per-sistent such ideas can be. To the historian the developments are less surprising when seen against the backcloth of the 'Age of Reason' which, in France, can be seen free from the very English tendency to view nature theologically. By exalting man and his reason the authors of the *Encyclopédie* succeeded better than they knew in relegating religion to the museum. The radical scepticism – and despair – generated by the *ad hoc* exclusion of God except as First Cause might justify a new ascription: The Age of Benightenment.

Of course there were reactions to the cult of reason. In literature the Romantic revival was exactly that. The 'age of prose and reason' was to give place to the poetry of Wordsworth and Coleridge. Reactions may even be perceived in changing attitudes to garden layout, mountain exploration and to scenery (see ch.9).

In religion itself Newtonian natural theology was not so much opposed directly as challenged by more biblical alter-natives. Two may be mentioned.

One was the *natural philosophy of John Hutchinson* (1674–1737), Steward to the Duke of Somerset.[28] Deeply interested in Hebrew originals of the Old Testament as well as in palaeon-tology, he produced an alternative synthesis of science and theology that differed in several ways from Newton's. He had a strong Trinitarian emphasis, thinking the three Persons of the Trinity might correspond to fire, light and air; he denied that space was God's 'sense-organ' (as Newton had suggested), believing it rather to be filled with an ethereal fluid through which action was transmitted; he stressed the transcendence of God and so avoided the suggestion of pantheism present in Newton's thought; he emphasized the sovereignty of God behind *all* phenomena, not least in the incarnation.

Hutchinsonianism became well known in the 1730s and was favoured by many of High Church persuasion. These constituted the majority of English clergy (though not bishops) and were also strong in the episcopal church in Scotland. Hutchinson's teaching, with its emphasis on revelation and experience, resonated well with the Augustinian theology that was at that time dominant in the High Church. It offered a more attractive blend of science and religion than Newtonian natural theology, though its apologetic utility was much less.

As a major force in history, Hutchinsonianism bears no comparison with the other movement to challenge the pretensions of natural theology. This was the *evangelical revival* associated initially with the names of Whitefield and the Wesleys. What intellectual argument could not begin to do, the preaching of these men accomplished on a truly awesome scale. Multitudes of ordinary men and women who had probably never heard of the argument from design, and certainly knew nothing of universal gravitation, were drawn into the kingdom of God by an even greater attraction. Amongst many other things the revival meant a rediscovery of Scripture, both by the learned and the ignorant.

The Wesleys did not spend much time combating the religion of nature. John had early been advised by a Moravian friend, Peter Bohler, 'this philosophy of yours must be purged away', though he confessed 'I understood him not'.[29] This has been suggested as 'an emphatic repudiation of natural theology'.[30] Like Calvin, he accepted man's reason was sinfully corrupt for 'sensual appetites, even those of the lowest kind, have, more or less, the dominion over him. They lead him captive; they drag him to and fro, in spite of his boasted reason'.[31] As for nature, Charles Wesley saw little hope in that:

> Long my imprisoned spirit lay
> Fast bound in sin and nature's night;
> Thine eye diffused a quickening ray,–
> I woke! The dungeon flamed with light;
> My chains fell off, my heart was free,
> I rose, went forth, and followed Thee.[32]

Yet for all the irrelevance of natural theology for his life work John Wesley was far from unsympathetic to science. He was familiar with the writings of Hutchinson and his followers, he read widely in *Philosophical Transactions* and other scientific literature; after seeing experiments performed by the Anglican minister of Teddington, Stephen Hales (a pioneer in plant physiology), he exclaimed, 'How well do philosophy [science] and religion agree in a man of sound understanding!'[33]

As for natural theology, it took an important new turn in response to the evangelical revival. The agent for this change was an Anglican minister, James Hervey (1713–58),[34] who came under the influence of Whitefield and the Wesleys while at Oxford, and in 1741 became a convinced evangelical. Much attracted to Newtonian natural theology (he once concluded gravitation 'is only another name for the action of God our Saviour upon all matter in the universe'), he now began to modify his ideas in a series of best-selling books. These included such titles as *Reflections on a Flower Garden, A Descant on Creation, Contemplations on the Starry Heavens,* and others with similar themes. Although verbose and florid in places his writing has plenty of detailed allusions to the world of nature. Like any other natural theologian he exclaims, 'The heavens are nobly eloquent of the Deity, and the most magnificent heralds of their Maker's praise.'[35] But a glance at almost any page will reveal a radical new departure. He writes:

Stephen Hales (1677–1761), Perpetual Curate of Teddington, and natural theologian William Paley (1743–1805).

If the goodness of God is so admirably seen in the works of nature, and the favors of Providence, with what a noble superiority does it even triumph in the mystery of redemption![36]

For Hervey nature is no mere demonstration of a Designer's skill; it is a rich repository of spiritual truth. So the opening of flowers to the sun is a parable of the Christian's turning to God, and the 'immense expanse' of the heavens a reminder of the divine condescension to man. Ingeniously, the diurnal and annual motions of the earth suggest a compatibility between the religious and worldly concerns of the believer! Most remarkably Hervey's treatment is thoroughly Christo-centric. Speaking of the flowers he says Christ made them, recovered them (after the fall), upholds them and actuates them.[37]

If Hervey was not the first to give this new turn to natural theology, at least he thought that some might regard it as 'unprecedented' to represent God's attributes as 'shining with more distinguished lustre in the wonders of redemption than in the works of creation'.[38] The old-style natural theology persisted a surprisingly long time, but from now on this particular use of science was decreasingly important for those Christians committed to a biblical and evangelical under-standing of the world. Matters had certainly changed since the days of Boyle.

4. *The abuse of natural theology*

Until recently it has been fashionable in some places for claims to be made that natural theology was primarily pursued for socio-political, as opposed to religious, ends. In so far as that might be true it would be a travesty of natural theology as depicted by St Paul or advocated by Robert Boyle and kindred spirits. To that extent it is, therefore, an abuse. The prior question, however, is whether it ever happened. Since the matter has been recently discussed elsewhere[39] the briefest outline will follow here.

It has been suggested by Margaret Jacob that the Boyle Lectures were used by the 'Latitudinarians' of the Church of England to underpin the social order after the Restoration.[40] While it is widely agreed that many of these churchmen were ardent Newtonians, and that the social and natural orders are sometimes connected in their works, that is not sufficient evidence for her claim. That claim is repeated many times and with increasing confidence, but definitive evidence is not merely thin; it is simply not there. Indeed she undermines her whole case by an admission that she finds it incomprehen-sible either that the debate was 'centred essentially on intel-lectual issues' or that it was 'only simple Christian piety that was at stake'. And why should that not be true? Only if such debates *must* be socio-political in essence – a position as arbitrary as that of any natural theologian and just as inclined to circularity. Until unambiguous evidence is available that does *not* depend on that presupposition we can assume the primary purpose – however misguided – was to use science to defend a faith under threat.

Natural theology books were also evident over a century later in the Mechanics' Institutes of Britain. Several writers have informed us that their purpose was to help intimidate and thus control the unruly masses who flocked to the Institute in the troubled years of the early nineteenth century. A study of nature, rather than of abstract theology, would awe into reverence and docility.

Such a suggestion is not quite as silly as it sounds, for references to the orderliness of creation abound in the surviving literature. One may wonder, however, what a working man would make of arguments of any degree of abstraction after a long day's toil. In fact there is some evidence that this role for science was viewed with some alarm. Lord Brougham (who brought out a new edition of Paley's *Natural Theology*) recognized concern 'lest the progress of natural religion should prove dangerous to the acceptance of the revealed'. And the London Mechanics' Institute refused to allow rooms to be used by the so-called Christian Evidence Society, presumably on account of its deistic character. In this case, at least, a socio-political function for natural theology, and thus for science, did not take place.

Notes for chapter six

[1] J. Swift, *Gulliver's Travels*, Pt.3, Ch.V.

[2] A. Raistrick, *Quakers in Science and Industry* (David and Charles, 1968), p.346.

[3] E. E. Hager, *On the Theory of Social Change* (Dorsey Press, Homewood, Ill., 1961), p.297. The figures assume 3% of the population groups as Catholic, Jewish, *etc.*

[4] There is an immense literature on the Industrial Revolution. The role of science is discussed in A. E. Musson and E. Robinson, 'Science and industry in the late eighteenth century', *Econ. Hist. Rev.*, 1960, *13*, (2), 222–244; A. Thackray, 'Science and technology in the Industrial Revolution', *Hist. Sci.*, 1970, *9*, 76–89; A. and N. L. Clow, *The Chemical Revolution* (Batchworth Press, 1952).

[5] R. E. Schofield, *The Lunar Society of Birmingham* (Oxford University Press, 1963), p.1.

[6] A. R. Hall in N. McKendrick (ed.), *Historical Perspectives: Studies in English Thought and Society* (Europa Publications, 1974), p.129.

[7] R. H. Tawney, *Religion and the Rise of Capitalism* (Pelican, 1948), p.270.

[8] John Wesley, *Sermons on Several Occasions*, First Series (Epworth Press, 1967), p.318.

[9] Cited in B. Trinder, *The Industrial Revolution in Shropshire* (Phillimore, 1973), p.198.

[10] C. Elliott, 'The ideology of economic growth: a case study', in E. L. Jones and G. E. Mingay (eds.), *Land, Labour and Population in the Industrial Revolution* (Arnold, 1967), pp.76–99.

[11] T. Sprat, *The History of the Royal Society* (1667), p.426.

[12] C. E. Raven, *Natural Religion and Christian Theology* (Cambridge University Press, 1953), p.110.

[13] J. Ray, *The Wisdom of God Manifested in the Works of Creation*, 9th edition (1727), p.344.

[14] Letter dated 10 December 1692, in *Four letters from Sir Isaac Newton to Doctor Bentley containing some arguments in Proof of a Deity* (1756), p.1.

[15] R. Bentley, *A Confutation of Atheism from the Origin and Frame of the World* (1693), pt.3, pp.32 and 38.

[16] W. Derham, *Physico-Theology: or a Demonstration of the Being and Attributes of God, from His Works of Creation*, New Edition (1798), vol.ii, p.396 (First edition, 1713).

[17] See D. W. Gundry, 'The Bridgewater Treatises and their authors', *History*, 1946, *31*, 140; 1947, *32*, 122; 1948, *33*, 125; and W. H. Brock, 'The selection of the authors of the Bridgewater Treatises', *Notes and Rec. Roy. Soc.*, 1966, *21*, 162.

[18] On natural theology and 'the demise of revelation' see J. Dillenberger, *Protestant Thought and Natural Science* (Collins, 1961), pp.133–190.

[19] J. Locke, *The Reasonableness of Christianity* (1695).

[20] W. Whiston, *Astronomical Principles of Religion* (1717), p.131.

[21] J. Ray, (ref. 13), pp.372–373, 374–375.

[22] *Ibid.*, p.142.

[23] W. Paley, *Natural Theology*, 18th edition (1819), p.376.

[24] Compare Wesley's reaction (p.97).

[25] B. Willey, *The Eighteenth Century Background* (Pelican, 1972), p.47.

[26] J. H. Brooke, 'Natural Theology in Britain from Boyle to Paley', Units 9–10 of O.U. Course AMST283, 'Science and Belief: from Copernicus to Darwin' (Open University Press, Milton Keynes, 1974), p.45.

[27] A. Richardson, *The Bible in the Age of Science* (SCM Press, 1964), p.38.

[28] See G. N. Cantor, 'Revelation and the cyclical cosmos of John Hutchinson' in L. J. Jordanova and R. Porter (eds.), *Images of the Earth* (British Society for the History of Science, Chalfont St Giles, 1979), pp.3–22; and C. B. Wilde, 'Hutchinsonian Natural Philosophy and Religious Controversy in Eighteenth Century Britain', *Hist. Sci.*, 1980, *18*, 1–74.

[29] Wesley's *Journal*, 18 February 1738.

[30] M. Schmidt, *John Wesley: a Theological Biography*, Eng. trans. by N. P. Goldhawk (Epworth Press, 1962), vol.i, p.235.

[31] J. Wesley, (ref. 8), p.509.

[32] C. Wesley, hymn 'And can it be . . . ?'.

[33] Wesley's *Journal*, 3 July 1753.

[34] Hervey's natural theology is discussed in C. A. Russell, *Science and Social Change, 1700–1900* (Macmillan, 1983), pp.66–68.

[35] J. Hervey, *Meditations and Contemplations*, combined vol. (1820), p.330.

[36] *Ibid.*, p.370.

[37] *Ibid.*, pp.125–127.

[38] *Ibid.*, p.370.

[39] C. A. Russell, (ref. 34), pp.52–61 and 167–168.
[40] M. Jacob, *The Newtonians and the English Revolution 1689–1720*(Harvester Press, Hassocks, 1976).

7 Temporary flood warning: a geological interlude

When the caves of Kirkdale at last yielded their gruesome secrets to William Buckland in the 1820s, the delighted discoverer announced:

> The grand fact of an universal deluge at no very remote period is proved on grounds so decisive and incontrovertible, that, had we never heard of such an event from Scripture, or any other authority, Geology of itself must have called in the assistance of some such catastrophe, to explain the phenomena of diluvian action which are universally presented to us, and which are unintelligible without recourse to a deluge exerting its ravages at a period not more ancient than that announced in the Book of Genesis.[1]

It is not hard to understand his delight. This was the high point of natural theology and the era of the Bridgewater Treatises. Here was evidence of a most tangible kind that, literally by the barrow-load, could be wheeled into the arena and used to confound the forces of unbelief that still threatened to demean or even destroy the gospel. As Buckland's colleague, the Professor of Geology at Cambridge, Adam Sedgwick, was quick to realize, 'Geology, like every other science when well interpreted, lends its aid to natural religion.'[2] However, Buckland's pleasure, short-lived though it was to prove to be, stemmed also from much more specific considerations. The bones of Kirkdale, he believed, were visible evidence of a universal deluge of colossal proportions which must be identified with the biblical flood of Genesis 6 – 8. Here, then, was proof not merely of a *superintending* Providence and the presence of design in nature, but also of an *intervening* Providence and of purpose in history. More specifically still, the Kirkdale relics testified to the authority of Moses as a scientific commentator.

All these large issues were under debate at the time when Buckland first crawled through the narrow slits in the Kirkdale rock-face. None of them was new in principle, but all were given new urgency by two apparently quite unrelated circumstances. One was the emergence of a unified study of earth science to which the name 'geology' was becoming popularly attached; the other was an unwelcome onset of social instability in post-Revolutionary Europe and (especially) the England of the Industrial Revolution. Each in its own way was seen by some people as offering a challenge to the Christianity of the Bible. On one hand the compatibility of Genesis with geology was being seriously questioned, and on the other the relevance of Scripture to moral declension was being urged or denied. Thus, from whatever standpoint one looked, the authority and meaning of the Bible was once again emerging as more than an issue of academic theology. The revelations from Kirkdale focused these multifarious concerns on to one individual past event, the Deluge of Noah. In this chapter we look briefly backwards and forwards from Buckland to changing attitudes to this remarkable phenomenon.[3]

W. D. Conybeare's caricature of Buckland entering Kirkdale Cavern.

The rise of 'flood geology'[4]

The age of the earth had been a matter of contention long before the advent of geological science. Certainly the seventeenth century had seen plenty of discussion on this question. In the absence of any other data, efforts were made to derive a possible age for the earth from chronologies of the patriarchs in the book of Genesis (plus a good deal of imaginative guess-work). On this slender basis James Ussher, Archbishop of Armagh, and John Lightfoot, Chancellor of Cambridge University, jointly concluded that the date of creation was 4004 BC – a piece of misinformation printed in successive editions of the Authorized Version of the Bible from 1701 onwards (and thereby given a quite spurious degree of authority).

The Flood concludes this 'first age of the world'. Not for the first time it was seen as a watershed in the history, not only of mankind, but also of the world. Even in that century, however, doubts had been expressed about so recent a date for the creation of the earth. The Rev. Thomas Burnet, for example, in his *Sacred History of the Earth* (1681, 1684) regarded the six 'days' of the Genesis creation account as long periods of time. He too saw the Flood as a cataclysm which swept away the golden age of the patriarchs, one of several crises which periodically overwhelmed the earth and including a coming conflagration. His views reflected the millenarian expectations of the time and postulated an alternation of catastrophe and period of quiescence. Nevertheless it was some considerable time before any scientific evidence was adduced for challenging the so-called 'Mosaic chronology'.

Burnet was only one of many writers in the seventeenth and eighteenth centuries to produce a 'history' of the earth that gave great prominence to the Flood of Noah. It was once customary to dismiss these accounts largely as pious fantasies, where scientific progress in geology was repeatedly thwarted by theological obscuranticism. In several respects this is misleading. Geology as a coherent science hardly existed before the nineteenth century; there was no consensus as to *how* theology should constrain theories about the earth; and the speculators included not merely ingenious clerics but some of the most familiar names in science, including Newton, Hooke, Halley and Ray.[5]

The two great problems were the nature and occurrence of fossils and the shape of the earth's crust. It was by no means clear around 1700 that these required the same kind of answers, or that the phenomena were linked. The very nature of fossils was far from agreed.[6] Not everyone in the eighteenth century thought they came from once-living creatures, though as time went on the organic view began to predominate. Even then the problem was how to classify them: by geometrical form, by analogy with known forms of life, or by specific gravity? As the century progressed the wide variety of landforms became more fully appreciated with the growth of foreign travel. The archetypal Englishman crossing the Alps could be relied upon to express awe and wonder at the immense forces that had once helped to shape the surface of the globe. The difficulty was to know how this had happened.

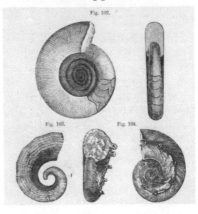

Fossil illustrations from Hugh Miller's Testimony of the Rocks *(1857). He believed that 'geology, rightly understood, does not conflict with religion'.*

In theories about the origin of the earth the Deluge of Noah played a prominent part. It was widely regarded as having been universal in coverage. But there the agreement ended.

The *causes* of the Deluge were in dispute. Halley thought it resulted from a shift in the earth's centre of gravity; Burnet believed it had been initiated by a contraction of the earth's crust; Whiston attributed it to the approach of a comet. Others, such as Woodward and Keil, declined to accept a naturalistic explanation and considered the whole event a miracle.[7] Nor was there unanimity as to its *effects*. At one extreme some people deemed the Genesis Flood to have been so brief and quiet that it could not have forced living creatures into the solid rocks. Others, such as the Cambridge physician John Woodward, were convinced that the fossils had been deposited in sediments from a cataclysmic flood and these had later hardened into the rock strata of today. Woodward's *Essay toward a natural history of the earth* first appeared in 1695. Years later, in 1724, his friend and former colleague in the Duke of Somerset's service, John Hutchinson (see p.120), attributed all major landforms to the Flood, during which the entire earth had been reduced to atoms and then recreated. On the other hand, the Lincolnshire clergyman, Abraham de la Pryme, thought (partly from his observations of coastal erosion, fen drainage and so on) that a major effect of the Flood had been to raise the sea-bed and depress land levels, so effectively exchanging positions between land and sea.

In these and many other ways the Deluge of Noah was used as an explanatory framework for the increasing mass of observational data through the eighteenth century, occasioned by the increase in travel and the growing mania for 'collecting' in natural history (which included rocks and fossils). Yet, as Roy Porter has argued, 'Empirical evidence was weighed in order to decipher the "real" meaning of traditional wisdom', and that included the biblical records as well as accounts in classical and other ancient sources. By this evidence Burnet was led to an allegorical interpretation of the creation and Flood stories in Genesis, while others drew different conclusions. Porter adds, 'These theories were not exercises in Biblical exegesis, but rather many-sided projects of the mind attempting to bring order out of cosmogonical chaos.'[8]

Towards the end of the eighteenth century a movement developed that was, it seems, innocent of theological motivation of any recognizably orthodox kind. This was a much-sharpened belief in the potent geological action of water, whether once for all in a remote past or at any time now. It became known, not unreasonably, as Neptunism. By far the most influential of the early Neptunists was A. G. Werner, a professor of mineralogy in Saxony. Many of the rocks in this area are indeed sedimentary and their formation could be credibly interpreted in Wernerian terms.

Werner postulated an enormous mass of water covering the whole earth and containing in solution materials which would crystallize out as granite and other primitive rocks. At later stages chemical precipitation would occur, the water level would drop, land would appear and further alluvial strata would be deposited. During these events life had concurrently appeared, but volcanoes were quite recent.

There were, of course, considerable difficulties attached to such views even at that time. How could one explain the steep inclinations of some strata? What about the cases where the sequence was inverted? Where did all the water go? Werner faced many of these problems, but not all his answers were convincing. But his influence on geological thinking was enormous. His own literary output was small, but his ideas were rapidly disseminated through his students and disciples. Many have felt that his Neptunist philosophy exerted a powerful retarding action on geological progress. Others, however, acknowledge the greater importance of his teaching methods with the emphasis on systematic observation and practical training. By all accounts his students thought the world of him, and he did give to mineralogy one of its first major conceptual frameworks.

Having thus spoken about Werner we must now dispel several misconceptions. He was not the first to think in Neptunist terms (one can cite de Maillet's *Telliamed* of 1748, to give but one example), nor, apparently, was he obsessed with the Deluge of Noah. But he was concerned with the primal geologic agency of water and he was the first to found an influential school to propagate (and extrapolate) his views. As d'Aubuisson observed (1819):

> One can say of Werner what has been said of Linnaeus, that his disciples have covered the earth and that from one pole to another nature has been interrogated in the name of one individual man.[9]

During the early years of the nineteenth century there must have been many who identified Werner's universal ocean with the Flood of Noah. Clear cases are hard to find, but one of Werner's most redoubtable champions, the Scot, Robert Jameson, felt it necessary to give an explicit denial to such an assumption. The point is that by now (1808) the whole Neptunist position was under attack and many geologists were relegating the universal ocean to the realms of mythology.

In 1813 an English translation of Cuvier's textbook *The Theory of the Earth* appeared complete with a preface by Jameson. Surprisingly, it claimed a correlation between geological findings and the Mosaic narrative in Genesis (holding that the 'six days' represented six indeterminately long periods). The view was enthusiastically taken up by the Scottish theologian Thomas Chalmers and then by John Sumner, Archbishop of Canterbury. When Buckland took up his Readership at Oxford in 1819 he too asserted a general harmony between his science and religion. Two years later the Kirkdale caves yielded up their age-old secrets. Diluvialism, it seemed, had triumphed, and so had Moses. His authority as a sacred historian was now unimpeachable.

It is important to note the *sense* in which Moses' authority was upheld. Few were in doubt that he was a 'sacred writer' or, for that matter, that he had personally written the book of Genesis. Those points were not in question. What was at stake was whether his writings about nature were to be taken in a totally literal sense. In specific terms this included six 24-hour days of creation and a Deluge that literally covered the whole of this planet.

The argument was no new one, even for earth science. In 1696 William Whiston had postulated 'the obvious or literal sense of Scripture is the true and real one where no evident reason can be given to the contrary'.[10] He also supposed that 'that which is clearly accountable in a natural way is not without reason to be ascribed to a miraculous power' – manifesting a deistic tendency that was later to land him in such trouble (see p.113). Even here a wooden literalism is avoided by the saving clause at the end. Others were not so sure even about that, and followed Burnet in his advice, "Tis a dangerous thing to ingage the authority of Scripture in disputes about the natural world, in opposition to reason.'[11]

So why were these battles being fought all over again? The most obvious reason was the recent accumulation of data that did not support diluvialism, arising from advances in mining, foreign travel and the amassing of vast 'collections'. Moreover, a new historical awareness was arising in Britain and elsewhere that made the past seem so much more important than many Enlightenment figures would have cared to admit. Again, as we have seen, natural theology was flourishing and the foundations of an ordered society were shaking; one recent writer has suggested that the foundation of the Geological Society in 1807 came about not because the earth was in decay, but because the founders thought that civil society was.[12]

We turn, then, to consider the rival movement which was to challenge not only diluvialism but also the traditional views of the age of the earth and the extent of Noah's Flood.

The ebbing of the waters

Increased travel in the eighteenth century led to a new, sometimes uncomfortable, awareness of volcanoes and earthquakes. The simple-minded natural theology which saw all things created for the benefit of man could not but be concerned by the power of these destructive agencies. Volcanoes, in particular, were to become a veritable battleground for two rather different encounters. One was between those who favoured water as a geological agent and those who espoused the cause of fire: the Neptunists v. the Vulcanists. The other was a controversy between those who saw earth history as largely peaceful, but punctuated by a small number of catastrophic upheavals, and others who believed in a continuum of activity at a much lower level and (therefore) over a much longer time. This argument had been characterized as that between Catastrophists and Uniformitarians. Neither controversy can be possibly equated with a conflict between science and religion, though each had considerable and complex theological overtones. Whether this was logically necessary or not, the historical fact is that here again theology and science were interlocked.

Perhaps it is as well to begin with Buffon. Having conducted a series of experiments in which spheres of different materials and different sizes were allowed to cool, he calculated how long it must have taken for the planets in our solar system to reach habitable temperatures from an (assumed) initial white heat. He concluded our earth to be nearly 75,000 years old. Buffon wove earlier ideas of the Genesis 'days' into his own scheme of seven long geological eras. In his *Epochs of Nature* (1778) he became the first to give clear articulation to the doctrine that the earth had its own history. Of course his figures by modern standards are absurdly out, but he had made a very significant point.

As the creation was pushed back ever farther into time, the Flood became the focus of attention. After all, *this* had taken place in historic time, and evidence for its occurrence (once you knew what to look for) was accumulating on all sides. Richard Kirwan in 1799 drew attention to an important part of that evidence, the fossil record: he argued that the 'promiscuous' occurrence together of shells belonging to very different parts of the world are 'the most unequivocal geologic proofs of a general deluge'.[13] This, of course, was Buckland's point, though he was talking of bones rather than shells. His excitement derived at least partly from the emergence of a contrary view of earth history associated with James Hutton (1726–97) of Edinburgh.

Hutton believed that there were two kinds of rocks, one of which (igneous) had a volcanic origin, while the other (aqueous) was laid down by water. They had reached their present form, however, by the combined actions of high temperature and pressures. In this way Hutton accounted for such phenomena as the extrusion of granite into limestone fissures. His commitment to a constant series of interactions involving water and heat led him to a momentous conclusion about his time-scale. Unlike his opponents he regarded the whole earth as being in a state of dynamism and thus requiring immense time. In his own words:

> Having, in the natural history of this earth, seen a succession of worlds, we may from this conclude that there is a system in nature; in like manner as, from seeing revolutions of the planets, it is concluded that there is a system by which they are intended to continue those revolutions. But if the succession of worlds is established in the system of nature, it is in vain to look for any thing higher in the origin of the earth. The result, therefore, of our present enquiry, is, that we find no vestige of a beginning – no prospect of an end.[14]

Not only did this attitude eliminate Noah's Flood as a cardinal point in a geological time-scale, it also raised the whole question as to whether such a time-scale could be determined. Hutton argued further that 'general deluges form no part of the theory of the earth, for the purpose of this earth is evidently to maintain vegetable and animal life, not to destroy them'.

Hutton's own writing came in for severe handling from his opponents. But in 1802 Hutton's opinions were rescued from the oblivion into which they were in danger of falling on account of his own turgid and repetitive style and the diatribes of his opponents. In that year the Edinburgh geologist John Playfair published his own *Illustrations of the Huttonian Theory*. Although dissenting from Hutton's denial of a Flood, Playfair was anxious to exonerate him from a charge of impiety:

> To assert, therefore, that, in the economy of the world, we see no mark, either of a beginning or an end, is very different from affirming, that the world had no beginning, and will have no end. The first is a conclusion justified by common sense, as well as sound philosophy; while the second is a presumptuous and unwarrantable assertion, for which no reason from experience or analogy can ever be assigned. Dr. Hutton might, therefore, justly complain of the uncandid criticism, which, by substituting the one of these assertions for the other, endeavoured to load his theory with the reproach of atheism and impiety.[15]

In fact, Hutton worked within a framework not of atheism but of deism. True to the spirit of much natural theology, he saw the earth as 'evidently made for man', 'wisely adapted' and a system of perpetual stability. A long, gradual development is consistent with these teleological presuppositions. Also, his residence in Edinburgh, with volcanic rocks all around and underneath him, coupled with a close acquaintance with that pioneer of heat studies, Joseph Black, would have impressed upon him the importance of heat as a geological agent. This tended to be neglected by the enthusiasts for catastrophic inundations, of whom more in a moment.

This philosophy came to be known as uniformitarianism: the earth owes its present shape to slow changes of the kind seen around us today (erosion, precipitation and so on) rather than to cataclysmic convulsions like the Flood. Its most articulate spokesman, Charles Lyell (1797–1875), published his views in his *Principles of Geology* which first appeared in 1830. Almost alone amongst uniformitarian geologists, Lyell assumed the rate of change to have been of the same order of magnitude as at present, and this meant an immense age for earth history. It is of some interest to note that, theologically, Lyell tended towards unitarianism, a position close to deism with its non-intervening God and built-in Design. Yet even Lyell admitted one great 'intervention' with the creation of the human race. Otherwise, he asked, 'How could man supervene?'

After Lyell little is heard of the Flood. On the new geological time-scale it was so recent an event that it could scarcely be credited with the major effects ascribed to it by the diluvialists. Lyell himself seems to have espoused a 'local flood' theory for the Deluge of Noah. He raised the question 'whether the deluge of the Scriptures was universal in reference to the whole surface of the globe, or only so with respect to that portion of it which was then inhabited by man'. Agreeing with Fleming's views also he said:

> There are no terms employed [in Genesis] that indicate the impetuous rushing of the waters...on the contrary, the olive-branch, brought back by the dove, seems as clear an indication to us that the vegetation was not destroyed, as it was then to Noah that the dry land was about to appear.[16]

These views were, of course, but a small part of Lyell's whole uniformitarian philosophy. Going beyond the actualism of Hutton's alternate activity and rest, he supposed that the present was the key to the past and that nature had *not* been 'parsimonious of time and prodigal of violence'. It would take us too far from our subject either to explore more deeply into Lyell's own philosophy of science or to assess its importance in history. It is sufficient to say that, in Gillispie's phrase, *The Principles of Geology* 'administered the *coup de grâce* to the deluge', that is, as a major geological agency.[17]

Lyell's sketch of Etna. The vast mass of the mountain on top of relatively young strata convinced him of the immensity of geological time needed to produce the present features of the earth's surface.

For all Lyell's commitment to a kind of deism the fact remains that by now empirical evidence had accumulated that made the case for a long earth-history look almost overwhelming. This arose especially from the fossil record. With the labours of William Smith ('the father of stratigraphy') it became possible to correlate strata in different parts of the land by means of the fossils they contained. Smith (1769–1834) was a surveyor in the West of England, much involved in the construction of canals that were beginning to criss-cross the country. His excavations laid bare the strata to an extent rarely if ever encountered before. He became the first to recognize that each bed of rock could be identified by the fossils within it. Thus, to give but one example, Charles Lyell in his journeys across Sicily was astounded to discover that the huge mass of Mount Etna was in fact on top of strata that were relatively young, from which he concluded that a vast era of time was necessary to form the mountain and therefore the underlying rock beds.

And what of the theologians? Buckland modified his views quite quickly as the new evidence became available. But the most spectacular case of a turn-around was Adam Sedgwick, Professor of Geology at Cambridge. In 1825 he asserted:

TABLE OF STRATIFIED ROCKS.

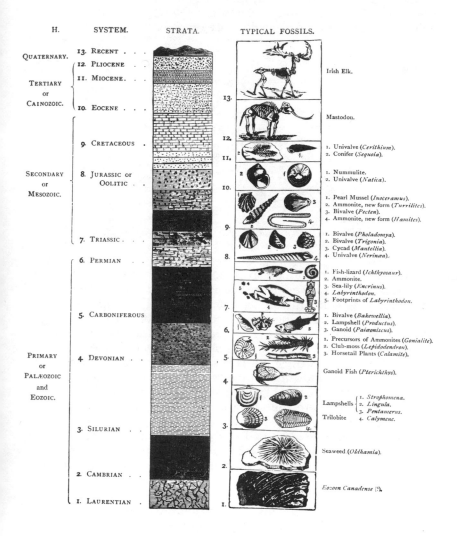

Table of geological strata (1888) showing how each is 'finger-printed' by the fossils it contains.

The sacred records tell us – that a few thousand years ago 'The fountains of the great deep were broken up' – and that the earth's surface was submerged by the waters of a general deluge; and the investigations of geology tend to prove that the accumulations of alluvial matter have not been going on many thousand years; and that they were preceded by a great catastrophe which has left traces of its operation in the *diluvial detritus* which is spread out over all the strata of the earth.[18]

Yet he, too, was mistaken. With great courage he admitted as much when, as President of the Geological Society, in 1831 he announced the following:

Having been myself a believer, and, to the best of my power, a propagator of what I now regard as a philosophic heresy... I think it right, as one of my last acts before I quit this Chair, thus publicly to read my recantation. We ought, indeed, to have paused before we first adopted the diluvian theory, and referred all our old superficial gravel to the action of the Mosaic Flood. For of man, and the works of his hands, we have not yet found a single trace among the remnants of a former world entombed in these deposits.[19]

Sedgwick did not deny the historicity of Noah's Flood; he most certainly did not abjure a deeply-held faith in Scripture and a commitment to biblical doctrines that realistically can be termed evangelical.[20] He simply abandoned an arbitrary determination that Genesis should be interpreted in certain specific ways with respect to natural phenomena and the circular argument for that interpretation from certain observations that *at the time* seemed convincing.

Notes for chapter seven

[1] W. Buckland, *Vindiciae Geologicae* (1820), pp.23–24.

[2] A Sedgwick, *A Discourse on the Studies of the University* (1833), p.22

[3] A brief account, from which some of the following is taken, is C. A. Russell, 'Noah and the Neptunists', *Faith and Thought*, 1972–3, 100, 143. It occurs as part of a Symposium of the Victoria Institute on 'The Flood'.

[4] L. E. Page, 'Diluvianism and its critics', in C. J. Schneer (ed.), *Towards a History of Geology* (M.I.T. Press, 1969), p.259.

[5] Roy Porter, *The Making of Geology: Earth Science in Britain, 1660–1815* (Cambridge University Press, 1977).

[6] M. J. S. Rudwick, *The Meaning of Fossils* (Macdonald, 1972).

[7] Roy Porter, (ref. 5), p.75.

[8] *Ibid.*, pp.64–66.

[9] J. F. d'Aubuisson de Voisins, *Traité de Géognosie* (1819), vol.i, p.xiv.

[10] W. Whiston, *A New Theory of the Earth* (1696), p.77.

[11] T. Burnet,*The Theory of the Earth* (1684), Preface.

[12] P. Weindling, in L. J. Jordanova and R. Porter, *Images of the Earth* (Chalfont St Giles, 1979), p.256.

[13] R. Kirwan, *Geological Essays* (1799), p.54.

[14] J. Hutton, *Trans. Roy. Soc. Edinburgh*, 1788, 1.

[15] J. Playfair, *Illustrations of the Huttonian Theory of the Earth* (1802), pp.119–120.

[16] C. Lyell, *Principles of Geology*, 3rd ed., vol.iv, p.148.

[17] C. C. Gillispie, *Genesis and Geology* (Harper & Row, New York, 1959), p.140.

[18] A. Sedgwick, *Ann. Phil.*, 1825, *10*, 34.

[19] *Idem, Proc. Geol. Soc.*, 1831, *1*, 313.

[20] V. P. Marston, 'Science, Methodology and Religion in the Work of Adam Sedgwick', Ph.D. Thesis, The Open University, 1984.

8 Troubled waters:
the evolution controversy

[Man] trusted God was love indeed
And love creation's final law –
Tho' Nature, red in tooth and claw
With ravine, shriek'd against his creed.

Alfred Lord Tennyson (1809–92), *In Memoriam*

We know that the whole creation has been groaning as in the
pains of childbirth right up to the present time.

Romans 8:22

'The troubled waters of evolution'

In 1974 a book with exactly that title was published by
Creation-Life Publishers of San Diego. The author, Henry M.
Morris, is one of the most outspoken and articulate critics of
the theory of evolution in post-war America. He and others of
the 'Institute for Creation Research' have crusaded tirelessly
for the right to challenge evolutionary theory in the public
(state) schools of the United States. They have sought a
balanced treatment in which evolution is accompanied (or
even replaced) by a literal reading of Genesis as a *scientific*
account of the origins of the world and of humanity. The
arguments have been associated with legal battles from the
Scopes trial of 1925 to the Arkansas case in the 1980s, but it is
not our purpose to discuss the current situation, confused as it
is by association with right-wing North American politics.
Nor is it necessary to attempt an assessment of the flood of
'creationist' literature which continues almost unabated. Partly
this is because it is a peculiarly American phenomenon (British
readers often wonder what all the fuss is about), partly because
it has been extensively criticized in several recent books,[1] but
mainly because it is best illuminated indirectly by historical
consideration of the earlier episodes associated with Darwin
himself.

Nevertheless we may be grateful to Henry Morris for a
phrase which accurately depicts not merely the contemporary

scene as he views it, but also the situation in the nineteenth century when Darwinism burst forth upon the world. That 'troubling of the waters' affected not merely the pace and direction of scientific progress of all kinds, but human life in its widest connotations. Ordinary men and women became aware of something new and strange,[2] literature, philosophy and even music were profoundly influenced by Darwinism, while politicians of left and right have confessed their debts to its author. All this and more has, not surprisingly, been reflected in an enormous literature. The 'Darwin Industry' has almost certainly surpassed in output that other most productive literary establishment concerned with Isaac Newton. A comprehensive bibliography would fill the remaining pages of this book.[3] Yet, as everyone knows, it is in one sphere above all others that Darwinism has been traditionally held to have created the greatest stir: the world of Christian religion. On this question Henry Morris would most surely agree, for it is by undermining Christianity that the theory of evolution is seen by the 'creationists' as responsible for all manner of social evils (in which they include 'communism' and 'fascism'). Most of this chapter is devoted to exploring in historical terms the evolution/religion controversy. But first we must glance briefly at the origins of evolutionary theory.

The origin of biological species had long fascinated generations of naturalists, most, though by no means all, regarding them as having existed as such from their first creation. The views of Buffon, Cuvier and Lamarck were early attempts to wrestle with the problem, especially in the light of the fossil record, and represented definite moves towards an evolutionary theory. But the decisive steps were taken by Charles Darwin. It is important to remember that *fixity of species* was a deeply-held conviction based not merely – or even mainly – on Genesis, but on a whole range of other considerations. It was a legacy of Aristotelian philosophy that had survived the tentative doubts of Buffon and the searching criticism of Cuvier. It was also associated, however mistakenly, with social stability which could be seen also to represent a 'fixity' of structural arrangements. Destroy one and you destroy the other was the fear, often hardly articulated but probably none the less real. If to us this all seems illogical and beside the point, it is worth remembering Sedgwick's words about a book by an earlier evolutionist, Robert Chambers (*Vestiges of the Natural History of Creation*, 1844). If the book were true and transformism of species were possible, 'religion is a lie, human law is a means of folly, and a base injustice; morality is moonshine...'. And in France, where Darwinism made very heavy going in the nineteenth century, transformism was often associated with fear of Revolution.

Charles Darwin (1809–82) was the son of a prosperous medical practioner in Shrewsbury and grandson both of the famous Erasmus Darwin and his eminent associate Josiah Wedgwood I. Eventually Charles was to marry Emma Wedgwood, another of Josiah's grandchildren. To an astute naturalist of Darwin's calibre the interbreeding in his own family, as in the Wedgwoods before him, must have been a subject of intense interest. He was as well-endowed financially as he was genetically, and was sent to Edinburgh to study medicine. Finding this not to his taste (he saw only two operations and rushed away before either was finished), he transferred to Cambridge with a view to entering the Anglican ministry. Here again his academic studies were, in his view, largely a waste of time, though studying Paley's works (including *Natural Theology*) gave him much delight. Spare time was so plentiful for an undergraduate in those days that he was able to indulge freely in his passion for collecting beetles. More fruitful was his growing friendship with J. S. Henslow, Professor of Botany and a great explorer of the surrounding countryside. Young Darwin became known as 'the man who walks with Henslow'. Not only Henslow, but several of his distinguished friends conversed with Darwin, including William Whewell (later Master of Trinity), and Adam Sedgwick (Professor of Geology), who took him on a fossil-hunting expedition in North Wales in the summer of 1831. On returning home he found a letter waiting for him. Henslow had written with an invitation that was to be the turning-point of his life.

Darwin was being offered the prospect of a two-year voyage round the world. Robert FitzRoy, Captain of a Royal Navy survey ship, H.M.S. *Beagle*, required a cabin-companion with a knowledge of natural history, partly to share the lonely meal-times and provide suitable conversation, but also to gather scientific data to support his own literal interpretation of Genesis. Thanks to Henslow's recommendation Darwin was able to accept the position and on 27 December 1831 they set sail for a voyage that was to last, not two, but nearly five years. It was, as he said, 'by far the greatest event of my life'.

The story of that epic journey has been told and retold times without number. It must suffice to say that, as he faced the dazzling variety of living creatures on the islands off the South

American coast, it began to dawn upon Darwin that the creation was more complex than had ever been suspected before.

HMS Beagle *beached for repairs at the mouth of the river Santa Cruz.*

Eventually he was to ask why, for example, did each of the Galapagos Islands have its own characteristic species of tortoises, mocking-birds, finches? Had each species been specially created just for one island? Why did they not *all* occur on islands apparently so similar? At the root of his difficulty lay the view that each species was immutable and created for appropriate conditions. If the conditions on one island were appropriate for species X, why did that particular species not occur under seemingly identical conditions elsewhere? Of course he could have taken refuge in multiplying such 'special creations' and merely acknowledging ignorance as to why God had made them. But he did not. The thought crossed his mind that 'from an original paucity of birds in this archipelago, one species had been taken and modified for different ends'.

More remarkable even than the living were the dead. This avid reader of Charles Lyell and former companion of Sedgwick was profoundly impressed by what he discovered of fossils embedded in a gravel beach of Argentina. One was the head of an extinct animal of immense size, yet curiously similar in some respects to the capybara, rodents about the size of sheep. Were these and other long-extinct species casualties of the flood (as FitzRoy maintained)? Or was there some other explanation? Had they perished long before the days of Noah, and if so why had this been allowed? There was also the disturbing fact that,

while some genera represented in the fossil-bed were un-
questionably extinct, others alongside them had survived,
largely unchanged until today. It was all most puzzling but, at
this stage, any convincing explanation eluded him and, in the
mean time, the sheer joys of collection and exploration were to
be savoured to the full.

After the voyage was over Darwin's career was settled. By
1838 matters were clear. Gone were thoughts of ordination.
His fame as a naturalist had travelled ahead of him, and that
was to be his life's work. Fortunately he did not need to 'earn'
a living in employment. By now he had struck up a close
friendship with Charles Lyell and he was to be, for three
years, Secretary of the Geological Society. A Pocket Book for
1837 records the following momentous announcement: 'In
July opened first note-book on Transmutation of Species.' He
had begun his assault on that bastion of the intellectual establishment: the fixity of species. The idea that they might evolve
was itself evolving in his own mind. We now know this was
happening far more quickly than he cared to acknowledge in
public.

Shortly after he returned home – in 1838 – Darwin started to
read a remarkable book by one of Paley's fellow-ministers in
the Anglican Church: Thomas Robert Malthus. In this sixth
edition of his *Essay on the Principle of Population* Darwin quite
accidentally picked up a vital hint for his own still-germinating
theories. No purveyor of Enlightenment optimism, Malthus
painted a grim picture of a future population explosion. The
human population naturally increased in a *geometric* progression, *e.g.* doubling each generation if each pair of parents
had four children (a small number in those days). But food
supplies increased only in an *arithmetic* progression. Hence
inevitably many offspring will not survive, irrespective of the
quality of medical care. Moreover there would soon be on this
planet, as the cartoonists depicted, standing-room only.

In fact, however, nature takes its own action to reduce the
population, especially by famine and disease. And so there
must be a struggle for existence, with all its attendant miseries
and privations. Even these, however, may be turned to good
account as human beings practise the virtues of moral restraint
in marriage and industrious application in agriculture. Future
benefits in the life to come will flow from these temporary
difficulties on earth.

Darwin's mind was still full of memories of Fuegians
struggling for their very existence in the inhospitable wastes

of South America, of natural disasters like the earthquake near Concepcion and of animals fighting to the very death. On reading Malthus, he said, 'it at once struck me that under these circumstances favourable variations would tend to be preserved, and unfavourable ones to be destroyed'.

In a world of Victorian capitalism this struggle for existence was familiar enough. In the context of an evolutionary theory it was almost without precedent. Species could change as environments changed, but only as the weakest went to the wall and the strongest survived. 'At last', he noted, 'I have a theory to work with.'

It would, unfortunately, take far too long to explore thoroughly the route by which Darwin arrived at his fully fledged theory, how he confided it to his notebook in 1842 and more fully in 1844, and how he spent fifteen years silently refining and expanding it. Indeed that theory itself was developed over the years after its first publication: *On the origin of species by means of natural selection*. Nor is it right to give all the credit (or blame) to Darwin. A very similar theory was propounded by Alfred Russel Wallace in 858, and it was the fear of losing his priority in print that goaded Darwin to publish *The Origin* in 1859. All 1,250 copies of the first edition were subscribed for on the day of publication.[4]

The full title of Darwin's book enshrines his central thesis. Individual species, according to him, do not each originate by a special creation but by a slow process which he called 'natural selection'. It presupposes three facts which are surely self-evident:

1. Organisms reproduce more offspring than can reach maturity, whether animals in a litter or seeds on the ground. This principle of nature's over-production is sometimes called *super-fecundity*.

2. A range of individual differences exists within any species (colour, size, speed of movement, *etc.*), and these are often inheritable. Such is the principle of *variation*.

3. Environments vary widely in terms of climate, food supplies and hostile organisms.

These three facts taken together ensure that a competitive struggle for existence is often to be found within a species and those members least favoured by inherited assets will survive a hostile environment least effectively. If food is to be found only high up in trees, giraffes with shorter necks will be at a disadvantage. So will their offspring if they inherit this 'deficiency', and so gradually the line will weaken, eventually being replaced by the strain that is better fitted to survive that particular environment. That process is 'natural selection', the immediate result of which is 'survival of the fittest'. Within any one species it is all most reasonable, but in Darwin's day it raised many eyebrows by virtue of his conclusion: if this went on *for a very long time* it could have three possible outcomes:

1. A species might continue more or less unchanged if conditions remained favourable.

2. Individuals might perish and the species become extinct.

3. Individuals might slowly change to become a new species.

This last possibility, transmutation of species, is often represented as Darwin's great break with tradition. In fact, the eighteenth-century naturalist Buffon had recognized that some species become extinct and had greatly reduced the number of species recognized. But transformation he would not allow. On the other hand his compatriot Lamarck believed in transformation, though natural selection was not implied. He held that evolution took place by the inheritance of characteristics acquired in an individual's lifetime, and he also allowed for spontaneous generation. In England an anonymous treatise, *Vestiges of the Natural History of Creation*, appeared in 1844 and advocated quite specifically a progression from one species to another. The writer was an Edinburgh publisher, Robert Chambers. Seeking to demonstrate the dominion of law in the universe he argued for evolution of the solar system as well as of living organisms, and compared the latter with the ways in which embryos develop in the womb. His lack of scientific training, however, permitted more than a few lapses in accuracy and these were seized on with delight by his opponents, who were many. The strength of the opposition derived more from social than explicitly theological objections and may well have been one reason for Darwin remaining silent for twenty years before *The Origin*. Otherwise he would have had to take on the intellectual establishment almost single-handed.

The other feature of Darwinism that was not new was its demand for an immensely long time for evolution to occur.

James Hutton had argued from the evidence of the rocks that 'we see no vestige of a beginning, no prospect of an end' (he did not say *there was* no vestige). Buffon had suggested 75,000 years as the minimum age of the earth, but the great surge in geological investigation from 1800 to 1850 led to a widespread acceptance of much longer times still for the emergence of life. The notion of a series of *catastrophes* in a relatively short timespan had been invoked before this period as an explanation for the irregular shape of the earth's crust. Now it became more acceptable to regard the causes as those which we see around us today (erosion, precipitation, even glaciation), in which case an immensely long time is needed to account for their effects. Lyell was prepared to allow Darwin 200 million years as a minimum for earth history. The theological implication of such a *uniformitarian* view will be considered shortly. Meanwhile we note that an 'old earth' was not invented for Darwin and certainly not by him.

Theological issues at stake

In a work of seminal importance[5] James Moore has discussed the wide range of responses to Darwinism made by Christians of Protestant persuasion. They ranged from implacable opposition to that strange compound the so-called 'Christian Darwinism'. The Roman Catholic Church, though more slowly and less colourfully, displayed a variety of attitudes, at least among individual members if not by official decree.[6] These facts should warn us not of the duplicity and gullibility of Christians, but that the issues are far from simple, and were seen as such when Darwinism was still news. At this distance of time it may be possible to disentangle some of the most important threads in the tangled skein of controversy.

1. The interpretation of Genesis

We start here, not because it was the most important issue at stake, but because it is the most obvious. By many Christians Darwinism was condemned simply because it was incompatible with a literal reading of Genesis chapters 1 – 3. The latter suggested a four-day period for the whole of organic creation, a specific order of events, a specific creation of man from the dust, a separate creation of woman, and so on.

This objection featured prominently, though not exclusively, in some of the earliest outbursts against Darwin. The Bishop of Oxford, Samuel Wilberforce, who had forsaken the evangelicalism of his father for Anglicanism of the High Church variety, declared that 'the principle of natural selection is absolutely incompatible with the word of God'. Charles Perry, Bishop of Melbourne, was not to be outdone: Darwin and other proponents of evolution were out 'to produce in their readers a disbelief of the Bible'. From the American branch of the same church came the ultimate in *non sequiturs*: 'If this hypothesis [evolution] be true, then is the Bible an unbearable fiction', while Paul's remark in 1 Corinthians 15:39 is marshalled in support ('All flesh is not the same flesh'). Examples along these lines can easily be multiplied, though to little purpose. They would, however, strengthen an extraordinary paradox.[7]

It might be supposed that objections to evolution on the grounds of its conflict with a literal interpretation of Scripture would be found most stridently among those with a strong *a priori* commitment to the authority of the Bible. These would be the orthodox and, especially, the evangelicals of Anglican or Free Church persuasion. What is truly remarkable is that it was members of this group who offered *least* opposition to Darwin. Indeed Moore's detailed analysis leads him to conclude that 'it was only those who maintained a distinctly orthodox theology who could embrace Darwinism'.[8] One cannot fail to be reminded of the parallel case in geology (see p.139).

Samuel Wilberforce, the Bishop of Oxford between 1845 and 1869.

In the early days of the Darwinian controversy some evangelicals did oppose evolution on the grounds of its incompatibility with a literal rendering of Genesis. Thus the Rev. T. R. Birks (a co-founder of the Evangelical Alliance) assailed evolutionists precisely for this failure to take into account biblical evidence. In America the Princeton theologian Charles Hodge inclined to the same opinion, holding that the biblical view of man as created in the image of God was irreconcilable with the Darwinian concept of a developed ape. However, he recognized that 'science has in many things taught the Church how to understand the Scripture', and accepted (for example) that each 'day of Genesis may represent a far longer period than 24 hours'. This was a much more characteristic attitude for nineteenth-century evangelicals than a point-by-point refutation of Darwinism simply by treating Genesis as though it were a scientific textbook. Concerted opposition to evolution on those grounds had to wait until the 'fundamentalist' movement after the First World War. The acceptance of Darwinism by many of the Princeton School of Theology has been recently stressed.[9]

For the comparative silence from evangelicals there must surely be an explanation. Indeed there is, and it is a simple one. So far as literal interpretation of Genesis was concerned Darwin raised no new issues of principle. The evolution controversy promised to be a re-run of the arguments over the age of the earth and the demise of 'flood geology'. It was not that they failed to take Scripture properly into account. Because they took it so seriously they declined to saddle it with arbitrary interpretations that flew in the face of empirical evidence. And precisely because they stood in the direct line of Augustine, Calvin, Boyle and the rest they accepted a scriptural mandate to do science and were not prepared to read a contradictory message in Genesis and in geology or biology. Certainly there were aspects of 'evolution' with which they were not happy, but this was not usually one of them.

Furthermore many Protestants, at least, had seen the Darwinian furore as likely to repeat the mistakes of the Galileo affair. From that, at least, they had learnt that in giving us Scripture the Holy Spirit might 'accommodate' himself to the understanding of mere men and that Scripture was not a source-book for science.

That being the case, it is remarkable to find the following historical judgment from a modern 'creationist':

So here is the difference between Darwin and Galileo: Galileo set a demonstrable *fact* against a few words of Bible poetry which the Church at that time had understood in an obviously naive way; Darwin set an unprovable *theory* against eleven chapters of straightforward history which cannot be reinterpreted in any satisfactory way.[10]

While we must always be careful about drawing historical parallels, in this case it would not take many pages to refute such a set of misconceptions; but because it is widely circulated some brief comments are in order.

1. Galileo produced no 'facts' which incontrovertibly established Copernicanism. That had to wait over two centuries (see p.39).

2. Darwin, on the other hand, had marshalled quite literally thousands of facts which, while certainly not 'proving' his theory, made the old six-day creation model look almost incredible.

3. The church's understanding of 'a few words of poetry' may have been 'naive' but at the time it was not *obviously* so.

Charles Darwin.

4. That the first eleven chapters of Genesis, like all Scripture, are straightforward history was not obvious then and is not obvious now, partly because they have a manifestly moral and spiritual lesson to impart, partly because they deal with such unique phenomena that we have no parallel history with which to compare them, and partly because the literary form (whether liturgically intended or not) far more resembles ancient Babylonian poems than modern history.

5. It is not clear why 'eleven chapters' should be more significant than 'a few verses'.

6. The Genesis narrative, with its reference to 'firmament', 'windows of heaven', 'waters under the earth', 'waters above the heaven', *etc.*, is thoroughly geocentric in form, though not in teaching. It uses the language of appearance. If Galileo may challenge its literal interpretation, why may not Darwin?

This digression was necessary to establish a concordance between the attitudes of Galileo and some Darwinians over the interpretation of Genesis. That being so it is not hard to see how this particular problem was the least, not the most, they had to face.

When *The Origin* was published in 1859 the Bible as a whole had been under attack from numerous quarters. The so-called 'Higher Criticism' from Germany had caused little more than a few ripples in England, until a new historical approach to Scripture was advertised in the multi-authored *Essays and Reviews* of 1860. The book received the doubtful compliment of a hostile review from Samuel Wilberforce (who was having a busy time in those days). One commentator remarked that the row over *The Origin* would have been much noisier had it not been for the greater row engendered by *Essays and Reviews* (R. W. Church). But the two cannot have been unrelated and one can understand the reactions of biblical literalists (amongst others) as part of a more general alarm over the authority of Scripture. As it happened, both storms blew over but each left a trail of devastation in its wake.

2. *Elimination of purpose in nature*

Charles Darwin was heir to a long tradition of natural theology. Everything had a purpose in nature: final causes might be discerned in every organism, however humble, and all testified to the masterplan of an infinitely wise and powerful Designer. But now, it seemed, design was gone. A giraffe's neck was long not because a wise Providence intended it so, but simply because possession of such a feature was a necessary condition for survival. Short-necked ancestors of the animal could be found only in the fossil record.

Here in truth was a challenge to accepted beliefs. What was called in question was not whether Genesis was about six days' work, or about the spiritual facts of God's sovereignty and man's dependence and sinfulness. The issue here was nothing less than the reality of God's superintending Providence. Said Darwin:

> There seems to be no more design in the variability of organic beings, and in the action of Natural Selection, than in the course which the wind blows.[11]

Whereas the natural theologians had proclaimed 'design' and 'purpose' in every part of the natural world, Darwin was to protest this was really wishful thinking. The 'design' is illusory and the patterns in nature of no more significance than (say) the random arrangement of tea-leaves at the bottom of a cup. Huxley used the metaphor of pellets from a shotgun, some of which happen to hit the target.

For those steeped in natural theology this was a hard pill to swallow. For many ordinary unlearned men it was as much against common sense as had been the proposal of a spherical earth. For Christian believers it stretched credulity to the limit, for, if God were truly in control of the world, would not the signs of that control be manifest everywhere in nature? As we shall see they had a point, but it was more complex than that simple question implies. To answer it we need to see what Darwin had actually done to the design argument. It used to be said that he had broken completely with the natural theologians, but since the 1960s new work has disclosed a rather different relationship. Walter Cannon pointed out a remarkable congruence between the ideas of Darwin and natural theology, identifying no less than ten points of apparent indebtedness.[12] Three will be sufficient to consider now.

Many of the more perceptive writers of natural theology had recognized purpose in nature quite unconnected with the welfare of man. Their universe was not anthropocentric, even if their arguments may have been. Neither was that of Darwin, who would certainly have deplored a suggestion that all things are for our human benefit. Then again, the notion of adaptation to conditions was freely canvassed by Paley and his co-authors. It hardly needs to be stressed that Darwin did the same. Thirdly we can note the commitment of some (though not all) natural theologians to a view of history that stressed its unrepeatability. (Of course the further they distanced themselves from revealed theology the weaker was their incentive to do this; a fully incarnational theology is the strongest antidote to believing that 'history repeats itself'.) Darwin also, in contrast to Lamarck, held that evolution precluded any cyclic view of life history. Cannon himself went so far as to assert that the success of Darwinism was nothing less than 'the triumph of a Christian way of picturing the world over the other ways available to scientists', and Robert M. Young has said that Darwin took Paley's answers and turned them into questions.[13]

Whether or not Darwin was so indebted to Paley, there is sufficient evidence to make us question whether contemporaries saw his elimination of design as inherently contradictory of Christian belief. There was, for example, real doubt as to Darwin's own commitment, at the emotional if not the intellectual level. He himself wrote:

> I am conscious that I am in an utterly hopeless muddle. I cannot think that the world, as we see it, is the result of chance; and yet I cannot look at each separate thing as the result of Design.[14]

When he wrote his famous treatise on *Orchids* (1862) he thought it was rather 'like a Bridgewater Treatise'. In a private conversation many years later with the Duke of Argyll, orchid fertilization was mentioned as an example of purposive design. Darwin replied, 'Well, that often comes over me with overwhelming force; but at other times it seems to go away.'[15] Quite apart from Darwin's own ambivalence there were writers, like the American botanist Asa Gray, who embraced Darwinism for the paradoxical reason that apparent waste in nature could now be seen as part of a larger scheme of Design. Thus in 1861 Gray could write *Natural Selection not inconsistent with Natural Theology*, a tract warmly approved by Darwin himself.

These and other instances show that even Darwin's handling of the Design argument was not automatically seen as subversive to religion. The theological nerve that Darwin had undoubtedly touched lay even deeper than that. Some would argue that at the deepest level the threat was seen to the stability and fabric of society itself.

3. Man in society

From the current association between right-wing politics and 'creationism' in prominent anti-evolution crusaders in the USA, it might be tempting to infer that Darwinism was chiefly opposed for its subversive effects on established society. It would, however, be unhistorical to extrapolate back a century or more, though there is in fact a continuous stream of political interpretations of evolution from the days when Karl Marx wrote politely of it to Darwin, and Spencer spawned his version of Social Darwinism. What is truly remarkable is that versions of evolution have been used in arguments by Left and Right, from Marx to Hitler. As Bernard Shaw observed, Darwin 'had the luck to please everybody who had an axe to grind'. In the early days, however, it was precisely for its socially subversive implications that some opponents called Darwinism into serious question.

Two of the first objectors were men to whom Darwin owed much. Charles Lyell was never able to go the whole way with Darwin, unable to agree with any geologist who arrived 'at conclusions derogating from the elevated position previously assigned by him to man'. The status and dignity of man as perceived by Lyell could not be squared with an animal ancestry. It has been argued that this reluctance to accept progressive development in general sprung from his concern for 'the high genealogy of man'.[16] This position seems to have been held for reasons that were basically intuitive and aesthetic. But why?

Sentimental pride is an unlikely motive. Merely to place man on a par with the brutes was no new thing. Rousseau had alleged that 'it is only in degree that man differs in this respect [ideas] from the brute', and Voltaire told him his book 'makes one long to go on all fours'. This was common talk in the Enlightenment. For Lyell to react as he did there must have been something very specific about Darwinism which troubled him. What more likely candidate than the Malthusian concept of deadly struggle manifest in a nature 'red in tooth and claw'? If man was like the animals *in this respect*, what hope was there for Victorian industrial society where competition was already the order of the day, and the population of Britain's crowded cities was increasing alarmingly? Not for Lyell was any hope to emerge from the Christian good news of the power of Christ which could transform a person, irrespective of his origin, and could 'turn the world upside down'. Lyell by this time was well into the Unitarian camp to whom, of course, such comfort and hope were usually denied.

In the case of Darwin's other reluctant friend, Adam Sedgwick, the basis of opposition is much clearer. He noted that Darwin had not taken into account the link between moral and material. If that link were to be severed, 'humanity, in my mind, would suffer a damage that might brutalize it, and sink the human race into a lower grade of degradation than any into which it has fallen since its written records tell us of its history'.[17]

Ludgate Hill, from Gustave Dore's London, *showing the kind of over-population predicted by Malthus.*

Sedgwick, too, feared degradation and anarchy. Unlike Lyell he recognized a greater Power that could forestall it, but saw that for this to happen a condition must be a restoring or reaffirmation of moral categories – a denial of man's ape-like character.

It is easy to assert that Sedgwick's deepest hostility came from a determination to conserve existing social structures, and that Darwinism was opposed for political rather than religious reasons. That is to neglect the known strength of Sedgwick's theological views. Admittedly he was not to know that Darwin had confided to his private notebooks that 'The Devil under form of Baboon is our grandfather', though he was perfectly capable of reading between the lines of *The Origin* and seeing the clear implication of Darwin's thinking. The real error of *The Origin*, in Sedgwick's opinion, lay in its implied relegation of moral issues to mere epiphenomena, by-products, of matter. Thus Sedgwick could write of Darwin's book, 'From first to last it is a dish of rank materialism cleverly served and cooked up.' The same charge of 'rank materialism' he had previously levelled at Chambers' *Vestiges*, and for the same reason.

This brings us to the level at which Darwinism and Christianity came into the deepest conflict. However threatened some people may have felt from an undermining of traditional natural theology or the destruction of social stability, the heart of the opposition was that Darwinism seemed to be the agent of materialism. If so, morality was restructured, the spiritual world abandoned and God himself eliminated.

4. *The elimination of God*

It was on the relationship between God and his creation that Darwin touched the most sensitive theological nerve. Of this he was acutely aware. His early notebooks testify to a materialism of sorts, though he was careful not to reveal it too plainly to the public, partly out of deference to his wife's religious sensitivities, perhaps. The conventional portrait of Darwin makes much of the 'secularization' of his thought, from the days of *The Beagle*, when he first doubted, to his old age when he confessed that it had stripped him of all the finer things of life, such as musical and artistic appreciation, and left him an agnostic zombie, incapable of anything save the endless processing of scientific data. On this view his occasional references to God or the Creator were merely formal rhetoric, or even deliberate misrepresentation.

Recent scholarship has questioned this age-old view of Darwin himself, though it has been fostered by his friends (like Huxley) and enemies (so-called 'creationists' in modern times). The facts are much too complex for such a simple view to be sustained. So contradictory do some of them appear that one writer has referred to 'two Darwins' – an agnostic visionary on one hand and a theistic scientist on the other.[18] Paradoxes of this kind may have a variety of explanations: the difference between a man's private and public views, a change in attitude with time, or simple human inconsistency. In Darwin's case all of these were manifestly true, but in addition he was impaled upon the horns of a genuine dilemma: how could he at one and the same time deny special creation of individual species and yet preserve the rationality of science for which God had hitherto been the guarantee? Writing of later followers of Darwin who eliminated God from their world-view, S. L. Jaki expressed the dilemma in these terms:

> Their work is a life-long commitment to the purpose of proving there is no purpose. Every Darwinist is a living refutation of a philosophy, Darwinism, for which purpose is non-existent.[19]

Thus we find Darwin on occasion veering towards deism with a God at the beginning who can for all practical purposes be left out of consideration now. Sometimes his privately-held materialism suggests that even that kind of God is without meaning. Frequently 'nature' is a verbal replacement for a deity who might or might not exist. Yet at other times Darwin crusades for a nobler image of a Creator who is not the author of cruelty or waste in nature, does not tinker with the cosmos once made, and will not mislead the honest enquirer after truth. Such a God would supervise his world by the operation of general laws, including those of natural selection. Other evidence suggests a deeper religious commitment than appears at first sight, manifest in cordial relations with committed Christians, financial support for missionary enterprises, and association in published works with writers like Gray and Kingsley. There is even a story of his late conversion with some circumstantial evidence but, tantalizingly, none that is direct and unequivocal. All that can be said with certainty is that for much of his life after 1850, or a little earlier, he was a muddled theist.

That, however, is not how the public saw him. Contemporary assessments of his theology were as confused as those of later historians. As we shall see (p.165), some Christian leaders such as Charles Kingsley repudiated any notion of atheism implicit in Darwin's thought. Even Huxley argued that his theory had 'no more to do with theism than the first book of Euclid has'. Later in the century a former President of the Baptist Union, John Clifford, made the remarkable decision to include Darwin in his book *Typical Christian Leaders* (1898), citing his reference in *Animals and Plants under Domestication* to the omnipotent and omniscient Creator, who ordains everything and foresees everything. Yet, especially at first, the prevailing impression was that Darwin was really set to undermine belief in God himself. The Roman Catholic Church, in Britain and abroad, reacted strongly in this way. Joseph Bayma, a Jesuit priest who taught science at Stonyhurst College, Lancashire, declared:

> Mr Darwin is, we have reason to believe, the mouthpiece or chief trumpeter of that infidel clique whose well-known object is to do away with all idea of a God.[20]

No less trenchantly Charles Hodge answered his own question 'What is Darwinism?' with the words 'This is atheism to all intents and purposes, because it leaves the soul as entirely without God, without a Father, Helper, or Ruler as the doctrine of Epicurus or of Comte'.[21] He did not say, however, that Darwin himself was an atheist. For him, and for many Christians afterwards, the crucial issue of Darwinism was not a finely-judged assessment of its precise theological status, but rather the fact that *in practice* it seemed to eliminate God from the world. That this simple evaluation obscured other important issues we shall see later (see p.162).

Scientific doubts

By no means all the heat generated by Darwinism sprang directly from religious concern, even if that is interpreted in the broadest possible ways. Scientific objections there certainly were, misguided though they may or may not have been. Reviewing Darwin's *Descent of Man* (1871), *The Times* pointed to a circularity of argument in the concept of 'survival of the fittest'; this was tantamount to saying 'survival of those who survive' and was merely a tautology. It also suggested that Darwin's argument for *natural* causes was predicated on a hidden assumption that *that is all there were*. Later, Lord Kelvin showed on the basis of known sources for the earth's heat, and of its current rate of cooling down, that insufficient time was available for evolution. Darwin was exceedingly worried, but he need not have been; Kelvin did not know of heat generated by terrestrial radioactivity (see p.199). Neither of those objections was theological in inspiration and it would be wholly false to suggest that the entire scientific community found Darwinism an acceptable position. What also needs to be stressed is that for many people scientific and theological issues were closely related.

This is particularly noticeable with a group of late-nine-teenth-century writers advocating what Moore describes as 'Christian anti-Darwinism'. These included the Yorkshire clergyman F. O. Morris, the Essex physician C. R. Bree, the Canadian geologist J. W. Dawson and the American lawyer C. T. Curtis, all of whom attacked Darwin on the grounds of scientific methodology. Although each held the Bible in high esteem, none used a conflict with Genesis as the chief ground from which to launch his assault. Instead Darwin was chided for his lack of logic and 'hopeless chaos of thought' (Morris), for his 'false mode of reasoning and inability to produce inequivocal proof' (Bree), and for his 'arbitary arrangement of facts in accordance with a number of improved hypotheses' (Dawson). Similar scepticism was displayed by Curtis who, with all the crushing rhetoric of a skilled advocate, undermined Darwin's credibility by pointing to the multitude of 'missing links' in his chain of evidence.[22]

Because Darwin was dealing only in *probabilities* he failed to come up to the standards of Baconian rigour expected of a scientist (especially an English one). This was exactly the point made years before by Adam Sedgwick when he wrote to Darwin, acknowledging receipt of *The Origin* (Nov. 1859):

> You have *deserted* – after a start in that tram-road of all solid physical truth – the true method of induction, and started us in machinery as wild, I think, as Bishop Wilkins's loco-motive that was to sail with us to the moon. Many of your wide conclusions are based upon assumptions which can neither be proved nor disproved, why then express them in the language and arrangement of philosophical induction?[23]

In the following decades such difficulties were largely unresolved, as indeed they had to be. The time-honoured
methodology of physical science, replete with mathematical
rigour and instant experimental tests, was not necessarily
applicable to concepts like those with which Darwin was
grappling. Geology, with which Sedgwick had been concerned, occupied an intermediate position between physical
and biological science, and it is of more than passing interest
to note that Lord Kelvin asked, 'Is not geology a branch of
physical science?' and sought to make it so. In Scotland natural
history was given an inferior status to natural philosophy
(physics), and physical scientists like Kelvin and Maxwell, as
well as their colleagues in England, viewed the scientific pretensions of Darwinism with some coolness. Certainly by the
end of the nineteenth century it was possible for the American
anti-Darwinian theologian L. T. Townsend to announce that
'scores of men eminent in the field of natural science' do not
support the Darwinian hypothesis, regarding it as mere
speculation.[24]

How far the scientific opposition comprised merely
rhetorical arguments to cover up a theological objection it is
hard to say. For some Christians opposing Darwin, scientific
difficulties posed by evolution were quite as real as any others,
and they cannot be discounted. It is likely that where religious
and scientific considerations led to the same conclusion the
one would have reinforced the other. What is clear is that
many Christian anti-Darwinians appealed to science, not the
Bible, in stating their case. Had they wished to invoke evidence
from Scripture they could most surely have done so, and had an
even more appreciative readership into the bargain. We may
infer from their silence that, for them, the primary issues were
not overtly theological but scientific.

In the celebrations of 1909, commemorating the centenary
of Darwin's birth, a perceptive comment was made by the
American psychologist John Dewey:

> Although the ideas that rose up like armed men against
> Darwinism owed their intensity to religious associations,
> their origin and meaning are to be sought in science and
> philosophy, not in religion.[25]

These were, as James Moore has pointed out, the quest for
absolute certainty and a belief in the fixity of species. Both
notions are pre-Christian in origin and each sat rather uneasily

beside some specifically Christian convictions. The demand for certain knowledge ignores human fallibility and sinfulness. The notion that species were not transmutable was characteristic of the neo-Platonism then thriving in German Romantic philosophy, and allotting to humanity a supremacy and divinity that would have scandalized the writers of the New Testament. Recourse to biblical texts like 1 Corinthians 15:39 and the phrase 'according to their kind' (see Genesis 1:11, 12, 21, 24, 25) suggests a prior commitment to the fixity of species whose eternalism seems to be at odds with a biblical view of history and temporality.

Bridge over troubled waters

Despite all the Darwinian controversy and the acrimonious spirit of the partisans, it is very easy to extrapolate to a scenario in which all is conflict and battle, both for science and religion in the nineteenth century. However, scant justice is done to what we now know of that period to depict it all as *Sturm und Drang*. The whole story of heroic warriors and inflamed passions has been reduced by Charles Raven to a mere 'storm in a Victorian teacup'. That possibly goes too far the other way, but it is sufficiently provocative to prompt an enquiry as to how distinguished and ordinary people alike contrived to avoid embroilment. That many did so is certain, and it is of some interest to see how they managed to construct a bridge over the troubled waters of evolutionary argument. Two methods stand out. One was to seek a synthesis between Darwin's theories and Christianity. The other was to suspend judgment and, in effect, to sidestep the controversial issues and wait for further light.

1. Attempts at synthesis

As we have seen (p. 153), a clear concordance existed between some of Darwin's ideas and concepts that might be termed Christian. It is not surprising, then, that many should attempt some kind of synthesis between biblical and evolutionary thought. That their efforts involved controversy goes without saying; but they were not involved in the head-on collision between evolution and Christianity, and it is not too much to claim that as well as bridging those troubled waters they may have been able to diminish the tumult in some measure.

In a book already mentioned (p.148), J. R. Moore has distinguished two kinds of synthetic response.[26] The 'Christian Darwinians' were men who stood where Darwin stood, but unlike him they saw the hand of God sovereignly at work in natural selection. They included the Scottish theologian James Iverach, the Anglican clergyman A. L. Moore, the American Congregational minister G. F. Wright and the Harvard Professor of Natural History, Asa Gray. All these were of orthodox theological views. A firm belief in the Trinity enabled them to perceive in Jesus Christ the continuous and rational Upholder of the universe (Colossians 1:17 was cited by Iverach) and to deny the validity of mere deism. The two American writers were fortified in their synthesis by a strong commitment to Calvinism. Said Wright: 'If only evolutionists would incorporate into their system the sweetness of the Calvinistic doctrine of Divine Sovereignty, the church would make no objection to their speculations.'

A second category, the 'Christian Darwinists', accepted evolution but not strictly on Darwin's terms. They may, for instance, have reverted to Lamarckian views and their theology was more often liberal than orthodox, with some kind of immanent power of God at work in the natural world. They included the future Archbishop of Canterbury Frederick Temple, the Eighth Duke of Argyll, George Henslow, son of Darwin's former mentor, and the Roman Catholic zoologist St George Mivart, and two well-known preachers, H. W. Beecher in America and George Matheson in Scotland. Often their writings were tinged with German Romanticism and with the social extrapolations of Darwinism associated with Herbert Spencer.

If it should still seem strange that Christianity could have had any concourse with the thoughts of Darwin, the following opinion of Charles Raven may be salutary. Speaking of those who first opposed Darwin he said:

> It is one of the ironies of history that Christendom which by its own Scriptures was committed to belief in an ever-working God (*e.g.* John 5:17), in a progressive revelation still incomplete (John 16:13), in suffering as the characteristic of the creature (Romans 8:18–23), and the means to perfection (Hebrews 2:10), and in fuller life as the divine purpose (John 10:10) should have so signally failed to maintain this belief when faced with the challenge of Darwinism.[27]

Let us look briefly at two men whose Christian beliefs were integrated with evolution. Henry Drummond (1851–97) was a remarkable man who mixed theology and science even during his training for the Free Church of Scotland ministry at New College, Edinburgh. At the age of only 32 he was appointed Lecturer in Natural Science at the Free Church College, Glasgow, where he remained for the rest of his short life. Brief though it was, his career made an immense impression on the English-speaking world, not least by his books. His exposition of Paul's definition of 'love', *The Greatest Thing in the World*, was a booklet prepared for Christmas 1889, of which 330,000 copies had sold by his death. More substantial was his *Natural Law in the Spiritual World* (1883) which completed 119,000 copies and had been translated into French, German, Dutch, Norwegian and other languages. This, together with his *Ascent of Man* (1894), placed before the public a synthesis of Christian and evolutionary thought as bold as it was original.

Natural Law maintains that the laws which govern biological life are identical with those that govern spiritual life. Thus with such themes as biogenesis, degeneration, growth, death and so on the preacher is furnished with instant analogies. An unusual example is 'parasitism', where this very biological concept is applied to the heart of church-going! 'Even the most perfect church affords to all worshippers a greater or less temptation to parasitism.... His senses now stirred by ceremony, now soothed by music, the parasite of the pew enjoys his weekly worship – his character untouched, his will unbraced, his crude soul unquickened and unimproved.'[28]

He had a point. But when he pressed his argument so far as to identify the cosmic process of redemption with evolution, the critics had a field day.[29]

Drummond's *Ascent of Man* developed these views even further, stressing the role of altruism in the final stages of the evolutionary process. This is one of his more famous purple passages:

Up to this time no word has been spoken to reconcile Christianity with Evolution, or Evolution with Christianity. And why? Because the two are one. What is Evolution? A method of creation. What is its object? To make more perfect living beings. What is Christianity? A method of creation. What is its object? To make more perfect living beings. Through what does Evolution work? Through Love. Through what does Christianity work? Through Love.

Evolution and Christianity have the same Author, the same end, the same spirit. There is no rivalry between these processes. Christianity struck into the Evolutionary process with no noise or shock; it upset nothing of all that had been done; it took all the natural foundations precisely as it found them; it adopted Man's body, mind, and soul at the exact level where Organic Evolution was at work upon them; it carried on the building by slow and gradual modifications; and, through processes governed by rational laws, it put the finishing touches to the Ascent of Man.[30]

In forming Drummond's strange amalgam of science and religion were two very different influences. One was a close friendship with the American evangelist D. L. Moody, whom Drummond met during a campaign in Edinburgh in 1873 and accompanied on many other occasions later. His concern for evangelism became the master-passion of his life and remained so to the end.

The other major formative influence on Drummond was the 'Social Darwinism' of Herbert Spencer. Indeed he went a step further. Spencer had tried to apply biological concepts to society; Drummond extended the process to the spiritual world. Spencerian wishful thinking about human progress permeates *The Ascent* from start to finish, and not infrequently surfaces as specific quotation here and in *Natural Law*. Such views brought Drummond on a charge of heresy before the General Assembly of the Free Church of Scotland in 1895. After some argument he was acquitted. Yet the very fact that twelve charges had been brought suggested more than a touch of heterodoxy and such was indeed the case. An ardent evangelist who retained Moody's affection though not his agreement, Drummond had, in truth, decidedly 'liberal' views and a tendency 'to place charity above all doctrine, and to carry the principle of evolution to a somewhat startling length'.[31] Clearly a Darwinist rather than a Darwinian, Drummond could elevate evolution to a cosmic principle (which he then Christianized) precisely because he sat lightly to the historic biblical doctrines which, in other men, restrained and modified their allegiance to any principle of universal progress.

Not very different from Drummond's in some respects was the case of Charles Kingsley (1819–75), Rector of Eversley in Hampshire and Canon of Chester and Westminster. He too was a highly successful author, of *Westward Ho!*, *The Water*

Babies and other tales, together with much poetry and several works of scientific and theological interest. Above all he could write engagingly for the young and his works enjoyed an enormous circulation. Like Drummond he was an enthusiastic naturalist and like him he saw no religious difficulty in the idea of evolution. To Darwin he wrote to acknowledge a copy of *The Origin of Species*: 'All I have seen of it *awes* me; both with the heap of facts and the prestige of your name, and also with the clear intuition, that if you be right, I must give up much that I have believed and written. In that I care little. Let God be true, and every man a liar!'[32]

However, in his synthesis of Christianity and evolution Kingsley was poles apart from Drummond. No evangelist in the Moody tradition, he found the temper of 'personal religion' bequeathed by Wesley and Whitefield 'unfavourable to a sound and scientific development of natural theology'.[33] Wesley, he thought, might have been a great High Churchman had he been a Victorian![34] That, in fact, was Kingsley's position, though it tells us little of his attitudes to the Bible or nature.

Kingsley was in some ways more orthodox than Drummond. As a young man he wrote: 'I wish to read hardly anything but the Bible, for some time to come', and in later years he was active in defending the Athanasian creed on which he preached 'from the pulpit in season and out of season',[35] and concerning which he held 'a very strictly orthodox doctrine'. Unlike some synthesizers of religion and evolution he was an ardent Trinitarian:

> Some things I see clearly, and hold with *desperate* clutch. A Father in Heaven for all, a Son of God incarnate for all – (That incarnation is the *one* fact which is to me worth all, because it makes all others possible and rational, and without it I should go mad,) – and a Spirit of the Father *and the Son*...who works to will and to do of His own good pleasure.[36]

In conformity with the view that the religious alternative to a biblical view of nature was one derived from German Romanticism (see p.180) it is interesting to read: 'Vital religion ...with me is synonymous with a belief in the main facts of the Bible. If they are taken away I have no alternative but the modern Neo-Platonist School, which I do not believe in; or to turn a jolly Greek Pagan again.'[37] Similarly, Kingsley was anxious to avoid an anthropocentric view of nature, again contrasting strongly with Romanticism and indeed with Drummond himself. Writing of coral-reefs and other ancient wonders, he remarked that even if no human eyes had seen them there was no need to be sorry:

Was there not a Father in Heaven who was enjoying their enjoyment, and enjoying too their beauty, which He had formed according to the ideas of His Eternal Mind? Recollect what you were told on Trinity Sunday – That this world was not made for man alone: but that man, and this world, and the whole Universe was made for God; for He created all things, and for His pleasure they are, and were created.[38]

So how did a man with these theological views reconcile them with evolution? First he was quite clear about the contention that evolution was contrary to Scripture:

I must beg very humbly, but very firmly, to demur to that opinion. Scripture says that God created. But it nowhere defines that term. The means, the How of Creation, is nowhere specified. Scripture, again, says that organised beings were produced each according to their kind. But it nowhere defines that term. What a kind includes, whether it includes or not the capacity of varying (which is just the question in point), is nowhere specified. And I think it a most important rule in scriptural exegesis, to be most cautious as to limiting the meaning of any term which Scripture itself has not limited, lest we find ourselves putting into the teaching of Scripture our own human theories or prejudices.[39]

Nor was it true that evolution undermined natural theology:

Not in the least. We might accept all that Mr Darwin, all that Professor Huxley, has so learnedly and so acutely written on physical science, and yet preserve our natural theology on exactly the same basis as that on which Butler and Paley left it. That we should have to develop it, I do not deny. That we should have to relinquish it, I do.... Of old it was said by Him without whom nothing is made: 'My Father worketh hitherto, and I work'. Shall we quarrel with Science if she should show how those words are true? What, in one word, should we have to say but this? – We knew of old that God was so wise that He could make all things; but behold,

He is so much wiser than even that, that He can make all things make themselves.[40]

Whereas Hodge and others had distinguished between 'physical causes' and 'operations of the divine mind', Kingsley deplored the antithesis and argued that God could just as easily create forms capable of self-development as he could intervene by special creation each time a new species was required. In Mother Carey's famous words in *The Water Babies*, 'anyone can make things if they will take time and trouble enough: but it is not everyone who, like me, can make things make themselves.'

Thus what might look like 'an immensely long chapter of accidents' may really be 'a chapter of special Providences of Him without whom not a sparrow falls to the ground, and whose greatness, wisdom, and perpetual care I never understood as I have since I became a convert to Darwin's views'.[41]

Writing to his old mentor, F. D. Maurice, in about 1863, Kingsley commented that 'Darwin is conquering everywhere', and that people now had a stark choice before them: 'Now they have got rid of an interfering God – a master-magician, as I call it – they have to choose between the absolute empire of accident, and a living, immanent, ever-working God.' For him this posed no problem. 'Verily, God is great, or else there is no God at all.'[42]

Had the radical Christian theism of a Kingsley been coupled with the evangelistic zeal of a Drummond, one wonders if evolution might ever have been a problem for the Victorian church.

2. Suspended judgments

With convictions like these many devout Christians felt reassured and left troubled waters of controversy far below them. But there was another strategy which also avoided confrontation between Darwin and the Bible. That was to ignore the issue altogether. Sometimes, of course, this happened out of ignorance or obscuranticism, or merely indicated a 'head-in-the-sand' attitude in the hope that the problem would go away in time. But there were other, and nobler, reasons for declining involvement in conflicts. One was a belief that as Darwinism was – and is – 'only a theory', a resolution of the apparent conflict with Scripture might be available in the future, so one had to adopt a policy of 'wait and see'. The case for suspended jugment was strongly put in 'The Declaration of Students of the Natural and Physical Sciences' of 1864/5.

This manifesto (which now rests in the Bodleian Library at Oxford) arose out of the controversies over Darwinism and *Essays and Reviews*. There were 717 signatories of whom 66 were Fellows of the Royal Society, some 350 others were members of other scientific institutions, and a considerable number, students at the Royal College of Chemistry. Representing 'ordinary' and theologically unsophisticated people, their Declaration is of special interest:

> We, the undersigned Students of the Natural Sciences, desire to express our sincere regret, that researches into scientific truth are perverted by some in our own times into occasion for casting doubt upon the Truth and Authenticity of the Holy Scriptures. We conceive that it is impossible for the Word of God, as written in the book of nature, and God's Word written in Holy Scripture, to contradict one another, however much they may appear to differ. We are not forgetful that Physical Science is not complete, but is only in a condition of progress, and that at present our finite reason enables us only to see as through a glass darkly; and we confidently believe, that a time will come when the two records will be seen to agree in every particular. We cannot but deplore that Natural Science should be looked upon with suspicion by many who do not make a study of it, merely on account of the unadvised manner in which some are placing it in opposition to Holy Writ. We believe that it is the duty of every Scientific Student to investigate nature simply for the purpose of elucidating truth, and that if he finds that some of his results appear to be in contradiction to the Written Word, or rather to his own *interpretations* of it, which may be erroneous, he should not presumptuously affirm that his own conclusions must be right, and the statements of Scripture wrong; rather, leave the two side by side till it shall please God to allow us to see the manner in which they may be reconciled; and, instead of insisting upon the seeming differences between Science and the Scriptures, it would be as well to rest in faith upon the points in which they agree'.[43]

Thus the policy for scientific and scriptural data, to 'leave the two side by side', is exactly that of suspended judgment.

Much the same kind of attitude (though without the self-advertisement) appears to have been true for the many distinguished physical scientists who, while maintaining a Christian commitment, were careful not to comment in public on these matters. Biology was not their field, in any case, and their predilection for strong proofs would also lead them to keep an open mind. Except for Kelvin (who argued over the age of the earth on thermodynamic grounds) little may be found on this controversy in printed papers and published biographies. Faraday, Maxwell, Stokes, Rayleigh and others kept their own counsel in public, though privately nurtured deep suspicions on many aspects of evolutionary theory. Lord Rayleigh, for instance, confessed as late as 1906 that he could not quite 'swallow' natural selection as an explanation for evolution.[44] As one historian has observed, 'some of the most strenuous opponents of a wholly mechanistic biology have been physical scientists.'[45] In the later nineteenth century their scepticism led most of them to bypass the controversies and pursue their own work in untroubled serenity.

If distinguished men of science could largely avoid engagement in religious controversies over evolution, so also could large numbers of Christian ministers, and for similar reasons: they had their own work to do, and the issues were far from settled even among scientists. One example of this detachment from controversy will be sufficient. For several reasons the case of Charles Haddon Spurgeon is specially instructive.

C. H. Spurgeon (seated, right) *with his first London deacons.*

Spurgeon (1834–92) was a Baptist who from 1861 to his death ministered at the Metropolitan Tabernacle in South London to a Sunday congregation regularly reaching 12,000 and, by an enormous literary output, to multitudes throughout the world. Known in his day as 'The Prince of Preachers' he exercised an incalculable influence on Victorian nonconformity, and especially his own denomination. His 'Pastors' College' (which still flourishes) further disseminated his distinctive evangelicalism, and scores of chapels throughout the country owed their foundation and growth to his work. Innocent of any formal academic training, he nevertheless became an omnivorous reader, and dozens of new books were reviewed by him in his monthly magazine *The Sword and The Trowel*, which had a circulation of 25,000 copies. Source material for his views is abundantly available.

For all these reasons his influence was such that he is an appropriate figure to consider. But there is another, more powerful, reason for seeing how Spurgeon dealt with Darwinism. Not merely did he minister at the height of the controversy. As a man who was not prepared to bow to prevailing tendencies in 'modern' theology, he opposed root and branch the 'liberalizing tendencies' which he called the 'down-grade' of biblical authority in his own denomination. In 1887, though minister of the largest Baptist church in the country, he resigned from the denomination. Thus it might be expected that a man so out of tune with contemporary religion, and so committed to the high authority of Scripture, would be deeply concerned to counter the pretensions of Darwinism. That expectation would be enhanced by much contemporary portrayal of Spurgeon as a theological backwoodsman.[46] The actuality was surprisingly different.

At first sight Spurgeon reacts as might be anticipated. His magazine reprinted occasional articles or extracts highly critical of evolution.[47] In 1886 he himself writes: 'Too many Christian people have been fascinated by the puerile hypothesis of evolution, and it is well that they should know how easily the whole mass of nonsense can be reduced to nothing.'[48] This looks conclusive enough, but it is clear that what he objects to is evolutionary *philosophy* with its gnostic overtones. The new 'Cosmic Philosophy' of Spencer is dismissed as an academic's dream for 'an all-embracing unified science', based upon dubious 'evidence'. But it is not condemned on any other ground.[49]

On more specific points, Spurgeon commended 'an inter-

esting argument against the theory of Mr Darwin' which
'proclaimed man a special creation',[50] and observed that 'the
unfounded idea of evolution, *with reference to man*', was in
conflict with evidence from geology.[51] On natural theology he
exclaimed, 'If Darwinism does not exclude, it does not fully
include, the argument of Design'; again he is troubled by lack
of 'the clearest demonstration'.[52]

Spurgeon's most pungent comments are reserved for the
various attempts to synthesize evolution and Scripture. However, one medical man who, like Drummond, blended Scripture and Spencer in evangelistic addresses, was gently handled
in a review of his book, and reminded 'We look upon
"evolution" as a questionable hypothesis. It is not yet an
ascertained or acknowledged truth of science, and assuredly
the time has not come to incorporate it with our faith in
revelation'.[53] And he runs to defend Drummond's *Natural
Law in the Spiritual World* from ill-informed criticism.[54] What
he could not sympathize with was Drummond's emasculation
of the gospel, particularly his small emphasis on the atone-
ment.[55] Theological liberalism was a major stumbling-block to
attempted syntheses between Christianity and Darwinism.
The other difficulty lies in what Spurgeon sees as the essentially
speculative character of much evolutionary thought:

> The dishonour cast upon Christianity by putting it side by
> side with the scientific dream of evolution is one which we
> resent in the strongest language within our reach. The only
> conclusion we can draw from this attempt [a series of articles
> from *The Homiletic Magazine*] is, that so far as any form of
> Christianity coincides with evolution, it may be pronounced
> to be false; and so far as it is not in accordance with it, it is all
> the more likely to be true.[56]

Heady stuff, indeed. Yet again it is clear that he chiefly objected
to coupling the Christian message with a concept as vague and
unverified as 'evolution', used in different ways and without
definition by several authors in the one volume.

Given this undoubted scepticism towards evolution, why
did he not condemn it totally and directly? One reason is that
he had a high regard for science and the study of nature. To his
students and ministerial colleagues he gave this advice:

> The presence of Jesus on the earth has sanctified the whole
> realm of nature; and what He has cleansed, call not you

common.... The paths of true science, especially natural history and botany, drop fatness. Geology, so far as it is fact, and not fiction, is full of treasures.... Every portion of God's dominion in nature teems with precious teachings.[57]

In one who was called 'the last of the Calvinists' such a predilection for science is not surprising. What he objected to was the degradation of science to 'the method by which man tries to conceal his ignorance'.[58] A respect for true science was allied with the Calvinist belief in the sovereignty of a creator God and this, as we have noted, is readily compatible with at least some degree of evolution. It is interesting that nowhere does Spurgeon seem to question transmutation of species. He even seems to have perceived science as an ally in his fight against liberal theology. Writing of J. W. Dawson's *Modern Science in Bible Lands* he exclaimed: 'when "modern criticism" seeks to steal the Bible from us, "modern science"...takes up arms on our behalf.'[59]

Spurgeon rarely preached on the first chapters of Genesis. In 1865 he referred to Genesis 1:1–5 as 'no doubt, a literal and accurate account of God's first day's work in the creation of the world',[60] but ten years later introduced a sermon on Genesis 1:4 with the words:

We shall this morning leave all discussion as to the creation of the world to those learned divines who have paid their special attention to that subject, and to those geologists who know, or at any rate think they know, a very great deal about it. It is a very interesting subject, but this is not the time for its consideration: our business is moral and spiritual rather than scientific.[61]

Clearly he was now less inclined to adopt a dogmatically literal interpretation of the text.

Thus to sum up: then as now orthodox Christian believers were often suspicious of evolution because others were trying to base so many unorthodox opinions upon it. But the opposition to evolution was by no means universal, and amongst the more Calvinistic Christians with a high view of science and of God's providence there were many who inclined to be more positive or at least open on the matter. The same situation continues in the present with only minor variations. Some at one extreme saw a threat of atheism not only in evolution but in almost all scientific advance which provides a scientific *explanation* for what previously was commonly spoken about (or argued for) in terms of God's plan, design or direct activity. They often brought into the debate the most dogmatic interpretations of certain key Bible passages, as did the opponents of Galileo. At the other extreme were those who tried to read the Bible through the spectacles of evolution. In so doing they forced Christianity into a very different shape from what we find in the New Testament. In between were those who, because their orthodox faith was strong, either asked for a suspended judgment, or failed to find any real conflict because they regarded all scientific knowledge and theories, however useful, as somewhat temporary compared with what is clearly revealed.

Apart from any ideological reasons for Spurgeon's failure to launch a sustained onslaught on evolution, there was one supremely practical consideration that eliminated the subject almost completely from sermons, articles and books. To all the major evangelistic and pastoral concerns of his life it was, quite simply, a total irrelevance. With evident approval he reprinted some words of his American colleague T. de Witt Talmage, who was a strong opponent of evolution.

> Try your scientific comfort on those parents who have lost their only child. You come in, and you talk to those parents about 'selection', and about the 'survival of the fittest'...Try that consolation...The American people are finding out that worldly philosophy and human science as a consolation in time of bereavement are an illimitable, outrageous, unmitigated, and appalling humbug.[62]

It was a matter of priorities. In Spurgeon's own case the issue was simple:

> Some like to talk of Darwin and Tyndall and Huxley in their sermons; it gives a show of learning. But I like to mention Paul and Peter and Jesus Christ.[63]

In truth the bridge that Spurgeon was building did more than cross the troubled waters of evolution. He was not particularly interested in that. The gospel as he understood it was the only bridge that could span the chasm between troubled, sinful man and the God by whom he was so fearfully and wonderfully made.

Notes for chapter eight

[1] *E.g.* D. B. Wilson (ed.), *Did the Devil make Darwin do it?* (Iowa State University Press, 1983); P. Kitcher, *Abusing Science: the Cause against Creationism* (Open University Press, Milton Keynes, 1983).

[2] *E.g.* A. Ellegard, *Darwin and the General Reader: the Reception of Darwin's Theory of Evolution in the British Periodical Press, 1859–1872* (Goteborgs Universitets Arsskrift, 1958); W. Irvine, *Apes, Angels and Victorians* (Weidenfeld and Nicolson, 1955).

[3] A single – but excellent – example must suffice: D. R. Oldroyd, *Darwinian Impacts* (Open University Press, Milton Keynes, 1980).

[4] The secondary works generated by this one event would fill a small library. Extensive bibliographies may be found in Oldroyd, (ref. 3); M. Ruse, *The Darwinian Revolution* (University of Chicago Press, 1979); W. Karp, *Charles Darwin and the Origin of Species* (Cassell, 1968); A. Moorehead, *Darwin and the Beagle* (Penguin, 1971); J. H. Brooke, *Darwin*, Course Unit No. 13 in O.U. Course 'Science and Belief: from Copernicus to Darwin' (Open University Press, Milton Keynes, 1974).

[5] J. R. Moore, *The Post Darwinian Controversies: A study of the Protestant struggle to come to terms with Darwin in Great Britain and America 1870–1900* (Cambridge University Press, 1979). This contains an extensive bibliography.

[6] B. C. A. Windle, *The Church and Science* (Catholic Truth Society, 3rd edition, London, 1924); B. Ramm, 'The Catholic approach to Bible and Science', *Bibliotheca Sacra*, 1954, 3, 204–212; H. W. Paul, *The Edge of Contingency: French Catholic reaction from Darwin to Duhem* (Florida University Press, 1979).

[7] All these – and more – cited by A. D. White in his *History of the Warfare of Science with Theology in Christendom*, 2 vols. (1895 and subsequent editions).

[8] J. R. Moore, (ref. 5), p.303.

[9] Even then several notable contributors to *The Fundamentals* were sympathetic to evolution: B. B. Warfield G. F. Wright and James Orr. On Hodge and his successors see D. W. Livingstone, 'The Idea of design: the vicissitudes of a key concept in the Princeton response to Darwin', *Scottish J. Theol.*, 1984, 37, in the press.

[10] D. C. C. Watson, *The Great Brain Robbery* (Moody Press, Chicago, 1976), p.46.

[11] In F. Darwin (ed.), *Charles Darwin: his life told in an autobiographical chapter, and in a selected series of his published letters* (Murray, 1902), p.59.

[12] W. Cannon, 'The bases of Darwin's achievement: a re-evaluation', *Vict. Stud.*, 1961, 122.

[13] R. M. Young, 'Malthus and the Evolutionists, the common context of biological and social theory', *Past and Present*, 1969, No. 43, 109–145 (125).

[14] Cited with other examples in N. C. Gillespie, *Charles Darwin and the Problem of Creation* (University of Chicago Press, 1979), p.87.

[15] See G. Basalla, 'Darwin's Orchid Book', *Proc. Tenth Int. Cong. Hist. Sci.* (Ithaca and Philadelphia), 1962, 971–974 (973).

[16] M. Bartholomew, 'Lyell and evolution: an account of Lyell's response to the prospect of an evolutionary ancestry for man', *Brit. J. Hist. Sci.*, 1973, 6, 261–303.

[17] In F. Darwin, (ref. 11), p.217.

[18] N. C. Gillespie, (ref. 14), p.146.

[19] S. L. Jaki, *Angels, Apes and Man* (la Salle, Illinois), p.63.

[20] J. Bayma, cited in A. D. White, (ref. 7), p.72

[21] C. Hodge, cited *in extenso* in J. Dillenberger, *Protestant Thought and*

Natural Science (Collins, 1961), pp.237–245 (243). But see also note 9, above.
    [22] These and other examples are cited by J. R. Moore, (ref. 5), Ch.9.
    [23] F. Darwin, (ref. 11), p.216.
    [24] J. R. Moore, (ref. 5), p.199.
    [25] *Ibid.*, p.193.
    [26] *Ibid.*, Part III.
    [27] C. E. Raven, *Christianity and Science* (Lutterworth, 1956), p.31.
    [28] H. Drummond, *Natural Law in the Spiritual World* (1894), pp.351, 354.
    [29] In a much briefer biography than the standard one by George Adam Smith, Cuthbert Lennox cites 21 books and pamphlets written against *Natural Law*, excluding hostile reviews in periodicals (*Henry Drummond*, 1901, pp.233–235.
    [30] H. Drummond,*The Ascent of Man* (1894), pp.438–439.
    [31] John Watson in C. Lennox, (ref. 29), p.154.
    [32] F. Darwin, (ref. 11), p.228.
    [33] C. Kingsley, *Scientific Lectures and Essays* (1890), p.316.
    [34] C. Kingsley, *Life and Letters* (1877), vol.ii, p.221.
    [35] *Ibid.*, vol.i, p.114; vol.ii, pp.393–397.
    [36] *Ibid.*, vol.i, p.468.
    [37] *Ibid.*, vol.ii, p.187.
    [38] C. Kingsley, *Madam How and Lady Why* (Macmillan, 1907), p.175.
    [39] C. Kingsley, (ref. 33), pp.332–333.
    [40] *Ibid.*,pp.329, 332.
    [41] C. Kingsley, (ref. 34), vol.ii, p.175.
    [42] *Ibid.*, vol.ii, p.171.
    [43]See E. G. W. Bill 'The Declaration of Students of the Natural and Physical Sciences, 1865', *Bodleian Library Record*, 1956, 5, 262–267; W. H. Brock and R. MacLeod, 'The Scientists Declaration', *Brit. J. Hist. Sci.*, 1976, 9, 39–66.
    [44] R. J. Strutt, *John William Strutt, Third Baron Rayleigh* (Arnold, 1924), p.45.
    [45] D. M. Knight, *Studies in Romanticism*, 1967, 6, 76.
    [46] See Iain Murray, *The Forgotten Spurgeon* (Banner of Truth Trust, 1972), pp.139–190.
    [47] E.g. *Sword and Trowel*, 1882, 532; 1890, 187.
    [48] *Ibid.*, 1886, 290.
    [49] *Ibid.*, 1887, 361.
    [50] *Ibid.*, 1873, 523.
    [51] *Ibid.*, 1892, 674.
    [52] *Ibid.*, 1874, 337.
    [53] *Ibid.*, 1884, 88.
    [54] *Ibid.*, 1884, 292.
    [55] *Ibid.*,1891, 340.
    [56] *Ibid.*, 1888, 293.
    [57] C. H. Spurgeon. *An all-round Ministry* (Banner of Truth Trust, 1972), p.36–37 (originally published 1909).
    [58] *Ibid.*, p.97.
    [59] *Sword and Trowel*, 1892, 674.
    [60] Sermon preached 12 November 1865, No.660 in *Metropolitan Tabernacle Pulpit*, Vol.xi, p.637.
    [61] Sermon preached 29 August 1875, No.1252 in *Metropolitan Tabernacle Pulpit*, Vol.xxi, p.493.
    [62] *Sword and Trowel*, 1886, 417.
    [63] William Williams, *Charles Haddon Spurgeon* (R.T.S., London, n.d.), p.64.

9 Sacred stream: Romanticism and scientific naturalism

Many days have pass'd,
Beloved scene, since last my wet eyes saw
The moonbeams gild thy whitely-foaming waves.
Ambitious then, confiding in her powers,
Spurning the prison, – onward flew my soul,
To mingle with her kindred; – in the breeze
That wafts upon its wings futurity,
To hear the voice of praise; – and not in vain
Have these high hopes existed, – not in vain
The dew of labour has oppress'd my brow,
On which the rose of pleasure never glow'd;
For I have tasted of that sacred stream
Of science, whose delicious water flows
From Nature's bosom. I have felt the warmth,
The gentle influence of congenial souls,
Whose kindred hopes have cheer'd me; who have taught
My irritable spirit how to bear
Injustice; who have given
New plumes of rapture to my soaring wing
When ruffled with the sudden breath of storms,
Here, through the trembling moonshine of the grove,
My earliest lays were wafted by the breeze, –
And here my kindling spirit learn'd to trace
The mystic laws from whose high energy
The moving atoms, in eternal change,
Still rise to animation.
Beloved rocks! thou ocean white with mist,
Once more with joy I view thee;
Once more ye live upon my humid eyes;
Once more ye waken in my throbbing breast
The sympathies of nature. Now I go
Once more to visit my remember'd home,
With heartfelt rapture, – there to mingle tears
Of purest love, – to feel the ecstatic glow
Of warm affection, and again to view
The rosy light that shone upon my youth.

Humphry Davy, c.1800

They exchanged the truth of God for a lie, and worshipped and
served created things rather than the Creator ....

Romans 1:25

It is not common for scientists to write poetry, at least of any enduring quality. Yet, at the very end of the eighteenth century, the young Humphry Davy,[1] who had already distinguished himself in chemistry and had a glittering scientific career before him, penned the composition at the head of this chapter. Recollections mingled of the waves breaking on the coast of his native Cornwall, and of the sheer delight of scientific discovery shared with friends in Bristol. Of such heady pleasures he wrote:

> For I have tasted of that sacred stream
> Of science, whose delicious water flows
> From Nature's bosom.

Quite apart from any literary merits that the poem may have (and Wordsworth thought quite highly of Davy's verse), it is remarkable for its depth of feeling, its evident 'sympathies' with nature, and for two other features captured in the lines above. Science itself is now regarded as something holy and religious: it is a 'sacred stream'. And nature regains what long ago it had lost, a femininity, a personality, something approaching divinity. These two trends have roots stretching back to antiquity, but now they have a new visibility, a new prominence and they were to have profoundly important repercussions in the two centuries that followed. During all the years of the Darwinian controversies and right into our own day they represent ways of confronting nature and of thinking about science that were radical alternatives to those of the Newtonian mechanistic world-view. By the same token they depict the relationship between God and his universe in a rather new light. For Davy and those who shared his sympathies, divinity was an attribute of nature and of science – suggestions which would have scandalized Boyle, Newton and succeeding generations whose God was separate from nature and sovereignly in control of it. Theirs might be termed the 'classical' view of science. What was now emerging was its polar opposite: Romanticism.[2]

This has been described as predominantly 'a desperate rearguard action against the spirit and the implications of modern science'.[3] The simple fact was that much post-Newtonian science had forgotten its distinctively Christian origins and, as such, disclosed a universe that was not only unfriendly to man but was no longer able to convey a sense of God's continuing benevolence and love. Deism, actual or implicit, exacted heavy penalties from its adherents. From the comfortless, formal, deistically inclined Anglicanism of the day a way of escape appeared in the evangelical revival and the rediscovery of God's love and power available through the cross and resurrection. But not all would bring themselves to learn from Whitefield and Wesley. For many an alternative position was that associated with Romanticism, and this included nature within its world-view. First we look at this view of nature so eloquently announced (but not invented) by Humphry Davy.

Humphry Davy (1778–1829): poet, chemist, inventor of the miners' safety lamp, and founder of electrochemistry.

The worship of nature

It would take us much too far from our present purpose to enquire into the extent to which Davy was a true 'Romantic'.

The term itself is fraught with ambiguities, though is generally agreed to relate to certain cultural movements between about 1790 and 1830, associated first with Germany, then England and finally France. Romanticism was a reaction against that which could constrain and stultify the human imagination, whether in the form of literary rules, acceptance of ancient authorities and received wisdom, or using 'reason' as an ultimate arbiter.

So far as the Romantics were concerned, nature is not merely (or mainly) apprehended by scientific analysis. Said William Blake, 'Nature is imagination itself', and he accordingly held a low view of Bacon ('Bacon's philosophy has ruined England') and Newton ('May God keep us from single vision and Newton's sleep'). Nature was more to be appreciated and felt than to be measured and analysed. It was invested with such a potency to capture the imagination and speak to man at the deepest levels that in some respects, at least, it would be seen to pulsate with a life of its own, even with a divinity that could be worshipped.

All this, of course, is strongly reminiscent of the universe before Bacon. But there are differences. Romanticism arose from a specific social situation that included (in England at least) the growing Industrial Revolution. Blake also inveighed against the 'dark Satanic mills', and many Romantic poets held radical, if not subversive, political ideals. Then again this resurgence of nature-worship was a specific reaction against the mechanistic world-views promulgated right through the 'Enlightenment'.

Seen in this light Davy certainly participates in some of the characteristics of a Romantic. Because he was also a scientist he is well worth some further acquaintance. His Romanticism gains in significance when we recall that, during his Bristol period, he joined the circle of those who were later to be called the 'Lake poets': Southey, Wordsworth and Coleridge. At Wordsworth's request he saw through the press *Lyrical Ballads*, and he revised Southey's lengthy poem *Thalaba*. Coleridge became his passionate admirer and attended his chemical lectures to improve his stock of metaphors.

The poem above testifies to the sensitivity of Davy's response to nature. But how did it begin? While only a teenager he wrote:

Today, for the first time in my life I have had a distinct sympathy with Nature. I was lying on the top of a rock to leeward; the wind was high, everything was alive, and myself part of the series of visible impressions: I should have felt pain in tearing a leaf from one of the trees.

It was not long before sympathy turned to worship:

> Oh! most magnificent and noble Nature!
> Have I not worshipped thee with such a love
> As never mortal man before displayed?
> Adored thee in thy majesty of visible creation,
> And searched into thy hidden and mysterious ways
> As Poet, as Philosopher, as Sage?

Most clearly his devotion emerges in a letter to his friend Thomas Underwood and dates from 1801:

> That part of Almighty God which resides in the rocks and woods, in the blue and tranquil sea, in the clouds and moonbeams of the sky, is calling upon thee with a loud voice: religiously obey its commands and come and worship with me on the ancient altars of Cornwall.[4]

Davy, it appears, has taken us right back to that most primitive of religious attitudes: pantheism. Even allowing for rhetorical exaggeration, or even a jocular caricature of his own real beliefs, we can hardly escape the conclusion that deep in his consciousness was some kind of identification of God with nature. And so it was with many another sensitive soul who recoiled in horror from the arid deism of much post-Newtonian science and the ugliness and degradation coming upon the new industrial urban society. Unfortunately many such people focused only on creation, not the Creator.

It is worth recalling that Davy was far from alone in this re-deification of nature, nor was it only 'romantic' coastal scenery that evoked such a response. In an important recent book on *Man and the Natural World* Keith Thomas discusses changing attitudes to nature in England from 1500 to 1800. He devotes one section to 'The Worship of Trees', showing how the fear of forests gradually became replaced by awe and reverence.[5] Pagan beliefs of great antiquity associated with yew-trees and mistletoe persisted despite official disapproval of 'sacred groves'. Trees were increasingly cherished in the eighteenth century, both for their utility as structural materials and for making charcoal for iron-smelting; but, as Thomas points out, their symbolic value also became increasingly appreciated.

Thus when William Cowper contemplated a vast and venerable oak in Yardley Chase he confessed that to worship it was idolatry, but 'idolatry with some excuse' at least for his Druid ancestors. (Incredibly it was under that very tree that he is supposed to have written 'God moves in a mysterious way'!) Years later Wordsworth reported the case of a yeoman advised to cut down 'a magnificent tree' in order to make a profit. 'Fell it?' he exclaimed, 'I had rather fall on my knees and worship it.' And for the Romantics, the analogy between Gothic architecture and a forest grove was deeply significant.

As for trees, so it was with mountains.[6] Regarded in the early eighteenth century with aversion and fear, they were frequently given the overworked adjective 'horrid' (the same word used by Bishop Butler for Wesley's 'pretending', and for a similar reason: both Wesley and mountains were incomprehensible to the tidy rationalism of the 'Enlightenment'). Yet fear became replaced by fascination and in 1792 the Langdale Pikes were first climbed for pleasure; eight years earlier a new word entered the English vocabulary: 'scenery'. And in the early days of Lake District exploration natural theology gained new devotees and fresh arguments.

Thomas West, whose *Guide to the Lakes* appeared in 1778, confessed, 'Whoever takes a walk into these scenes, must return penetrated with a sense of the Creator's power, in heaping mountains upon mountains, and enthroning rocks against rocks.' The artist William Green maintained that 'in a survey of the scenes surrounding him the spectator cannot but contemplate with religious awe the wonders of his beneficent creator'. As Arnold Lunn showed, over a century later, the mountain cult is rational only within the framework of a theocentric philosophy.[7]

With the coming of the Romantics these conventional expressions of natural theology tend to be replaced by direct interactions with nature herself. Wordsworth, who at Tintern Abbey in 1798 had declared himself 'so long a worshipper of Nature', confessed to feeling:

> A presence that disturbs me with the joy
> Of elevated thoughts: a sense sublime
> Of something far more deeply interfused,
> Whose dwelling is the light of setting suns,
> And the round ocean and the living air,

> And the blue sky, and in the mind of men:
> A motion and a spirit, that impels
> All thinking things, all objects of all thought,
> And rolls through all things.

For him the mountains of his native Lake District came to symbolize 'the living principle of things' and 'in the mountains did he feel his faith'. One Wordsworth scholar, introducing his *Guide to the Lakes* (1835), said that Wordsworth's love for the area was possible only 'because he conceived of Nature as herself endowed with life, and capable herself of both inward and responsive joy'.[8] Many others reacted in a similar religious way, as Ruskin who supposed 'there is a mountain brotherhood between the Cathedral and the Alp'.

One other illustration must suffice of this divinization of nature: 'the rainbow'. An interesting recent paper has shown how attitudes to this familiar phenomenon dramatically changed between about 1600 and 1800.[9] From being a symbol of God's covenant with man it became a subject of scientific analysis, successfully accomplished by Newton. The poets had a field-day. Newton is often seen as triumphing over nature as, in feminized form, she yields herself to him. Wrote Thomson (1727):

> Nature herself
> Stood all subdued by him, and open laid
> Her every latent glory to his view.

A contemporary poet, Richard Glover, enquired of the sun in similar vein:

> How Newton dared adventurous to unbraid
> The yellow tresses of thy shining hair?

Decades later the Romantics tended to decouple the image of the rainbow from its Newtonian associations and to use it imaginatively in a variety of other ways. Wordsworth wrote coldly of Newton 'with his prism and silent face', but it was left to Keats to express most succinctly the Romantic horror of scientific analysis:

> There was an awful rainbow once in heaven:
> We know her woof, her texture; she is given
> In the dull catalogue of common things.

> Philosophy will clip an Angel's wings,
> Conquer all mysteries by rule and line,
> Empty the haunted air, and gnomed mine –
> Unweave a rainbow....

Here perhaps is the ultimate philistinism of the poet towards science. To propose that 'philosophy [science] will clip an Angel's wings' is to deny the plausibility of complementary approaches to any physical phenomenon. If a rainbow is explicable at a scientific level, that need no more diminish its aesthetic appeal than it need contradict its significance for a religious covenant. Logically Keats had no case at all. But the problem is that we are not dealing with logic but with feeling, not with reason but emotion. That is the essence of Romanticism, on which account it is odd to find it espoused by a scientist.

So we return to Humphry Davy. How did he manage at the same time to be ravished by a semi-divine nature and to become the leading chemist of his country? Several facts spring to mind.

The Royal Institution where Davy's lectures were so popular that, to avoid congestion of the audience's carriages, Albemarle Street became the first one-way road in London.

In the first place Davy's commitment to Romantic ideals was not total, and it was at its peak before his greatest scientific discoveries were made. Away from the Cornish cliffs and the congenial company of the Lake poets his commitment to a rational view of science increased as his poetic effusions diminished. In London it was not so much communion with nature as fame which became the spur. Then, secondly, a polarization between Romanticism and science was not as complete as might be imagined. Coleridge, Wordsworth and (especially) Shelley were all keen to study chemistry at some stage in their adult lives. This science, not as precise as physics in those days, posed less of a threat to the human imagination. Moreover it was much more useful, and Romantics tended to favour utility. Thirdly, a Romantic view of nature included a conviction as to its essential unity. Perhaps it was for this reason that Davy was able to over-ride conventional demarcation lines between chemistry and electricity and become, in fact, the founder of a new hybrid science, electrochemistry. And it may well have been the same innate conviction that impelled him to seek for a deeper unity of matter than the conventional view of the chemical elements suggested, and to wonder whether the several dozen elements then known might not be reducible to a much smaller number.

Yet it has to be said that Romanticism and physical science were odd bedfellows and, at the end of the day, Davy's chemistry seems to have suffered from the association. He did not like tightly-bound conceptual schemes, and was well known for his reluctance to elaborate a detailed theory of electrochemistry and to accept the atomic hypothesis of his famous compatriot John Dalton. His great rival, the Swedish chemist J. J. Berzelius, perceived in Davy another Romantic characteristic: a tendency to think broadly and imaginatively without too much attention to detail. Had his approach been more disciplined, thought Berzelius, Davy 'would have advanced chemistry by a whole century. But as it was, he only left brilliant fragments'. Berzelius was similarly critical of the Romantic movement in Germany (*Naturphilosophie*) whose simplistic generalizations were of little value in chemical theory. The great German chemist Liebig also regretted an early period of his life wasted with such concerns. Those discoveries that were formally within the context of *Naturphilosophie* by Ritter and Oersted can be readily understood as products of a 'normal science' tradition imbibed long before their absorption of Romanticism.[10]

In fact a Romantic view of a nature personified, if not deified, persisted as an undercurrent in many streams of Victorian thought. Nor is it dead today, and we shall meet it in connection with the environmental reaction against science and with a systems approach to ecology. Most obviously it is enshrined in memorable phrases like 'The living planet', 'Nature's cures' and 'Friends of the Earth'. How far it had – or will have – a relevance for humanity as a whole could well depend upon its precise theological orientation.

The rejection of a deistic world-view by the Romantics is clearly compatible with biblical teaching and indeed is positively encouraged. So also is the capacity to appreciate beauty and power in nature that owes nothing to human manipulation or planning. We may even argue that a balanced biblical theology asserts not only God's transcendence but also his immanence in nature: the Psalmist asked where he could fly from God's presence (Psalm 139:7), God is said to fill heaven and earth (Jeremiah 23:24) and not to be far from any of us (Acts 17:27), even having knowledge of the sparrow that drops forgotten to the ground (Matthew 10:29). There might be some evidence for locating a special presence of God in extraordinary situations, though that is confined to the Old Testament, not the New (Exodus 3:5; 19:18; 1 Kings 19:11–12, *etc.*). And as we have seen (p.114), there are strong reasons for inferring the glory of God from natural phenomena.

One may go even further than this by recalling the Romantics' conception of the historical process. They reacted strongly against the essentially static universe implied by an unchanging hierarchical view of a nature governed solely by Newtonian mechanics. Such a view denigrated history and offered no hope to mankind for the future. This contrasts with the biblical insistence on hope and the continuing parading of the facts of Israel's history before a forgetful people. The adoption of an essentially evolutionary world-view, with 'higher' beings emerging from 'lower', might be deemed an interesting instance of Romantic writing echoing, consciously or otherwise, Christian values.

That, however, is not to equate other aspects of the Romantic and biblical world-views. Nature as an object of adoration in itself is foreign to biblical thinking, worshipping even images of natural objects (let alone the objects themselves) being forbidden categorically (Exodus 20:4), and a mark of spiritual declension (Romans 1:22–25). Moreover the hope enjoined by the New Testament is specifically hope in the gospel (Colossians 1:23) and in the Lord Jesus Christ (Colossians 1:27; 1 Thessalonians 1:3; 1 Timothy 1:1) and relates not merely to this life but to the resurrection of the dead (Acts 2:26; 23:6; 1 Corinthians 15:19) and the life of the world to come (Colossians 1:5; Titus 1:2; 2:13; 3:7). It is of a wholly different character from the woolly optimism of Romantic writing in general. Thus it is not surprising to find an element of theological heterodoxy in many Romantics.

Humphry Davy, though nominally an Anglican, did not care to display orthodox Christian views in his posthumous *Consolations in Travel,* even though religion figured prominently in the book. His private notebooks are more revealing. He opposed atheism, materialism and biological reductionism. Several times he expressed a hope (no more) in the immortality of the soul, and regarded investigation of the wonders of creation as a religious duty. The nearest he comes to a credal statement is a footnote reference in an early notebook to what he calls 'the simple and fundamental truths of the Christian religion'. These he defines as 'the unity of God, the necessity of morality and the future state of retribution founded on the resurrection'.[11] Just that. It is scarcely any advance on the emasculated deism to which the 'Enlightenment' had sunk so miserably. It is not surprising that Davy's religion brought him little joy as the years advanced or that his spokesman in *Consolations in Travel* confessed that religion really had nothing to do with ordinary life. However, his biographer records that at the very end Davy 'not only studied the doctrines of Christianity, but derived the greatest consolation from its tenets'.[12] If so it will have far eclipsed any 'consolations in travel'.

Of course Davy is only a single example, but his case does support the thesis that veneration of 'Mother Nature' and Christian orthodoxy were mutually exclusive. Such was also the case with the self-proclaimed materialist John Tyndall. He said:

> Some people give me little credit for religious feeling. I assure you that when I walk here and gaze at these mountains I am filled with adoration.[13]

It has been plausibly suggested that many Victorian agnostics found some kind of 'religious' consolation in the mountains.[14] When Coleridge moved to a much more biblical apprehension of Christianity he said that what he now disliked most in

Wordsworth was 'the vague, misty rather than mystic, confusion of God with the world and the accompanying nature-
worship'.

There was in fact no more specifically Christian reason for
writing poetry about the nature-goddess than there necessarily is today in subscribing to *The Field* or *Country Life*.
Writing about tree-worship Keith Thomas observed: 'Durk-
heim may have been wrong when he suggested that when
men worshipped God they were really worshipping society.
But he would have been very near the truth if he had said it
about the worship of the trees.'[15]

T. H. Huxley.

The worship of science

While the Romantic poets fell over themselves in their eager-
ness to idolize nature, science was, as we have seen, generally

unimpressed. Those scientists in the early nineteenth century who did permit themselves to write on theological matters generally did so in the context of natural theology, as in the Bridgewater Treatises. Their view was dramatically opposed to God-in-nature thinking. One illustration must suffice: the Bridgewater Treatise by William Prout, who trenchantly observes:

> The poor untutored savage 'sees God in every cloud, and hears him in the wind'. The complacent philosopher smiles at the credulity of the savage, and perhaps deifies 'the laws of nature!' Both are alike ignorant; nor is the imagined Supreme Being of the untaught savage in any degree more absurd than the imagined Pantheism of the philosopher.[16]

Before Darwin these sentiments were entirely typical of a British man of science – especially if he worked in astronomy, physics or chemistry. One of the most remarkable changes in the character of Victorian scientific discourse is that, once the half-century had passed, men of science are suddenly to be found reverting to the linguistic forms hitherto the prerogative of poets and speculative thinkers. Something really quite remarkable had happened.

Of this new movement the most eloquent (and aggressive) spokesman was T. H. Huxley. Having been deeply impressed by the writings of Goethe, he admitted in 1856 (when he was 31) that for him 'living nature is not a mechanism but a poem'. Thereafter this English biologist and popularizer of science could never completely shake off the influence of *Naturphilosophie*. In the first issue of the scientific journal *Nature* he proffered his own translation of Goethe's rhapsody on 'Nature' which concludes:

> She has brought me here and will also lead me away. I trust her. She may scold me, but she will not hate her work. It was not I who spoke of her – No! What is false and what is true, she has spoken it all. The fault, the merit, is all hers.[17]

Somewhat lamely he denies that so to apostrophize nature is to indulge in pantheism (which the British public detested). That was in 1869. Years later he spoke easily of Dame Nature and continued to feminize, as well as personalize, the concept.[18] The usage is too persistent to be accidental, and if it is not intended can only be what a recent commentator has styled 'the trick of speaking from both corners of the mouth . . . , performance worse than a blunder'.[19]

Huxley did not blunder. He knew what he was about, and he was far from alone in reverting to an organismic, pre-Christian view of nature. His friend the physicist John Tyndall thought of the world not as a machine but as an ever-growing tree.[20] His Presidential Address to the British Association, delivered in Belfast in 1874, not merely rocked public opinion for its advocacy of materialism, but also expressed sympathy with the Renaissance mystic Bruno, in his belief that matter is not that 'mere empty *capacity* which philosophers have pictured her to be, but the universal mother who brings forth all things as the fruit of her own womb'.[21] And in 1869 the Metaphysical Society was founded with many leading scientists amongst its members. The first meeting included a reading of a poem by Tennyson. Its title was 'The Higher Pantheism'.

So why did science revert to that which it had seemingly abandoned after a brief flirtation around 1800 and from which it had been liberated 150 years before that? To answer that question it is necessary to recall some new elements in the social context. Most notable of those was the growing unpopularity of the Established Church in England. Even in rural parishes anti-clerical feeling had been markedly on the increase from about 1750. There was growing discontent with the tithes exacted by clergy from farmers; the system of enclosure made many country parsons into prosperous farmers, and this was not conducive to a spiritually edifying ministry; and the new breed of clerical magistrate or squire-parsons ('squarsons') at the end of the century alienated still further the rural labourers from the church.[22]

Add to this the general declension of spirituality in the Church of England before the time of Charles Simeon and we have a wholly understandable aversion to the Established Church by much of the population. If that were not enough, the tiny but growing scientific community was regarding that Church with increasing disfavour for reasons that had nothing whatever to do with interpretations of Genesis.

For centuries Britain had been governed by a largely hereditary aristocracy. With the Industrial Revolution this became unmistakably joined by a new aristocracy dependent on talent, intellect and enterprise. The new leaders of urban society often sought to use science as an aid to social progress – hence in part the burgeoning of local institutions where

Darwin. As James Moore aptly put it, 'Darwin had stormed the holy of holies with a naturalistic creed.' The message of those who manipulated the whole macabre event, removing Darwin's body from its intended village resting-place, was clear to all: 'an imperial mandate to rule over "men and their intelligences" belongs to the favoured few who follow the conquering naturalist of Downe.'[26]

It would seem that the sacralization of science – and the secularization of society – had been accomplished. '...that sacred stream of science' was now a reality, if not a mighty river that would purge society of its ills and even its sin. If ever Huxley and his friends really believed that was a possibility, they would have been appalled by the subsequent course of history. The euphoric haze of unlimited optimism associated with Spencer and his followers was swiftly dispersed by the two World Wars that followed. The contours of Victorian scientific naturalism melted away in the face of twentieth-century science in its rejection of a closed, determinate universe. In our own day the supreme irony is that the very world-view from which naturalism sprang – a Romantic view of nature – is amongst the most hostile opponents of science itself (ch.11).

We must not, however, be misled by a one-sided assessment of the situation even in Victorian times. Those who shout loudest do not necessarily make the strongest impression. By no means did all men of science count themselves in with Huxley and his friends. Many leading physical scientists from Faraday to Kelvin counted themselves members of a greater church than the 'church scientific' (and many were not Anglicans). Nor must we be dazzled by circulation figures for *Nature* or the 'heavy' periodicals of the day. Immense numbers were reached by humbler organs like *The English Mechanic,* which had a straightforward no-nonsense approach to science free from ideological naturalism.

Today our judgment must be that, if Romanticism liberated the arts, neither it nor its offspring Victorian naturalism did anything for science *as a way of understanding nature.* Eichner could hardly have put it better:

> The real scientists of the last two hundred years...took no notice of Romantic theory and carried on in the spirit of Copernicus, Harvey, Newton and even La Mettrie....

After slight adjustment and 'a few sleepless nights caused by the uncertainty principle' Galileo would 'feel completely at home at M.I.T.'. On the other hand, 'Schelling would have to be brainwashed'.[27]

Sacred streams often turn into muddied rivers, and such was the case with Victorian 'sacralized' science. As an ideological tool it accomplished much in its time, though even then it is doubtful if many turned from a Christian faith on account of science. It has left us the baleful legacy of a 'military metaphor' which still confuses the layman and ensnares the would-be Christian apologist. And it obscured the fact that the whole value and purpose of science depends, not on a divine nature, but on a divine creation and a divine mandate to study it.

Notes for chapter nine

[1] Recent book-length studies on Davy include Sir Harold Hartley, *Humphry Davy*, 2nd ed. (S.R. Publishers, 1971); A. Treneer, *The Mercurial chemist. A life of Sir Humphry Davy* (Methuen, 1963); S. Forgan (ed.), *Science and the Sons of Genius: Studies on Humphry Davy* (Science Reviews Ltd., 1980).

[2] A variety of papers on 'Romanticism and Science' in *Studies in Romanticism*, 1977, *16*; see also D. M. Knight, 'The physical sciences and the Romantic movement', *Hist. Sci.*, 1970, *9*, 54; *idem*, 'The Scientist as Sage', *Studies in Romanticism*, 1967, *6*, 65.

[3] H. Eichner, 'The rise of modern science and the genesis of Romanticism', *Proc. Modern Language Assoc.*, 1982, *97*, 8.

[4] These three citations occur in Treneer, (ref. 1), pp.54–55; J. Davy (ed.), *Fragmentary Remains of Sir Humphry Davy* (1858), p.14; and Treneer, (ref. 1), p.80. There are many similar examples in these sources.

[5] K. Thomas, *Man and the Natural World* (Allen Lane, 1983), pp.212–223.

[6] On attitudes to mountains see M. H. Nicolson, *Mountain Gloom and Mountain Glory: the development of the aesthetics of the infinite* (Ithaca, 1959); E. W. Hodge, *Enjoying the Lakes* (Oliver and Boyd, 1957).

[7] A. Lunn, *A Centenary of Mountaineering 1857–1957* (Allen and Unwin, 1957).

[8] E. de Selincourt, Introduction to Wordsworth's *Guide to the Lakes* (5th ed. 1835, reprinted Oxford University Press, 1973), p.xxiii.

[9] J. L . Epstein and M. L. Greenberg, 'Decomposing Newton's rainbow', *J. Hist. Ideas*, 1984, *45*, 115.

[10] H. Eichner, (ref. 3), pp.23–24.

[11] MS Notebook 13e, Royal Institution, London.

[12] J. Paris, *Life of Sir Humphry Davy* (1831), vol.ii, p.362.

[13] J. Tyndall, cited in A. Lunn, (ref. 7), p.46.

[14] R. W. Clark, *The Victorian Mountaineers* (Batsford, 1953), pp.18–24. Clark's suggestion that many clergy turned to the mountains because of 'the impinging of science on religious thought' (p.112) is refuted by A. Lunn, (ref. 7), (p.47) as 'derived from the folklore of Victorian freethinkers'.

[15] K. Thomas, (ref. 5), p.223.

[16] W. Prout, *Chemistry, Meteorology, and the Function of Digestion, considered*

with reference to *Natural Theology* (London, 3rd Ed., 1845), p.495.

[17] *Nature*, 1869, 1, 10.

[18] O. Stanley, 'T. H. Huxley's treatment of "Nature"', *J. Hist. Ideas*, 1957, *18*, 120–127.

[19] S. L. Jaki, *Angels, Apes and Men* (Sugden, Illinois, 1983), p.89.

[20] J. Tyndall, *Fragments of Science*, 9th ed. (1896), Vol.ii, p.337.

[21] *Rep. Brit. Assoc. Adv. Sci.*, 1874, p.xcii.

[22] E. J. Evans, 'Some reasons for the growth of English rural anti-clericalism, c.1750–c.1780', *Past and Present*, 1975, no.66, 84.

[23] On the X-Club see J. V. Jensen, *Brit. J. Hist. Sci.*, 1970, *5*, 63; and R. M. MacLeod, *Notes and Records Roy. Soc.*,1970, *24*, 181.

[24] See E. E. Daub, 'Demythologising White's Warfare of Science with Theology', *The American Biology Teacher*, 1978, *40*, 553–556 and many other references in this book. One notable example of 'conflict historiography' must suffice: the idea that massive religious opposition to the introduction (by J. Y. Simpson) of chloroform anaesthesia for obstetrics in 1847 on the basis of Genesis 3:16. Recent work has shown the opposition that has been reported in dozens of historical accounts was 'virtually non-existent' (A. D. Farr, *Ann. Sci.*, 1983, *40*, 159–177).

[25] C. Fraser, *Nature*, 1871, *4*, 120.

[26] J. R. Moore, 'Charles Darwin lies in Westminster Abbey', *Biol. J. Linnean Soc.*, 1982, *17*, 97 (111).

[27] H. Eichner, (ref. 3), pp.24–25.

10 Powerful currents: crisis in Newtonian physics

At quite uncertain times and places,
    The atoms left their heavenly path,
And by fortuitous embraces,
    Engendered all that being hath.
And though they seem to cling together,
    And form 'associations' here,
Yet, soon or late, they burst their tether,
    And through the depths of space career.

James Clerk Maxwell (1831–79), Poem *Molecular Evolution*, written at the British Association Meeting in Belfast, 1874.

'In the beginning, O Lord, you laid the foundations
        of the earth,
    and the heavens are the work of your hands.
They will perish, but you remain;
    they will all wear out like a garment.
You will roll them up like a robe;
    like a garment they will be changed.
But you remain the same,
    and your years will never end.'

Hebrews 1:10–12

The new scientific revolution in the physical sciences

There is absolutely no way in which scientific developments over the last century can be summarized, let alone discussed, within one short chapter. Perhaps this does not matter too much, since there is an abundance of accessible literature covering everything from quantum theory to sociobiology.[1] What can be done is to indicate, however briefly, a few of the critical turning-points in human thought which appear as major discontinuities with the past and can by almost any criterion be termed a new 'scientific revolution'. Of their practical consequences and implications we shall, in this chapter, say almost nothing. How, if at all, they are or were related to Christian theology will be our main concern, though even here the bibliography will be more informative than the text (and that, too, is highly selective). Even as Darwin was shattering many long-established beliefs about man and his probable ancestry, others working in the physical sciences were eroding even more incisively the very foundations of human understanding about nature itself and calling into question cherished assumptions about the whole enterprise called science. In the following account we shall confine ourselves to four developments in physics.

1. Atomic structure

From the Greeks to Newton atoms were seen as the ultimate units of matter and were, as their name implied, unsplittable. After John Dalton they were distinguished by characteristic weights for atoms of each element, and some doubts were entertained (by Prout and others) as to whether heavier atoms might not be composed of simpler ones. However, no evidence that could be seriously held to support this emerged until the end of the nineteenth century. Then the currents of change flowed swiftly and within two decades had swept away the atomic beliefs of 2,000 years.[2]

In 1896 the French chemist Becquerel was surprised to note the fogging of sealed photographic plates, and attributed it to the presence of uranium compounds in the same drawer. He soon established that air in the neighbourhood was also ionized. The subject was taken up by a young Polish girl for her doctoral thesis in Paris. In a few months Marie Curie (as she became on marriage) had named the phenomenon 'radioactivity' and isolated from pitchblende an element many times more active than uranium. She called it 'radium'. To the astonishment of the academic world she concluded that what was happening was nothing less than a spontaneous breakdown of heavy atoms to simpler ones, with emission of positively and negatively charged particles as well as short wave-length radiation. She further concluded that disintegration cannot be hastened or retarded, that each element had a definite half-life period and that new elements were formed. Thus was laid to rest not only the unsplittable atom of the physicist but also the immutable element of the chemist. Many years later man-made atomic fission and fusion became possible.

Meanwhile, in 1897, J. J. Thomson in the Cavendish Laboratory had been passing electric discharges through gases at low pressure (a favourite pastime for late Victorians). He obtained X-rays, streams of positive ions and 'cathode rays'; these turned out to be negatively charged particles with enough kinetic energy to rotate the sails of a miniature windmill in their path. They were identical whatever the source, and appeared to be a common constituent of all matter. He had discovered the electron. The negative 'rays' from radioactivity proved to be identical.

Eminent Professor. "AND SO YOU SEE, MY DEAR YOUNG LADY, THE ELECTRONS OR B PARTICLES WHICH ARE EXPELLED FROM THE ATOM LOSE THEIR KINETIC ENERGY BY IMPINGING ON THE GASEOUS MOLECULES, WHICH THEY IONISE, AND WHEN THEIR VELOCITY IS REDUCED SUFFICIENTLY ARE EVENTUALLY SWALLOWED UP."

Dear Young Lady. "OH, I *SEE*; BUT WHAT FEARFULLY ROUGH LUCK ON THE ELECTRONS!"

Mysteries of modern physics: Punch *cartoon, 5th March 1913.*

From these results Ernest Rutherford concluded that the atom consists of positive and negative electricity and, in his nuclear theory of 1911, proposed a nucleus of positive electricity, surrounded by a shell of (negative) electrons. Subsequent experiments revealed that much of the atom must be empty space. Charged helium atoms ($\propto$-particles) could pass through thin sheets of lead. Experiments in a cloud chamber enabled tracks of particles to be followed visually. From the extreme rarity of deflections it appeared that the atom must be comparable to the solar system in its porosity.

The Rutherford atom was soon modified by Bohr, Somerfeld and others, but its main contention remained. The 'hard, massy solid particles' of Newton were as removed from reality as were the eternally unchanging atoms of Lucretius. From the electronic structure of the atom emerged powerful new explanations of chemical bonding at the hands of Lewis, Langmuir and others. But it was physics rather than chemistry that underwent the most profound changes as the billiard-ball image of the atom disappeared from sight for ever.

2. Thermodynamics

It is sometimes said that the Newtonian, mechanistic view of the universe was destroyed by Einstein in the twentieth century. In fact the challenge began half a century earlier with the emergence and development of thermodynamics.[3] The famous First Law, otherwise known as the Law of Conservation of Energy, was established in the late 1840s by J. P. Joule, the Manchester physicist, who determined the mechanical equivalent of heat and is commemorated by a plaque in Westminster Abbey and by the modern SI unit for work and energy, the Joule.

The Second Law of Thermodynamics is about the *availability* rather than the *conservation* of energy and is a far more revolutionary concept. Its formulation is variously attributed to the French engineers N. L. S. Carnot and E. Clapeyron and the German physicist R. J. E. Clausius. A paper by Clausius to the Berlin Academy in 1850 may be said to have been the first effective exposition of both laws, making use of the dynamic theory of heat: that heat is not a weightless fluid (caloric) but a motion of particles. Many engineers had been intrigued by the steam-engine, in which work is obtained from heat, and Carnot had concluded that the amount obtainable depended on the quantity of heat transmitted from a hot body to a cold one and the difference in their temperatures. On this basis Clausius was to announce a fundamental generalization that heat cannot, of itself, pass from a colder to a hotter body. This is one formulation of the Second Law of Thermodynamics. Like the First Law, it was of course an act of faith, but it has never yet been disproved. To those unfamiliar with physical science it comes as something of a shock to realize that this apparently pedestrian statement of the obvious, together with the First Law, lies at the root of most physical chemistry and much physics and engineering also. Its implications for philosophy and theology have similarly been perceived as immense.

In 1865 Clausius invented the term *entropy* as a measure of the extent to which heat is unavailable for conversion to mechanical energy. It is really a mathematical concept, and can be understood as that quantity which increases during an irreversible change (such as heat flowing from a hot to a cold body). The total entropy of the universe, therefore, is constantly increasing whereas its total energy stays constant.

On the basis of all this work William Thomson (later Lord Kelvin) developed his own dynamical theory of heat, which included his absolute scale of temperature (1851) and the conclusion (1852) that the dissipation of mechanical energy in nature was so inevitable that eventually, at maximum entropy, the whole universe will succumb to a 'heat death' with everything uniformly at a very low temperature.

Apart from the chilling prospects of such a universal fate, there were other reasons to question the absolutist character of the Second Law. Amongst the more resolute sceptics was James Clerk Maxwell, who determined to test the matter with a now-famous 'thought experiment'. Accepting that the molecules of a gas at given temperature would not all have the same velocity, he supposed that their velocities would have a probabilistic distribution, as indicated below (I). At higher temperatures the curve would be skewed to the right as in (II):

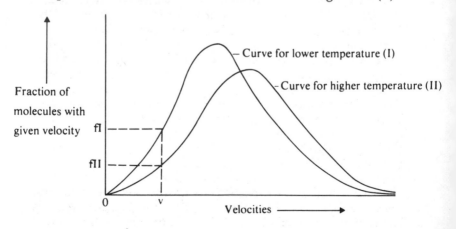

He imagined a two-compartment box containing a gas, with the temperature in B greater than that in A. Because of the statistical distributions of velocities some molecules (a minority) in A would have speeds exceeding the average in B. Between the two compartments is a partition with a hole just big enough for one molecule at a time to pass through, but capable of being opened or closed at will. Now, he said, 'conceive a finite being who knows the paths and velocities of all the molecules by simple inspection, but who can do no work except open and close a hole in the diaphragm by means of a slide without mass'. He might have imagined the experiment as follows:

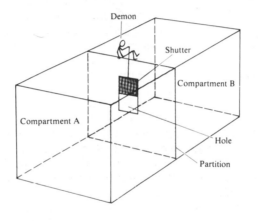

This 'finite' being was called by Kelvin a 'demon' (meaning 'spirit' or 'intelligence') and Maxwell's Demon has survived ever since. His job was to open the hole to let faster-than-average molecules pass from A to B, and slower-than-average molecules go in the opposite direction. Thus, if we could take the place of the Demon, we could actually make the temperature in B rise further at the expense of that in A, thus confounding the Second Law ('only we can't, not being clever enough').

In this way Maxwell gave a light-hearted demonstration of what was a serious proposition: that the Second Law of Thermodynamics has statistical validity only. If true, this would mean that the laws of science derived from it would share this limitation. Though overwhelmingly probable, they would lack the 100% certainty hitherto attributed to physical laws (at least in an ideal sense).

At first Maxwell appears to have inclined to the view, as old as Lucretius, that molecules (or atoms) moved in a totally random fashion. From this extreme position, with its atheistic associations, he soon drew back, and distinguished between the molecular world ('a region where everything is certain and immutable') and our own world of experience where 'chance and change' appear to reign. For his Demon molecular motions would need to be knowable, so the question of 'randomness' reduces itself to an apparent disorder, stemming from our own limited knowledge. And if that were not enough Maxwell and others (notably L. Szilard in 1929 and L. Brillouin in 1951) extended the application of the Second Law to information-gathering: knowledge can be acquired only at a cost – an increase in entropy (disorder) in the surrounding system. Practically, this has been used in the theory of computer programming; ideologically it tells us that the Second Law is different in kind from all other laws of science and affects not only our knowledge of nature but also the way in which we acquire it. At the very least thermodynamics enabled Kelvin to attack Darwin and the geologists for postulating too great an age for the earth, even though additional evidence was later to provide partial vindication for an older earth. At most thermodynamics represents a decisive break with the clock-work image of the universe inherited from Boyle, where *everything* was, in principle, predictable; and the concept of irreversibility and unidirectional time (where entropy is 'time's arrow') was as foreign to Newtonian physics as was the statistical formulation of physical laws.

3. Relativity

Thermodynamics was only the beginning of the new post-Newtonian physics. More familiar to the layman, though no easier to explain, were the theories of relativity enunciated by Albert Einstein early in the present century.[4]

The notion of light as wave-motion was demonstrated by Thomas Young and others early in the nineteenth century. Since waves occur only in a medium, an aether was postulated which filled all space but was undetectable by all known methods. From 1856 onwards, Clerk Maxwell was able to include light with electric and magnetic forces in one great unified theory of electromagnetic radiation. Equations were produced for the waves which are transmitted with the speed of light through the aether. Spectacular verification of this view was afforded by Hertz's demonstration, in 1888, of what we now call 'radio waves'. However, in the previous year, the famous Michelson-Morley experiment had conclusively proved that the speed of light was the same in the direction of the earth's orbital movement through the aether *and* at right angles to it. One may compare the situation with the different speeds of bullets fired from a moving car along the line of motion or perpendicularly to it. To account for this anomalous result various *ad hoc* expedients were tried, notably by H. Lorentz, and Maxwell's field equations modified accordingly. In so far as they were successful it was at the cost of some arbitrariness, not least in the mathematical process known as 'co-ordinate transformation', one technique being used for mechanics and another for electromagnetic radiation.

James Clerk Maxwell (1831–1879), founder of the electromagnetic theory of light.

Against this situation Einstein reacted and, in 1905, produced his first paper on what was to be later called Special Relativity. He was then an unknown 26-year-old, working in the Swiss Patent Office in Berne. Dealing with 'the electrodynamics of moving bodies', he attacked with astonishing rigour and vigour some of the basic concepts of Newtonian physics. Taking issue with Newton's 'absolute space' and 'absolute time', he contended that all laws of physics take exactly the same form in any inertial frame of reference (*i.e.* co-ordinate system in which Newton's laws are obeyed). Also, the speed of light is a constant whether or not the source is moving. The aether, always undetectable, is now a superfluous concept. Questions of measurement are raised, and it becomes clear that it is meaningless to talk of two events being absolutely simultaneous.

In a short following paper Einstein published his famous equation connecting mass (m) and energy (E) of an object with the velocity of light (c):

$$E = mc^2$$

thus connecting mass and energy. On the basis of this relationship nuclear energy becomes a reality. But Einstein did not finish there. Spurred by a desire to unify theories of electromagnetism and gravitational phenomena, and to express them as partial differential equations, he arrived in 1915 at a General Theory of Relativity. Rejecting Newton's idea of gravity as a force between two bodies, he recast it in terms of a 'field' arising from distortion of a 4-dimensional space-time continuum itself induced by the presence of matter. On earth the practical consequences are usually negligible (unless speeds approach the velocity of light, as in a nuclear accelerator). But astronomical phenomena may be more accurately predicted and explained by Einstein than by Newton. A small deviation in the orbit of Mercury was exactly accounted for in relativistic terms. The bending of starlight by the sun was predicted, and during a total solar eclipse of 1918 was triumphantly recorded by Arthur Eddington: the Einstein-shift. Relativity was vindicated and the homely, easily-grasped Newtonian mechanics superannuated except for quite parochial calculations and experiments here on earth.

4. Quantum theory

The quantum theory arose from a study by the Berlin physicist Max Planck of the radiation emitted by a 'black body' (*i.e.* a perfect 'radiator').[5] Unlike earlier workers, who had also noticed the energy was not uniform but had a maximum value at definite wave-length, Planck supposed that the energy is emitted not continuously but in 'bundles' or *quanta*. The energy (E) of each quantum is related to wavelength (λ) by

$$E = h/\lambda$$

where h is a universal constant known as Planck's constant. Shortly afterwards (1905) Einstein suggested that radiation is propagated through space in quanta with this energy and these became known as *photons*. Light itself could behave as though it were particulate, so posing a considerable dilemma for those who had long held it to be essentially wave-motion. This construction received added confirmation from the Compton effect (1923). When X-rays (another form of electromagnetic radiation) were scattered by electrons, the pattern of scattering was explicable only if the 'X-rays' actually possessed momentum, *i.e.* if they behaved like particles.

Now the difficulty arose as to whether light, X-rays, *etc.* were really waves or really particles. It was compounded by a comparable problem for electrons. These had been known since 1897. They behaved like particles in a number of ways and their mass had been determined with some accuracy. Yet there were problems.

For example, it had long been known that when atoms were 'excited' (by heat or other ways) they emitted light of definite frequencies which constituted a spectrum characteristic for that one element. But why? Improving on the simple nuclear atom of Rutherford, the Danish physicist Neils Bohr said that electrons could exist in several permitted orbits, each of which was associated with a specific energy. Hence, if an electron could 'jump' from one orbit to another the difference in energy would be always the same, and as

$$E = h/\lambda$$

there would be one specific wavelength of light associated with each such leap. That, however, still leaves unresolved the question as to why only certain orbits were permitted. A daring solution was proposed in 1923 by Louis de Broglie, who suggested that if electrons were thought of as waves rather than particles and that if the wave chased itself round the nucleus, only at certain wavelengths would interference be impossible and the crests on successive revolutions all coincide. This bold suggestion was triumphantly confirmed four years later when C. P. Davisson and L. H. Germer obtained diffraction patterns when a beam of electrons impinged on a nickel crystal, and when G. P. Thomson successfully diffracted an electron beam through four very thin films of metal. Such behaviour was entirely characteristic of waves and not at all of particles.

Thus quantum theory had landed modern physics in yet another dilemma. Light and electrons could behave as either particles or waves, so what on earth *were* they? To say, with Bragg, that one view is held on Mondays, Wednesdays and Fridays, and the other on Tuesdays, Thursdays and Saturdays merely emphasizes the problem. Nor did it help much to characterize the entities as 'wavicles'! One wonders how the self-assured and self-proclaimed scientific naturalists of Victorian times could conceivably have come to terms with such a shaking of the very foundations of their mechanistic creed. Yet, from that point of view, there was worse to come.

The wave-particle duality was dramatically symbolized in the enunciation by W. Heisenberg in 1927 of his famous Uncertainty (or Indeterminacy) Principle. Suppose one wishes to determine the position of an electron; one could illuminate it with short-wavelength radiation and observe where the latter interacted on impact. But at that very moment the electron would receive a large input of momentum from the high momentum photons. So in determining the electron's position we throw away any chance of finding its momentum. To discover the latter one could use low energy (high-wavelength) radiation, but that would have greater diffraction in a microscope so no precise information would emerge concerning the position of the electron. Thus it is impossible to know at one and the same time the position and momentum of a sub-atomic particle like an electron. A similar relation exists between its energy and time of measurement: they cannot be known with certainty. Thus built into the very fabric of the micro-world of nature was an apparently impenetrable barrier to that ultimate goal of scientific humanism: certain knowledge. And with that restriction went another, expressed by Heisenberg as follows:

Since all experiments obey the quantum laws and consequently the indeterminacy relations, the incorrectness of the law of causality is a definitely established consequence of quantum mechanics itself.[6]

So the next casualty is causality! That lynchpin of scientific materialism was wrenched from its socket and cast away. At the sub-atomic level of electrons and photons it is simply impossible to calculate future events from present data, even in principle. This Heisenberg and most of his colleagues stoutly maintained. But there was one doubter. As his name was Einstein his doubts had to be taken seriously. Yet each argument he produced was, eventually, refuted by Bohr or his colleagues and he found himself increasingly isolated. In 1944 he wrote to Born:

You believe in the God who plays dice, and I in complete law and order in a world which objectively exists, and which I, in a wildly speculative way, am trying to capture. I firmly *believe*, but I hope that someone will discover a more realistic way, or rather a more tangible basis than it has been my lot to find.[7]

So far no-one has discovered that other way. The fact that two giants of physics could so disagree on a fundamental matter is a salutary reminder of the limitations on scientific knowledge imposed by nature, or by God himself.

Ideological imperatives

So dramatic was the transformation of physical science by the 1920s that a late Victorian scientist would have difficulty in recognizing familiar landmarks, while an early Victorian would have rubbed his eyes in sheer disbelief. Gone were the hard immutable billiard-ball atoms of Dalton, and in their place were minute planetary systems consisting largely of empty space. Gone was the long-familiar aether in which light waves fluctuated and even the waves could as well be spoken of as particles. Gone, too, was the comforting absolute time and space of Newton, their replacement being an unimaginable 4-dimensional continuum. Worst of all, gone for ever was the deterministic universe where nothing was unknowable in principle and where causality had reigned unchallenged by all except a few religious fanatics. Inevitably one asks: why did all this happen? By no means all was due to the unanswerable challenge of new experimental data. The answer can be found only in one place, in the deeply held ideologies that informed, nudged, inspired, cajoled or drove the participants to wrestle with nature until at length they felt one more mystery of the universe was solved.

It should be said at once that no single ideological explanation has yet been proposed to account for all the cataclysmic changes in physical science. By analogy with the first Scientific Revolution one might expect Christianity to have played a prominent part. In the earlier stages, and especially in Britain, this appears often to have been the case. Joule, Maxwell and Kelvin are examples.[8]

James Prescott Joule (1818–89) was the son of a wealthy Salford brewer, and was able to devote most of his time to scientific research in the Manchester of John Dalton and the Industrial Revolution. In a succession of papers unfolding the First Law of Thermodynamics (1843, 1845 and 1847) he makes repeated reference to God, arguing in support of his views (that force or energy cannot be annihilated) that 'power to destroy belongs to the Creator alone'. Twenty years later he was one of the most distinguished of the 717 signatories of the 1865 'Declaration' asserting the authority of Scripture (see p. 169). If Scripture did not lead him directly to the First Law, it certainly provided the framework for his thermodynamic speculations.

James Clerk Maxwell (1831–79) was a Scot who today is remembered as the founder of the electromagnetic theory of light as well as a pioneer in thermodynamics. Despite the brilliance of his contributions to physics, he maintained throughout his life a Christian faith with great conviction. As his short career drew to an end he confessed, 'I have read up many queer religions: there is nothing like the old thing after all', and 'I have looked into most philosophical systems and I have seen that none will work without a God'. Echoing an earlier natural theology he affirmed that 'Christians whose minds are scientific are bound to study science that their view of the glory of God may be as extensive as their being is capable of'. Brought up in the Presbyterian kirk, and marrying a girl from the Episcopalians, Maxwell sat lightly to denominational allegiances. In the same way he declined to commit himself to highly specific (and transitory) attempts to harmonize science and Scripture.[9] But of the depth of his theological convictions there can be no possible doubt.

Maxwell's repudiation of materialism and suspicions of a completely deterministic view of physics are undoubtedly linked to his Christian ideology. An interesting paper by Daub on 'Maxwell's Demon' argues that this 'creature' is a product of Maxwell's theology, and that he regarded it rather as Newton regarded God in his omniscience and omnipotence.[10] It is noteworthy that Maxwell never used its 'demonic' title, which is hardly appropriate as even a partial symbol for some of the attributes of the Deity. However this may be, Christian theism informed all his activities. As he said in 1875, 'Men of science as well as other men need to learn from Christ.'

William Thomson, later Lord Kelvin, about 1859.

A scientist of the towering reputation of Lord Kelvin (1824–1907) has unsurprisingly attracted the attention of many scholars, including several who have focused on his theology.[11] As a result it is now possible to write with considerable confidence of his views and, more significantly, of their connection with science. Rejecting any attempt to separate his theology and science, Crosbie Smith reminds us that Kelvin 'saw a continuous inter-relation between theology and nature as mutually supporting enterprises'. He goes on to locate Kelvin in the theological tradition of the University of Glasgow where he matriculated and eventually became Professor of Natural Philosophy for 53 years. Here – as his own notebooks record – were those who held unequivocally to a biblical theism that saw God 'as the active Governor of the Universe, maintaining and sustaining His creation through the continued exercise of His Will, acting either directly, by intermediaries or by His ordained laws'.[12]

While Kelvin's mentors and predecessors held these views, it does not follow that he necessarily accepted them. Yet the evidence is clearly that he did. In 1887 he stated that 'I believe that the more thoroughly science is studied, the further does it take us from anything comparable to atheism'. A manuscript note on 'the dynamical theory of heat' (1851) argues that only the Supreme Ruler has the power to destroy energy or to turn back the thermodynamic clock. An Introductory Lecture to his class in natural philosophy urges study of scientific laws as 'the noblest privilege which he [God] has granted to our intellectual state'. It also refers to the 'gifts and constant care' of the Creator showered upon man as well as the production and maintenance of the physical powers of the animal world.

Kelvin strenuously rejected a reductionist view of life, observing that 'here scientific thought is compelled to accept the idea of Creative Power'. A bitter opponent of Darwin for his rejection of design, Kelvin refused to accept ascription of life to 'a fortuitous concourse of atoms' and as late as 1903 confessed to be persuaded by 'that excellent old book' Paley's *Natural Theology*. He did not, however, subscribe to a literal view of the six days of creation and believed in a relatively old earth (though not old enough for Darwin). There is some evidence also that Kelvin linked the 'heat death' of the universe with specific passages of Scripture (as Isaiah 51:6).

In these three great British physicists of the nineteenth century the evidence for a biblical faith informing their science is unambiguous (though much more could be said about the ways in which this worked). Much the same is true of some compatriots whose 'contributions' to science were on a lesser scale, though still considerable. One may cite Professors P. G. Tait (Edinburgh) and Sir George Stokes (Cambridge).

Yet not only were all these British (and often Scottish), but each had his locus within the nineteenth century. As one moves beyond 1900 and away from Britain a very different impression is received. Most of the other 'great names' in physics are German, many are Jewish as well, and not one gives any obvious impression of working at a science under-girt by a Christian or even a theistic ideology. Do we conclude, then, that in modern physics a theistic impetus was solely to be located in Victorian Britain?

It would certainly seem to be the case. But on close examina-tion a wide spectrum of attitudes may be perceived which militates against any simple interpretation. There is, for example, the case of Ernest Rutherford (1871–1937), the founder of nuclear physics. Born in New Zealand he worked at Cambridge with J. J. Thomson, whom he eventually suc-ceeded in 1919 after occupying Chairs at McGill (Montreal) and Manchester. Although not a Briton by birth he worked within the British scientific tradition. Yet he appeared to eliminate theology from his thinking in what had been up to that time a decidedly un-British tendency. His only outward concession appears to have been the habit of loudly singing, slightly off-key, 'Onward Christian soldiers' while moving round his laboratory. In fact his friend and biographer A. S. Eve confessed that he had never heard religion discussed or found 'one line of writing connected with it'.[13] There was no hostility to Christianity, merely a total unawareness of its relevance, it seems. Rutherford was, as a recent biographer calls him, a 'simple genius'[14] and he genuinely seems to have felt no need for metaphysics of any kind. In a lecture in 1932 he announced that science 'still goes marching on', calling out to the metaphysicians 'There are more things in heaven and earth than are dreamt of in your philosophy'.[15] It was also said that his musical tastes were confined to military bands, preferably loud. All of which is consistent with a view of himself as a foot-soldier in the triumphant army of science who was not going to be diverted from the immediate battle ahead. He was once heard to declaim, 'Don't let me catch anyone talking about the Universe in my department!'[16] His was no grandiose strategy for plumbing the depths of reality. Nor was it one of personal advancement (despite his knight-hood (1914), OM (1921), peerage (1931) or Nobel Prize in 1908). He worked alongside junior colleagues all his life and indignantly exploded when friends referred to him as 'Lord'. His apparatus was as simple as his conceptions. In that respect he was heir to an important element in the traditions of

Cambridge physical science from the last century. Had he but troubled to look, he would surely have seen that in his quest for science, his conviction of the rule of law, his openness to new revelations of nature, and his dedication to experiment, he was also heir to the Christian rationale for science so powerfully developed and articulated in the Cavendish. But for the man who discovered α-particles, erected the nuclear theory of the atom, predicted the neutron and artificial radioactivity and fulfilled the age-old dream of the alchemists by witnessing the transmutation of the elements, there simply was not enough time. That was Rutherford's strength. It was also his misfortune.

Sharing some of Rutherford's convictions about a causal universe, but differing profoundly in other ways, was Albert Einstein (1879–1955). He *was* concerned with 'the Universe' and he did write on 'religion and science', most memorably in the *New York Times Magazine* in 1930. Yet this was written under some duress and his religion was essentially a private affair, so private that nothing may be found on it in the autobiographical notes which he left. By the 1930s Einstein had returned to what he called the 'deep religiosity' he had felt while very young. His 'cosmical religion' was, however, unorthodox in a Christian sense, though it owed something to the Judaism of his race. It is inseparable from his philosophy of science, in which sense he is the polar opposite of Rutherford. It also changed with time.

At first Einstein inclined towards the positivism of the German chemist, F. W. Ostwald, and (especially) the German physicist Ernst Mach, whose challenge to Newton's absolute space and time was taken up and extended in Relativity. But Mach's limitation of colours, space, tones and so on as the only realities, and his critique of the mechanistic world-view, led to increasing disenchantment in Einstein. By 1905 Einstein was committed to investigating microscopic reality in the structure of liquids. The positivist philosophy that would deny God as unobservable by the same token denied atoms as a meaningful concept. But of course by then radioactivity was rapidly eroding this philosophical dogma and positivism was having to shift its ground. As a modern commentator has suggested, such positivism is 'the necessary sword for destroying old error, but it makes an inadequate plowshare for cultivating a new harvest'.[17] And a new harvest was Einstein's objective, nothing less than a final solution to the mystery of the universe. To know beyond the laws of nature their inner rationale is to violate the very spirit of positivist philosophy. No wonder that Einstein admitted to being 'guilty of the original sin of metaphysics'.

If Einstein was to penetrate nature's secrets as no man had ever done before, he needed to be armed with convictions that could not themselves be deduced from nature. Three of these can readily be identified. Deeply impressed by the 'ordered regularity' of the universe, he sought a unifying theory that would be valid across all natural processes. Maxwell had created a precedent in bringing light within the rule of electromagnetic equations. Einstein wanted to go much further. A second conviction was that a physical reality exists independent of any observer and that this should be explicable in terms of great mathematical simplicity. Thirdly, from 1909, he pursued research in the settled conviction that not particles but fields constitute the ultimate physical reality.

Einstein's brand of philosophical realism lay at the root of his celebrated disagreement with Bohr and his colleagues in Copenhagen. Nominally this was about causality, Einstein deploring its absence in a strict sense in the statistical interpretation of quantum mechanics. He considered complementarity a 'tranquillising religion' but 'a dangerous game'. As he often said, 'God does not play dice.' For Einstein God seemed at times almost synonymous with an orderly system working according to laws discovered by science. That he felt the quest would eventually be rewarded may be inferred from another of his memorable phrases, 'God is clever but he is not dishonest.'

Albert Einstein (1879–1955).

Although he had not been brought up as a practising Jew, it was to Judaism that he turned as a youth seeking meaning and purpose in life. He found himself unable to accept any transcendental elements in this Jewish faith, just as he had already rejected much of the Christian's Bible. In an oft-quoted sentence he declared belief in 'Spinoza's God who reveals himself in the harmony of what exists not in a God who concerns himself with the fate and actions of men'. This affirmation elicited the remark from a prominent New York Rabbi that 'Einstein's theory if carried out to its logical conclusion would bring to mankind a scientific formula for monotheism'.[18] Whether Einstein ever pursued that logic to the end we cannot know. However, he once burst out to the Jewish philosopher Martin Buber that 'what we strive for is just to draw His lines after Him'. Years later he confessed, 'I want to know how God created this world...I want to know His thoughts, the rest are details.'[19] Even if he had come to believe in a personal God (and he certainly admitted the possibility) it would have been the awesome, omnipotent, remote Lawgiver of Mount Sinai. Such a Deity would not have provided him with the personal assurance and cosmic confidence embedded in Christianity, but he would have underwritten the quest for law, regularity and simplicity in the universe. Evidently for Einstein that was enough.[20]

The prominent part played by many Jews in the revolution in physics is surely suggestive. Apart from raising questions about their changing roles in European society, it also reminds us of the continuity between Judaean and Christian views of nature, each of which has notable resonances with the modern scientific world-view. Another notable physicist was Max Born (1882–1920) who, though a Jew by birth, never practised the Jewish faith but was brought up to value conscience and 'an understanding of human life within the framework of natural laws'. So lightly did he value 'religious professions' that he formally embraced Christianity at the request of his parents-in-law.[21] The echoes of Einstein's Spinozism can clearly be heard in his philosophy.

Though not a Jew, Max Planck (1858–1947) underwent a similar pilgrimage to Einstein. Of Lutheran stock he became an elder in the Lutheran church. Yet he too denied belief in a personal God and professed admiration for Spinoza. Perhaps for that very reason he sought the more ardently a total world-view. Like Einstein he opposed acausality in quantum mechanics and like him he broke with Mach's positivism, claiming of rival theories the 'ultimate, infallible test for distinguishing false prophets from true – "By their fruits ye shall know them"'. But unlike Einstein he was to go through an experience that stripped away his carefully maintained appearance of Spinozism. This was nothing less than the execution of his son Erwin by the Nazis in 1944. With his world shattered round him, the octogenarian physicist wrote simply to a friend:

> What helps me is that I consider it a favor of heaven that since childhood a faith is planted deep in my innermost being, a faith in the Almighty and All-good not to be shattered by anything. Of course his ways are not our ways, but trust in him helps us through the darkest trials.[22]

Thus the Nobel Prize winner discloses at his time of extreme need a very different conviction from that displayed in his public crusades for a metaphysical and ethical world-view. As Jaki has said, these 'made logical sense only if the world was the product of a rational personal Creator, a notion maintained by historic Christianity and from which the republic of science received crucial benefit'.[23] Perhaps the logic was perceived more clearly than anyone knew.

Much has been written concerning the ideologies underlying the quantum theory of the Copenhagen school centred on Bohr and Heisenberg. Max Jammer has linked the development of acausality with late-nineteenth-century philosophical ideas that were themselves a reaction to traditional views of mechanical determinism. He instances contingentism, existentialism, pragmatism and logical empiricism.[24] Paul Forman[25] has suggested that the challenge to causality may be connected with the climate of public opinion in Weimar Germany in the early 1920s. This climate included a certain anti-scientism, especially well exemplified in the much-circulated *The Decline of the West* by Otto Spengler. Forman's thesis – which is basically a sociological analysis – has been widely criticized. John Hendry notes (among other features) its neglect of religious attitudes.[26] In that connection it has been suggested that some of Bohr's scientific thinking may have stemmed from the writings of Kierkegaard, while the existentialist theology of Karl Barth was probably influential on at least some of the Weimar physicists. Much work still remains to be done and it is idle to speculate further. What may be said with confidence is that the quantum theory came to birth at a time when philosophy and theology were also experiencing a 'shaking of the foundations' and it is not unreasonable to assume some effect on science. And it is surely relevant that Germany itself was undergoing profoundly important social changes that stemmed from its defeat in World War I and were to culminate in the rise of Hitler.

Logically the quest for a rational understanding of the universe had its roots as firmly embedded as ever in the belief in a personal, rational God. The ample framework of biblical theism could as well accommodate the statistical 'acausality' of quantum theory as the traditional causality of Newtonian mechanics. That quarrels should have arisen by virtue of different philosophies simply demonstrates the extent to which a common biblical world-view had been eroded by the rising tide of secularism. It was the first major warning-sign that, for all its success so far, the future for science cannot be taken for granted.

Some theological impacts

Perhaps we should not be too surprised that the impacts of the new physics generally were not widely felt for many years. After all the concepts were (and are) difficult. Thermodynamics was the first area to be visibly linked to theology. In the Paris of the '1890s it became fashionable to espouse a positivistic philosophy which denied both God and atoms as unknowable. Since a thermodynamic description of a chemical reaction was independent of atomic terms, it was possible to make heat (or energy) rather than atoms the cornerstone of one's science. (Ostwald, a German in this tradition, even had his house called *Energie*.) Thus at the end of the nineteenth century thermodynamics became linked with a militant anti-religious (or, more accurately, anti-clerical) movement in France, its most influential leader being the chemist, and later Foreign Minister, M. Berthelot.

Some aspects of thermodynamics were, however, attacked by those not normally to be found on the side of religion. These usually involved the 'heat-death' prediction of the Second Law. The German biologist and advocate of a form of materialism, Haeckel, denied a beginning or end to the world on the basis of his own 'monistic' belief in the eternal conservation of matter and energy. (Thus he implicitly accepted the First Law and denied, or ignored, the Second.) Some of the later French positivists thought the Second Law of local and limited application, with perhaps entropy increasing only for one phase of an infinite series of fluctuations. But as the century advanced the grim prospect of a universal heat-death became generally accepted by scientists, amongst whom Sir Arthur Eddington and Sir James Jeans became the most effective proponents in the English-speaking world.

Eddington's book *The Nature of the Physical World* (1928) included a complete chapter on 'the running-down of the universe'. He regarded entropy as 'time's arrow', increasing as a pack of cards is shuffled, as stars grow old and die, or as Humpty Dumpty falls off his wall. 'Whoever wishes for a universe which can continue indefinitely in activity', he said, 'must lead a crusade against the Second Law of Thermodynamics.' Reluctant to tie this specifically to Christian theology, he nevertheless concluded 'the idea of a universal Mind or Logos would be a fairly plausible inference from the present state of scientific theory'.[27] Jeans went rather further and argued that 'from the intrinsic evidence of his creation, the Great Architect of the Universe now begins to appear as a pure mathematician'.[28]

Both Jeans and Eddington were heavily criticized by Susan Stebbing for their incursions into philosophy. Yet their influence was plainly visible in the writings of a theologian, W. R. Inge, Dean of St Paul's, and author of *God and the Astronomers* (1934). Switching his attention from the eugenics by which he had once hoped to effect some improvement in the human race, he now looks forward to the ultimate 'Twilight of the Gods' as depicted in Scripture (Hebrews 1:10–12):

'In the beginning, O Lord, you laid the foundations
   of the earth,
   and the heavens are the work of your hands.
They will perish, but you remain;
   they will all wear out like a garment.
You will roll them up like a robe;
   like a garment they will be changed.
But you remain the same,
   and your years will never end.'

Writing in the hungry 1930s, and disenchanted by naive liberal optimism and 'modernist' philosophy, he observes:

The idea of the end of the world is intolerable only to

modernist philosophy, which finds in the idea of unending temporal progress a pitiful substitute for the blessed hope of everlasting life, and in an evolving God a shadowy ghost of the unchanging Creator and Sustainer of the universe. It is this philosophy which makes Time itself an absolute value, and progress a cosmic principle. Against this philosophy my book is a sustained polemic. Modernist philosophy is, as I maintain, wrecked on the Second Law of Thermodynamics; it is no wonder that it finds the situation intolerable, and wriggles piteously to escape from its toils.[29]

Nor is it any wonder that Inge should have so openly used science (thermodynamics) in the service of theology. This latter-day disciple of Plato as well as of Christ believed in the unity of all knowledge, science and theology included. He wrote:

> Those Christians who despise or neglect science, as having no bearing on the probation of the soul in this life, are mistaken. The world that we live in is real, though our pictures of it are very unlike the reality. It is the work of God... it is the expression of His mind, and the field in which His thoughts and purposes are being actualised. Whatever we can learn about nature teaches us something about God.[30]

William Inge wrote between two World Wars. Another theologian, a German who lived through the horrors of *both* wars, wrote in 1962 of the choice set before us. Karl Heim recalls 'the radical hopelessness' of German nihilism offering only the prospect of universal heat-death. By contrast there is also the 'Easter faith', according to which the course of this world proceeds to a goal when the whole basic form of this world will be abolished to 'make way for a new form'. As he says, 'we all have to choose'.[31]

On relativity much theological and philosophical ink has been spilt. In addition to being held to discredit science by its emphasis on the limitations of common sense,[32] it has been variously thought to have led to atheism or to have promoted reconciliations between religion and science! That some should have found justification for applying relativity to ethics is indicated by Sommerfeld's attempts to refute that fallacy. Indeed, if anything, relativity lends support to the opposite view, for its chief point is the independence and objectivity of natural laws.[33] On specific theological matters relativity was an important catalyst for the views of A. N. Whitehead, in which 'processes' or 'events' were deemed more important than 'substances'. From this developed the 'process theology' of modern times.

Quantum theory has had a more obvious impact on theological thinking. Some have seen its dualistic view of matter a contributor to the downfall of materialism, though it is not very clear why waves could not replace particles in a materialist philosophy. But the chief focus has been on complementarity which has been extended far beyond quantum physics. Bohr himself considered that biological phenomena could be validly considered from complementary standpoints: mechanistic and organic. He also suggested that freewill and determinism may be similarly understood, in which he was followed by Eddington and others. Various writers have seen complementarity within theology, as in the divine and human natures of Christ, and in the age-old problem of freewill and divine providence. Others have thought of science and religion as complementary ways of looking at reality.[34]

Overall, perhaps the most profoundly important effect of these developments in science has been the administration of what one writer has called 'humility in modern physics'.[35] Heisenberg located this in 'the dissolution of the rigid frame of concepts of the nineteenth century'.[36] As a result the sheer inability of science to compass all the events in nature, for whatever reason, became obvious as never before. Yet the community of science did not merely experience shell-shock, but also a particular kind of exhilaration. Even if some kinds of knowledge were for ever beyond the reach of man (and not all agreed that that was the case), the whole of physical science was unified in a way and to a degree undreamt of in 1850. It was, as J. A. Thomson wrote, 'a picture of inexpressible grandeur, and yet, in a way, of extraordinary simplicity'.[37] He continued: 'this unification is congruent with the religious concept of a Creator.' Certainly for those who were predisposed to a Christian view of nature modern physics was far from discouraging. As we have seen, theistic conclusions can be reached from all manner of data, even some that is mutually contradictory. Bertrand Russell made the quip, not altogether fairly, that 'Sir Arthur Eddington deduces religion from the fact that atoms do not obey the laws of mathematics, Sir James Jeans deduces it from the fact that they do'. Eddington[38] was understandably riled, and expressed his total opposition to 'any proposal to base religion on scientific discovery'. As he said, much in the spirit of Clerk Maxwell:

> The religious reader may well be content that I have not offered him a God revealed by the quantum theory, and therefore liable to be swept away in the next scientific revolution.

The demolition of the old mechanistic, deterministic view of nature has prompted some misguidedly to announce that science can now permit miracles or can attribute free will to Heisenberg uncertainty. However neither miracles nor freewill depend for their credibility on particular scientific models of reality,[39] and it is unwise to put one's trust in the changing theories of science.

But for those whose faith was already in the Word made flesh as revealed in Scripture, the swift currents of modern physics posed no problems and actually swept away the last props of Victorian scientific naturalism which had for so long concealed the ways of God from man.

Notes for chapter ten

[1] One of the most comprehensible accounts may be found in R. Taton (ed.), *Science in the Twentieth Century* (Thames and Hudson, 1966).

[2] On atomism see H. A. Boorse and L. Motz (eds.), *The World of the Atom* (Basic Books, 1967); G. K. T. Conn and H. D. Turner, *The Evolution of the Nuclear Atom* (Iliffe, 1965); T. J. Trenn, *Transmutation Natural and Artificial* (Heyden, 1981).

[3] C. A. Russell, 'Time, chance and thermodynamics', Units 4 and 5 of O.U. Course A381, 'Science and Belief: from Darwin to Einstein' (Open University Press, Milton Keynes, 1981); S. G. Brush, *The Kind of Motion we call Heat* (North-Holland Publishing, Amsterdam, 1976).

[4] From the vast literature on Einstein the following can be specially commended: P. A. Schilpp (ed.), *Albert Einstein: Philosopher-Scientist* (Harper, N.Y., 1959); R. W. Clark, *Einstein, the Life and Times* (Hodder and Stoughton, 1973); P. M. Clark, 'Einstein: philosophical belief and physical theory', Unit 6 of O.U. Course A381 (ref. 3); A. Pais, *'Subtle is the Lord': the science and the life of Albert Einstein* (Oxford University Press, 1982).

[5] Much the best historical introduction to quantum theory is still B. Hoffmann, *The Strange Story of the Quantum* (Pelican, 1963). Also relevant are M. Jammer, *The Philosophy of Quantum Mechanics* (Wiley-Interscience, N.Y., 1974), and N. G. Coley and R. Stannard, Units 7 and 8 on quantum theory, O.U. Course A381 (ref. 3).

[6] W. Heisenberg, *Zeitsch. Phys.*, 1927, 43, 197.

[7] M. Born and A. Einstein, *The Born-Einstein Letters* (Macmillan, 1971), p.149.

[8] See ref. 3.

⁹ Further information is to be found in L. Campbell and W. Garnett, *Life of James Clerk Maxwell* (1882).

¹⁰ E. E. Daub, 'Maxwell's Demon', *Stud. Hist. Phil. Sci.*, 1970, *1*, 213–227.

¹¹ *E.g.*, C. W. Smith, 'Natural history and thermodynamics; William Thomson, "The dynamical theory of heat"', *Brit. J. Hist. Sci.*, 1976, *9*, 293–319; *idem*, 'William Thomson and the creation of thermodynamics 1840–1855', *Arch. Hist. Ex. Sci.*, 1977, *16*, 231–288; D. B. Wilson, 'Kelvin's scientific realism: the theological context', *Phil. J.*, 1974, *11*, 41–60.

¹² C. W. Smith (1976) (ref. 11).

¹³ A. S. Eve, *Rutherford* (Cambridge, 1939), p.402.

¹⁴ D. Wilson, *Rutherford, Simple Genius* (Hodder and Stoughton, 1983).

¹⁵ Address to the Royal Academy of Arts 1932, cited in D. Wilson, (ref. 14), p.594.

¹⁶ N. de Bruyne in J. Hendry (ed.), *Cambridge Physics in the '30s* (Hilger, Bristol, 1984), p.87.

¹⁷ C. Holton, 'Mach, Einstein and the search for reality' from *Daedalus*, 1968, 636–673, reprinted in C. Chant and J. Fauvel (eds.), *Darwin to Einstein: Historical Studies on Science and Belief* (Longman/Open University Press, 1980), p.252.

¹⁸ *New York Times*, 25 April 1929, p.60.

¹⁹ Cited in R. W. Clark, (ref. 4), p.33.

²⁰ On Einstein's religious beliefs see I. Paul, *Science, theology and Einstein* (Christian Journals Ltd., Belfast, 1982). Paul concludes 'in so many respects Einstein appears to have stood before the threshold of the Christian faith' (p.125).

²¹ M. Born, *Reflections of a Nobel Laureate* (Taylor and Francis, 1978), p.159.

²² Cited in S. Jaki, *The Road of Science and the Ways to God* (Scottish Academic Press, Edinburgh, 1978), p.179.

²³ S. Jaki, (ref. 22), p.80.

²⁴ M. Jammer, *The Conceptual Development of Quantum Mechanics* (McGraw Hill, New York, 1966), pp.166–167.

²⁵ P. Forman, 'Weimar Culture, causality and quantum theory 1918–1927 . . .', *Hist. Stud. Phys. Sci.*, 1971, *3*, 1–116 (reprinted in part in C. Chant and J. Fauvel, (ref. 17), pp.267–326).

²⁶ J. Hendry, 'Weimar culture and quantum causality', *Hist. Sci.*, 1980, *18*, 155–180.

²⁷ A. S. Eddington, *The Nature of the Physical World* (Cambridge University Press, 1928), pp.71–92, 324.

²⁸ J. Jeans, *The Mysterious Universe* (Cambridge University Press, 1930), p.134.

²⁹ W. R. Inge, *God and the Astronomers* (Longmans, 1934), pp.27–28.

³⁰ *Ibid.*, p.16.

³¹ K. Heim, *The World: its Creation and Consummation*, trans. by R. Smith (Oliver and Boyd, 1962), pp.110, 149.

³² R. Tobey, *The American Ideology of National Science 1919–1930* (Pittsburgh University Press, 1971), ch. IV.

³³ P. A. Schilpp, (ref. 4), p.99.

³⁴ I. G. Barbour, *Issues in Science and Religion* (SCM Press, 1968), pp.291–292. This gives full references and cautions against over-facile extensions of the idea.

³⁵ R. E. D. Clark, *Creation* (Tyndale Press, 1946), Ch. IV.

³⁶ W. Heisenberg, *Physics and Philosophy* (Harper and Row, N.Y., 1958), p.197.

[37] J. A. Thomson, *Science and Religion* (Methuen, 1925), p.87.
[38] A. V. Douglas, *The Life of Sir Arthur Eddington* (Nelson, 1956), pp.140–141.
[39] D. M. MacKay, *The Clockwork Image: A Christian perspective on science* (IVP, 1974).

11 Polluting effluent: science and the environment

All creatures of our God and King,
Lift up your voice and with us sing:
   Alleluia, Alleluia!
Thou burning sun with golden beam,
Thou silver moon with softer gleam:
   O praise Him, O praise Him,
   Alleluia, Alleluia, Alleluia.

Thou rushing wind that art so strong,
Ye clouds that sail in heaven along,
   O praise Him, Alleluia!
Thou rising morn, in praise rejoice,
Ye lights of evening, find a voice:
   O praise Him...

Thou flowing water, pure and clear,
Make music for thy Lord to hear,
   Alleluia, Alleluia!
Thou fire so masterful and bright,
That givest man both warmth and light:
   O praise Him...

Dear mother earth, who day by day
Unfoldest blessings on our way,
   O praise Him, Alleluia!
The flowers and fruits that in thee grow,
Let them His glory also show:
   O praise Him...

St Francis of Assisi (13th century), *Canticle of the Sun*,
trans. W. H. Draper

When I consider your heavens,
   the work of your fingers,
the moon and the stars,
   which you have set in place,
what is man that you are mindful of him,
   the son of man that you care for him?
You made him a little lower than the heavenly beings
   and crowned him with glory and honour.
You made him ruler over the works of your hands;
   you put everything under his feet:

Psalm 8:3–6

On 7 July 1855, Michael Faraday embarked upon a river steamer at London Bridge. His subsequent journey upstream to Hungerford Bridge was reported in a letter to *The Times*, and he himself enacted a minor drama which greatly affected contemporary society and was, in effect, an unintended parable of science itself. In those days the River Thames was the repository for all the untreated sewage and industrial waste of the metropolis. On that summer's day, with the river at low tide, Faraday could not but be impressed:

> The appearance and the smell of the water forced themselves at once on my attention. The whole of the river was an opaque pale brown fluid. In order to test the degree of opacity, I tore up some white cards into pieces, moistened them so as to make them sink easily below the surface, and then dropped some of these pieces into the water at every pier the boat came to; before they had sunk an inch below the surface they were indistinguishable, though the sun shone brightly at the time; and when the pieces fell edgeways the lower part was hidden from sight before the upper part was under water. This happened at St. Paul's Wharf, Blackfriars Bridge, Temple Wharf, Southwark Bridge, and Hungerford; and I have no doubt would have occurred further up and down the river. Near the bridges the feculence rolled up in clouds so dense that they were visible at the surface, even in water of this kind.[1]

Faraday was not of course the first person to be aware of Thames pollution, but he was one of the most influential men of science to make a fuss about it in the early Victorian period. His protests, as we shall see, were not entirely in vain. Yet pollution in general was to continue in industrialized countries for over a century with some government control, to be sure, but only a modicum of public outcry. Then, in the 1960s, it suddenly became a global ethical and political issue, involving in the furore swings against technology and science and bitter recriminations over their historic links with Christianity. The putrescent Thames of a century earlier had become symbolic of science itself. For some years various legislative measures (like Britain's Clean Air Act of 1956) had testified to Government awareness of a growing problem, but the event which is often said to have galvanized public awareness was the publication of Rachel Carson's *Silent Spring* in 1962. A searing indictment of chemical pesticides, the book majored on DDT which had been found in small quantities in dead birds, fish and animals. Use of such artificial aids to agriculture, Carson urged, meant profound alteration to 'the balance of nature', extinction of some species and irreversible damage to 'the environment'. At the same time the Environment Defense Fund of the U.S.A. was fighting a similar battle in the court-rooms. As a result, the world's worst pollution problem was solved by the American banning of DDT in 1972. By then everyone had heard of 'the environment'.[2]

A Punch *cartoonist's view, 21 July, 1855.*

This new environmentalist movement was already finding common cause with the student riots of the 1960s, the growing influence of oriental animistic cults, the rising popularity of Teilhard de Chardin's brand of mysticism and a general fear of dehumanized science. Groupings emerged like the self-styled Berkeley Ecological Revolutionary Organisation, appealing to groups like the following:

> Gnostics, hip Marxists, Teilhard de Chardin Catholics, Druids, Taoists, Biologists, Witches, Yogins, Bhikkus, Quakers, Sufis, Tibetans, Zens, Shamans, Bushmen, American Indians, Polynesians, Anarchists, Alchemists.[3]

Manifest at the same time in a dozen other ways from hippie culture to changing patterns of university entrants was the famous 'swing from science' that reached its peak (apparently) in the 1970s. It was against this background of anti-scientism and environmental concern – if not panic – that the American historian Lynn White addressed the American Association for the Advancement of Science in 1966. His theme was 'The historical roots of our ecologic crisis'.[4] He arrays before us 'the population explosion, the carcinoma of planless urbanism, the new geological deposits of sewage and garbage', commenting 'surely no creature other than man has ever managed to foul its nest in such short order'. He complains of the inadequacy of specific proposals ('ban the bomb, tear down the billboards, give the Hindus contraceptives and tell them to eat their sacred cows'). They are too palliative, too negative. Instead he urges upon his scientific congregation a reconsideration of the origins of science and technology. He concludes that modern technology is at 'least partly to be explained...as a realisation of the Christian dogma of man's transcendence of, and rightful mastery over, nature'. He thus locates the roots of our ecologic crisis in a Christian conception of nature and of man who has been put in charge of it. And he calls for a return to the ideals of that attractive mediaeval deviant who saw the animal world not as his slave, but as his brother, Francis of Assisi. 'I propose Francis as a patron saint for ecologists.'

Here indeed was a thesis that resonated well with the anti-scientific spirit of the time which, being anti-authoritarian in an even wider sense, was in no mood to truckle to biblical authority. White has been frequently quoted since that time, usually with a measure of approval. By blaming a specific

Christian view of nature for problems of pollution, he is deliberately setting the clock back three centuries and undermining one of the foundation structures of modern science, the biblical view of the relationship between man and nature. If he is right, moreover, accepted Christian interpretations of Scripture really have brought us all to our present predicament. Subsequent events (like the Three Mile Island near-catastrophe) have only emphasized the dangers, as have trends like the build-up of atmospheric carbon dioxide and consequent rise in global temperature (the 'greenhouse effect'); the slow destruction by aerosol sprays of ozone in the stratosphere which has hitherto shielded us from cosmic radiation; the addition of millions of tons of oil each year to our oceans ('the sinks of the world'); and the multiplicity of health hazards associated with lead in petrol, mercury in fish, fungicides, herbicides, insecticides and many other substances recently introduced to our ecosphere. It is more urgent than ever to disclose the underlying ideology which has rendered these hazards acceptable. Lynn White thinks he has found it, and points an accusing finger not merely at science-based technology but at what he conceives as the biblical theology by which it has been motivated. In no way can the matter be regarded as merely academic and unimportant. Nor is it even a case of high-powered theological or philosophical discussion. White's thesis is *historical* ('this is how things have happened'), rather than ethical or theological (how they should have happened), so historical methods must be used in its evaluation.

The case for the prosecution

This has been eloquently put by Lynn White himself. He asserts, reasonably, that 'human ecology is deeply conditioned by beliefs about our nature and destiny' and that we in the West 'have lived for about 1,700 years, very largely in a context of Christian axioms'. Focusing particularly on the Western (as opposed to the Eastern Orthodox) wing of Christianity, he briefly demonstrates that 'Western science was cast in a matrix of Christian devotion'. His brevity is entirely justified; this part of his thesis is virtually unassailable (see also pp.54ff.).

White now introduces a new consideration. He distinguishes between *science* and *technology*, though without defining either. He explains modern technology, at least in part, as a realization that Christian man is enjoined to be master over nature. He then continues:

> But, as we now recognise, somewhat over a century ago science and technology – hitherto quite separate activities – joined to give mankind powers which, to judge by many of the ecologic effects, are out of control. If so, Christianity bears a huge burden of guilt.

At this point a note of uncertainty enters the argument. He does not appear to object to the Christian basis of either science or technology on their own. It is only *when they combine* that the 'guilt' is engendered, only when they together exceed some kind of critical mass. The argument is most curious. Presumably the implication must be *either* that Christianity has somehow catalysed the combination (and is guilty for that reason) *or* that the ideological basis of each component is not as right as it seemed. Although the logic is tortuous it appears that the second position is being assumed. This follows from the final section of the article, which praises St Francis for trying to dethrone man from his lordship of the world and setting him rather on a level with all creation – hence 'Brother Ant', 'Sister Fire' and the rest. Only with such humility, mirrored in the incarnation itself, could man's arrogant determination to subdue nature have been restrained.

Thus traditional, Western Christianity is arraigned for complicity in our current ecological crisis. White does not dismiss Christianity in a general way; he confesses to being a 'churchman', and appears unsure as to whether to label Franciscan teaching as 'heretical' or just 'an alternative Christian view'. It matters little for his argument. He rests his case on the coincidence in space and time of the growth of technology and of a Christian conviction that man may dominate nature.

There are, however, other considerations that White does not mention which could be added to substantiate his claim. If his thesis is held to apply today, it may be pointed out that many contemporary environmentalist supporters in Greenpeace, Friends of the Earth and so on are hostile to biblical Christianity, and, conversely, modern evangelicals are not generally renowned for ecological concern. Obviously there are exceptions both ways, but the trend seems clear enough.

The case for the defence

At the outset it must be stressed that incontrovertible direct evidence either way is extremely hard to find. What might clinch the argument would be a quantitative correlation between known upholders of a 'dominion' view of nature and known exploiters and polluters, with as many individuals as possible. Such data may be available in the future, but certainly not now. Nevertheless there is much else that can be said in refutation of the thesis.

First, *it is highly dubious that science and technology came together only in the 1850s*. Depending on how the terms are defined, one could accept dates as early as 1800 or 1650. White himself admits the chemical industries were an exception, but it was precisely they which afforded the worst and earliest examples of man's pollution. However, this is a minor objection. A much more important one is as follows.

It has been remarked more than once elsewhere[5] that *despoliation of nature and massive pollution have often existed quite apart from any Christian ideology*. One can recall the foetid rivers of India near Madras or the suffocating air of Tokyo. Long before Bacon thirteenth-century Londoners were complaining of an atmosphere poisoned by smoke from burning sea-coal, and even before Christ the Mediterranean seaboard was being deliberately stripped of its forests by 'fire-drive' hunting methods and the Roman aristocracy were systematically poisoning themselves and their environment by accumulating and ingesting huge quantities of lead compounds. Until this century the peasants of Styria consumed arsenic in the hope of beautifying their complexions without, apparently, any theological motivation to do so. One could multiply examples without number in which the poisoning of the biosphere was brought about through greed, selfishness or ignorance and for which a theological explanation (in White's terms) is either implausible or impossible.

In the third place *it is simply incorrect to assume that environmentalist concern had no Christian mainspring in the past*. There are clear cases of a responsibility for nature being shouldered for explicitly biblical reasons. John Ray, for example, showed how birds were useful to man for food, medicine, feather-beds, adornment with their plumes for military purposes, quills to write with, and even feathers for brooms and dusters. All this is given by God who thus provides 'us employment most delightful to our natures and inclinations'. The present world, though not created solely for man, was intended to be used by him even if he would need to live ten times longer than Methuselah to explore its riches. Ray, like some of the Cambridge Platonists before him, found a strictly mechanistic explanation inadequate for living things, and assumed a 'plastic nature' or animating principle in addition. But in no sense was he advocating a 'brotherhood' with the brute animals which 'are not above consultation, but below it'.[6]

Ray's ideas were taken further by William Derham, who accepted that 'we can, if need be, ransack the whole globe' and that man was endowed with superiority over the animal world. In a classic treatise on natural theology these sentiments might seem at first sight more likely to confirm White's thesis than to refute it. But they are accompanied by others which drastically qualify the position. Derham becomes one of the first Christian writers on the 'uses' of nature to introduce quite explicitly the biblical concept of stewardship. Recalling Matthew 25:14 and Luke 16:2 he wrote:

> That these things are the gifts of God, they are so many talents entrusted with us by the infinite Lord of the world, a stewardship, a trust reposed in us; for which we must give an account at the day when our Lord shall call.[7]

Only in the light of our stewardship and of the biblical injunction to love our neighbour as ourselves could 'ransacking' of the globe be sanctioned. Carolyn Merchant has suggested his book might be called today an *ecotheology*.[8] Together with its successors it poses a serious challenge to the thesis of Lynn White, for here are biblical reasons being proposed for constraining as well as initiating technological change. And it may be justly observed that from that time onwards the note of responsible stewardship has rarely been silent in Christian writing, including even our own day.[9]

In White's polemic it is sometimes hard to distinguish between a disenchantment with the biblical interpretation undergirding the scientific enterprise and an attack on science itself. Yet a fourth reason for challenging his position lies in the *historic role of science itself in countering pollution*. For if science be correctly described as a product of Christian theology, the latter can hardly be blamed for pollution when science endeavours to restrict it. This was undoubtedly the case with the chemical industry which, in the early nineteenth century, had the doubtful distinction of originating 'acid rain'.[10] If the problem was caused by technology it was solved by science. Not only were acid gases like hydrogen chloride absorbed in tall condensing towers, but a battery of techniques for quantitative chemical analysis was developed in order to monitor progress. Admittedly this may seem like science/technology merely repairing the damage it had caused (and then not completely and under some duress from the Alkali Acts). But the same cannot be true for the transformation of the environment accomplished by the 'pure water' campaigns of Victorian Britain. Pollution of the rivers and of drinking-water, due largely to a rapid growth in urban populations, was countered by a complex set of measures in the fields of engineering, chemistry, biochemistry, bacteriology and medicine. Essentially the same methodology is used today by relief agencies in the Third World (often, one may add, for specifically Christian reasons). Thus the problem articulated by Faraday during his trip up the Thames was eventually solved by precisely the means abhorred by the more extreme followers of Lynn White. Speaking in another context of atmospheric pollution Faraday himself observed:

> None of these strange and injurious actions take place when we are burning, not merely a candle, but gas in our streets, or fuel in our fireplaces, so long as we confine ourselves within the laws that Nature has made for our guidance.[11]

If any man knew the difference between nature-worship and the worship of God, that man was Michael Faraday. Yet he, too, was able to reverence nature and learn from it. That meant science.

Finally, it is possible to identify *individuals who are (or were) a living refutation of the antithesis drawn by White between reverence for nature and control of it.* One could cite the cases of Derham, Faraday and many others. But perhaps the best example is one for whom traditional Christian theology was not very significant and who displayed an astonishing sensitivity to natural phenomena: Humphry Davy. We have already seen (see p.180) how he regarded nature with an almost numinous awe. It is perhaps surprising to find him (on more than one occasion) speaking of 'conquest' of nature, and of the noblest enjoyment of the mountains being connected with their 'uses and subserviency to life'. In 1802 this young man, who had but lately 'felt pain in tearing a leaf from one of the trees', committed himself to the following manifesto for progress through the control and manipulation of that same nature:

> By means of this science [chemistry] man has employed almost all the substances in nature either for the satisfaction of his wants or the gratification of his luxuries... He is to a certain extent ruler of all the elements that surround him; and he is capable of using not only common matter according to his will and inclinations, but likewise of subjecting to his purposes the ethereal principles of heat and light. By his inventions they are elicited from the atmosphere; and under his control they become, according to circumstances, instruments of comfort and enjoyment, or of terror and destruction.[12]

Yet any surprise at such a conjunction of reverence and manipulation is ill-founded. Only if 'Nature' is deliberately personalized is any such conjunction psychologically a puzzle. Otherwise there is no inherent inconsistency in the two attitudes, even taking into account the emotional overtones associated with the word 'exploitation'. If Davy, not overtroubled by fine details of Christian theology, could happily live with the paradox, it is unwise to suggest an either/or when it comes to technology on one hand and respect for nature on the other.

A provisional judgment

It must by now be clear that White's indictment of Christianity for our ecologic crisis is at best unproven and at worst rendered almost incredible. Writer after writer has pointed to one or more of the defects already mentioned. Some have suggested drastic modifications or alternatives.

L. W. Moncrief accepts an indirect Judaeo-Christian stimulus to the exploitation of nature, but only in so far as both capitalism and democratic values may be ascribed to Christianity in a general sense, and it is from these that urbanization and population growth emerged, with consequent damage to the environment.[13] But in Christianity he detects no ideological justification for the rape of nature. Neither does J. D. Hughes, who emphasizes the dependence of mediaeval ideas on classical as well as Christian traditions.

Public benefits due to science: from the Illustrated Times *(1858)*

Denying that ecological problems began in the 1960s, or in the Industrial Revolution, he affirms 'that the modern ecological crisis grew out of roots which lie deep in the ancient world, particularly in Greece and Rome'. As he observed, it was Protagoras who wrote 'man is the measure of all things', a far more anthropocentric sentiment than any in the Judaeo-Christian Scriptures.[14] Similarly, John Passmore locates the source of human arrogance towards nature specifically in the philosophy of the Stoics.[15]

Concerning possible solutions to the current dilemma,

White's rejection of 'more science and more technology' is vitiated by the very history to which he refers. That science and technology have contributed massively to reducing pollution has already been mentioned (p.232). It also happens to be true that ecology itself was from its Victorian beginnings conceived as a science, something for which a systems approach is appropriate. So far was this a consciously held attitude that from 1873 amateurs were systematically excluded from that part of ecology dealing with the plant world. As Charles Elton observed, 'ecology is scientific natural history'. To argue at the same time for suppression of science and promotion of ecology is to talk nonsense.

Today we need not less scientific research, but more and better. When Rachel Carson produced her *Silent Spring*, it was condemned by Norman Borlaug (Nobel Peace Prize Winner of 1970) as 'vicious, hysterical propaganda' against chemical pesticides, 'a diabolic, vitriolic, bitter, one-sided attack'. Why? Because the use of DDT, which demonstrably caused huge depradations of seabirds and other creatures, had also, according to the WHO Report for 1971, destroyed mosquitoes so effectively that in 25 years 1000m. lives had been saved from the risk of malaria.[16]

Sadly, a year after Borlaug delivered his speech his cause was lost and DDT was banned by the American Government (1972). As a result the Head of the British Conservancy Experimental Station concluded that 'on a world scale the effects of the American ban on DDT have been disastrous, as it has probably led to more deaths than the 1939–45 war'.[17] Whatever the facts, it is abundantly obvious that scientific research in its widest sense is urgently needed for this and many other problems relating to the environment.

However badly the Lynn White thesis has fared at the hands of its critics, it included one major proposition for which we may be profoundly grateful. White recognized that, ultimately, the roots of our trouble are religious, so 'the remedy must also be essentially religious'. Surely Derham had it right when he argued for the Christian concept of stewardship as a principle to undergird all else that was done in the name of science and technology. It was in that context, and that of the whole biblical view of nature, that the command to subdue the earth needed – and still needs – to be understood. Without that, science will continue to be a stream polluted by all the malodorous by-products of human selfishness and sin, whether individual or corporate.

Notes for chapter eleven

[1] *The Times*, 9 July 1855.

[2] T. R. Dunlap, *DDT, Scientists, Citizens and Public Policy* (Princeton University Press, 1981).

[3] Cited in A. R. Peacocke, *Creation and the World of Science* (Oxford University press, 1979), p.276.

[4] *Science*, 1967, *155*, 1203–1207.

[5] *E.g.* A. R. Peacocke in H. Montefiore (ed.), *Man and Nature* (Collins, 1975), pp.155–158.

[6] John Ray, *The Wisdom of God manifested in the Works of Creation* (London, Ninth edition, 1727), Part I.

[7] W. Derham, *Physico-Theology: or a Demonstration of the Being and Attributes of God, from his Works of Creation* (London, 1713).

[8] Carolyn Merchant, *The Death of Nature* (Wildwood House, London, 1982), p.248.

[9] See *e.g.* A. R. Peacocke, (ref. 3), pp.255–318; F. A. Schaeffer, *Pollution and the Death of Man* (Hodder and Stoughton, 1970); D. Morley, *The Sensitive Scientist* (SCM Press, 1978), pp.61–73; R. J. Berry, 'Alternatives and Accusations in Christians' Attitudes to the Environment', *Faith and Thought*, 1975, *102*, 131–150.

[10] C. A. Russell, *Pollution and the Pipes of Pan* (Open University Inaugural Lecture, 1983).

[11] M. Faraday, *The Chemical History of a Candle* (London, n.d.), p.126.

[12] H. Davy, 'A Discourse introductory to a course of lectures on chemistry' (1802) in *Collected Works* (1839), vol. ii.

[13] L. W. Moncrief, 'The cultural basis for our environmental crisis', *Science*, 1970, *170*, 508–512.

[14] J. D. Hughes, *Ecology in Ancient Civilizations* (University of New Mexico Press, Albuquerque, 1975), pp.149, 151.

[15] J. Passmore, *Man's Responsibility for Nature* (Duckworth, 1974).

[16] N. E. Borlaug, 'Ecology Fever', *Ceres*, 1972, *5*, 21–25.

[17] K. Mellanby, Review of T. R. Dunlap, (ref. 2), *Times Lit. Supp.*, 21 August 1981.

12 Floodtide

Make no mistake: if He rose at all
it was as His body;
if the cells' dissolution did not reverse,
   the molecules reknit, the amino acids rekindle,
the Church will fall.

It was not as the flowers,
each soft Spring recurrent;
it was not as His Spirit in the mouths and
   fuddled eyes of the eleven apostles;
it was as His flesh: ours.

The same hinged thumbs and toes,
the same valved heart
   that – pierced – died, withered, paused,
   and then regathered out of enduring Might
new strength to enclose.

Let us not mock God with metaphor,
analogy, sidestepping, transcendence;
making of the event a parable, a sign
   painted in the faded credulity of earlier ages:
let us walk through the door.

John Updike (b. 1932), Four of *Seven Stanzas at Easter*

Jesus answered ... 'Heaven and earth will pass away, but my
words will never pass away'.

Matthew 24:35

One of the most evocative pictures of crises in history is 'the
deluge'. The period from the eighteenth century of Madame
Pompadour ('after me, the deluge') to World War I (whose
history by Arthur Marwick was entitled simply *The Deluge*)
has conjured up apocalyptic visions of an inundation in which
all familiar features are swept away and civilization is submerged and all but destroyed, just as in the days of Noah.
Such an image has often been employed in conversations
about science in the twentieth century. The river has swollen
and risen to such an extent that at any time it may burst its
banks and engulf us all. Indeed in some respects the process
has begun already, and no-one is more aware of it than the
scientist himself or herself. The sheer volume of literature

creates such problems for storage that currently great scientific libraries in London and elsewhere are contemplating survival in their present form for only another five or six years. Microfilms and microfiches may solve the problem of space but not of access. Sophisticated abstracting services go some way to meet the difficulties, and computer terminals linked to central banks of information are already proving their usefulness. The prospect is not entirely disagreeable, but it represents an increase in availability of scientific information of a wholly new order of magnitude. Compared with this the deluge of information released by the new printed scientific journals of the seventeenth century was a mere trickle.

Important though the nearly exponential increase in scientific activity undoubtedly is, it pales into insignificance beside the effects which science has already had – or will have – upon the world in which we live, our dignity as human beings and our comprehension of God himself. Given understanding, and before the flood reaches its full force, we still have the opportunity for appropriate action.

Nuclear shadows

To enumerate even some of the beneficial effects of science in the last hundred years or so would read like a 'thirties style public relations exercise of one of the scientific institutions, anxious above all to enhance the prestige of its members' vocation.[1] But it is hardly necessary to do so, for surely everyone is to some extent aware of the unprecedented improvements in the quality of life in the West associated with new materials, advances in transport and communications, spectacular progress in agriculture, nutrition and medicine, and much else directly attributable to scientific research. Increasingly, people are also conscious of problems of pollution which, as we have seen (ch.11), if partly attributable to science, must also find in science a partial solution. Yet none of the evils attributed to modern science approaches in horror that ultimate tragedy for the human race, a nuclear holocaust. For the accumulated knowledge making possible the dropping of the atomic bomb on Hiroshima on 6 August 1945, science is openly and unequivocally responsible. The decision to develop, test and unleash the weapon was, however, that of the politicians, as must always be the case in nuclear warfare. Nevertheless men of science were involved in giving advice in

1945, though it was not always accepted. Since then the moral dilemma faced by successive generations of scientists has had several new features, most of which were as unwelcome as they were urgent.

First there is the fact that science could no longer be open. Secrecy had to be imposed for obvious reasons in any research with military potential. Not only would this violate the whole spirit of openness in which science had usually been conducted in the past; it would also breed suspicion and distrust among nations. As early as 1944 Niels Bohr had seen both Churchill and Roosevelt to express his fears on that score, and in 1950 he published his *Open Letter to the United Nations*, advocating international co-operation so as to avoid an arms race. His *Letter* came at a most inauspicious time and his words fell largely on to deaf ears. Of course this was not the first time that any scientific information had been suppressed. The alchemists kept fairly quiet if they thought transmutation was just round the corner, but now a greater transmutation demanded privacy on an infinitely larger scale. Occasionally questions of personal priority as well as commercial prudence militated against open discussion and publication. From now on, in many areas of science, this was to be the rule, not the exception.

Then again science was now much more strongly socialized. The atomic bomb simply could not have been made by an individual. It was a huge collective effort and in its early days demanded teamwork on an unprecedented scale. And of course this paid off. Never again will science be the individualistic thing it was in Victorian times or even later. One of the consequences of such a collectivization of science is the diminution of a sense of individual responsibility. As one member of the early research team remembered, 'There was a mesmeric quality about the bomb', and it was impossible to stop and consider what was actually happening.[2]

Such 'Big Science' was endowed by the state. Again this is only new in respect of scale.[3] In World War I the Government invested one million pounds as a major spur to research. This has been contrasted with a similar amount at the end of the Napoleonic Wars paid out for the building of new churches; now, in 1917 'a new deity was being enthroned'[4] and religion was visibly replaced by science. This indeed reflects another change that had imperceptibly come over science and was now displayed with a new clarity of focus: like society it had become secularized. The motivations of fear, greed and political ambition that had often been present in earlier days now became much more obvious, and the suggestion that science should be pursued to the glory of God would receive little more than a sympathetic (or pitying) smile in most quarters. But does it matter?

For a long time Marxists have been insisting that it does, and that the ideological framework within which science is pursued does affect the very nature of the science itself. Thus Steven and Hilary Rose have argued that much 'defence science', for example, is 'mission oriented', and that 'as a mission cannot be neutral, the science done in achieving it cannot be either'.[5] They go on to include *all* science in this category by invoking Thomas Kuhn's concept of 'paradigms', or intellectual frameworks, within which normal science operates until the framework can no longer sustain the weight of accumulated data or else for some other reason it collapses, as in the Copernican Revolution. These paradigms, the Roses argue, themselves embody the values of the scientific community, and so again the science pursued is value-laden. However, they are careful to add that they are not assaulting either the objectivity of science or its own internal logic. At this point Christians and Marxists must agree. If the course of science has been determined by theology, it is illogical to suppose that other value-systems could not have an analogous influence.

The question of the ethical neutrality of science is fraught with ambiguities, clouded by emotion and contorted by political polemic. Given that science does involve values to some extent at least, the problem is whether it *should* be pursued regardless of the good or bad uses to which it may be subsequently put. Yet again the problem predates the bomb, by which it is merely accentuated a thousandfold. In the 1920s a vocal but small group of scientists in England was publicly expressing doubts about the use of science for war purposes: J. Needham, J. D. Bernal, J. B. S. Haldane and a few others. Memories of scientific support for the 1914-1918 conflict were still vivid – 'the chemists' war', they called it. They also reflected the Marxist views of a Soviet delegation to the Second International Congress of the History of Science, held in London in 1931.

With the end of the 1939–1945 War and the realization of nuclear weapons these issues simply became far sharper. The 1960s, which witnessed a massive popular swing from science in Europe and America, saw also the founding of the British

Society for Social Responsibility in Science. Both were manifestations, at least in part, of mounting antipathy to the war in Vietnam. Before this, however, a growing number of responsible individuals in science had seen a greater catastrophe staring them in the face. In 1945, one month before the first U.S. atomic bomb was tested in New Mexico, seven American scientists sent a report to the Secretary for War urging that the weapon be not used against Japan on the grounds that an arms race would be precipitated – just as Bohr had argued independently. Other American scientists petitioned President Truman on similar lines. Their advice was not taken, more for diplomatic than military reasons, it seems.

During the next five years opposition to the use of nuclear weapons was stimulated by several prominent left-wing scientists, especially the British crystallographer J. D. Bernal and the French nuclear physicist F. Joliot-Curie, each of whom played an important role in the new World Federation of Scientific Workers. Behind the scenes other scientists shared their concern if not their political views. These included Bohr (as we have seen) and Einstein who, in the last week of his life, joined Bertrand Russell in the famous Declaration of 1955 that bears their two names and condemned the use of H-bombs as probable agents for the annihilation of civilization. From this came a long series of international gatherings of scientists to discuss disarmament and related issues, first held at Pugwash, Nova Scotia.

It must not be supposed that these attempts to de-neutralize science were conspicuously successful. When the Institute of Chemistry resolved to curtail correspondence in its *Proceedings* on 'science and war', maintaining that political controversy was 'beyond the province of a professional scientific institution',[6] it was merely setting a trend that has continued to the present day.[7] Nor must it be assumed that all the opponents of neutrality in science were of Marxist persuasion. Bertrand Russell was anxious to muster support from persons with widely differing political views. As an anti-communist he was anxious to collaborate with Joliot-Curie precisely because *he* was a communist.[8]

In the attempts to limit science for military purposes Christians active in science were not conspicuously visible. Certainly various clerical voices were raised in protest. As early as 1927 E. A. Burroughs, Bishop of Ripon, delivered a sermon at the Annual Meeting of the British Association and claimed that man's scientific powers had not been matched by comparable moral and spiritual progress. Since this 'ethical gap' posed a grievous danger to society Burroughs proposed – to the astonishment of his scientific audience – a ten-year moratorium on scientific research. The suggestion, though delivered tongue-in-cheek, caused a considerable stir. Charles Raven had long espoused a Christian pacifism and, as a theologian with a deep interest in science, became a vociferous opponent of its use for nuclear weapons. But Christians were not in the van of protest and it is worth asking why.

There never has been a Christian consensus on war, and nuclear war has been no exception (though in very recent times official pronouncements by Councils of Churches have been more forthcoming against atomic warfare than those by bodies of scientists). However, faced with a nuclear holocaust it is the materialist (dialectical or otherwise) who has most to lose. The world is all he or she has. Joliot-Curie's biographer suggests he was specially concerned lest he be deprived of the joy of scientific discovery, a joy that would instantly disappear if science were to be used as an instrument of mass destruction.[9] Doubtless an alliance with Marxists was abhorrent to some Christians. Some perceived in the Bible prophecies of a nuclear doom and resolved to accept the inevitable; Armageddon would be an atomic war. Yet others considered the task of political persuasion as hopeless and used their time in other more rewarding activities. This is not to defend (or attack) Christian inaction, but to try to understand why it existed. All these attitudes may be found in the abundant literature of the time.

There is little doubt that many Christians, whether in science or not, preferred to trust in God rather than in man. When the German chemist Ida Noddack suggested in 1935 that nuclear fission should be possible, neither Fermi nor Segre was able to discover it. The latter is reported to have said, 'The whole story of our failure is a mystery to me. I keep thinking of a passage from Dante: "O crucified Jove, do you turn your just eyes away from us or is there here prepared a purpose secret and beyond our comprehension?"'[10] Had these two distinguished physicists in Mussolini's Italy been successful, it is not unlikely that Hitler would have been able to threaten Europe with the bomb as early as 1939. One of Fermi's students commented, 'God, for his own inscrutable reasons, made everybody blind at that time to the phenomenon of nuclear fission.'[11] Obviously no-one at the time perceived how close humanity might have been to disaster. But it would not have been a surprise to Christians attuned to the historic faith in a God who acts in history as well as in nature. It is indeed a realized belief in the sovereignty of God that permits an unshakeable confidence for an age overshadowed by the bomb, or any other age whatever.

The dignity of man

If the advances of science appear to threaten the continued existence of this planet, or at least of civilization upon it, it is equally true that they have been seen to menace long-accepted values of human worth and dignity.[12] Even if nuclear war can be avoided, there remains the possibility that science may yet erode the belief that each man, woman and child has a special kind of value not shared with any other objects in the universe. Because this conviction, more than any other, underlies the universal abhorrence of nuclear obliteration, its erosion may be regarded as an evil greater even than atomic war. Over the last hundred years science has from time to time been roundly castigated for being an agent in the dehumanization of mankind. Since the 1960s its reputation has taken much harder knocks than previously, not simply because of military uses and environmental ruin but for its perceived assaults on the dignity of man.

The crude materialist attempts to reduce man to nothing but a mechanism, once the fashion among Victorian 'free-thinkers', are little heard of today. In the sense that, in principle, it may one day be possible to explain all human bodily activity in terms of chemistry and physics, this particular form of reductionism is almost beyond controversy. In the sense that that is all that can be meaningfully said about human bodies, it is scarcely credible at all, for it neglects altogether the concept of *function*. As for mental phenomena – let alone spiritual – it has nothing whatever to say. Thus at one level it is so trite as to be a truism. At any other it is simply irrelevant. These considerations were widely canvassed in the late nineteenth century. In Britain, for example, mechanical materialism was confronted by a revival of idealism as the century drew to a close. It was vigorously assailed on all sides by physical scientists like G. G. Stokes and P. G. Tait (who were orthodox Christians) and like William Crookes and Oliver Lodge (who sought for counter-evidence and personal comfort in the seances of 'spiritualism'). Amongst biologists the very concept of 'evolution' seemed to defy explanation in purely material, non-purposive categories. This was never more clearly seen than by A. R. Wallace, co-founder with Darwin of the doctrine of natural selection.[13]

If reduction of mankind to atoms and molecules was not a serious threat to human dignity, the same cannot be said of some post-war developments in ethology, the comparative study of animal behaviour.[14] The Austrian zoologist Konrad Lorenz had spent 35 years studying the behaviour patterns of animals and (especially) birds when, in 1963, he published his most famous work *On Aggression*. Comparing man with the animals he concluded that human aggression arose in part from instinct (as with carnivores), but mainly from his possession of greater power than his instincts could yet control. He saw in humanity a genetic decline similar to that in domesticated animals. His remedies, at first political and later at an individual level, were attempts to derive values from science that harked back to Herbert Spencer's social theories (the mis-called 'Social Darwinism') and foreshadowed more ominous developments in the near future.

In 1967 a highly popular book appeared in which the human/animal analogy was taken one step further. *The Naked Ape* by Desmond Morris began by observing that of the 193 living species of apes and monkeys only one (*homo sapiens*) was not covered by hair. The fact that man also has the largest brain and is 'the sexiest primate alive' does not emancipate him from 'all the basic laws of biological behaviour'.[15] From this it was but a short step to compare the whole of human biological activity with that of the primates and to infer that not only was man a naked ape, but he was nothing but a naked ape. By his genetic inheritance he is locked into a complex of behaviour patterns to which he can only submit in order to survive. If this really was the message of science, then it threatened not only man's destiny but also his dignity. Though well received for its entertainment value, *The Naked Ape* did not earn a great deal of scientific applause and it was criticized from several quarters for its reductionist philosophy.[16]

Stronger opposition was reserved for another book that appeared eight years later, in 1975. *Sociobiology* was written by E. O. Wilson, acidly but accurately described as 'a Harvard specialist in ants' who 'made himself a name by pontificating on man'.[17] From a study of insect societies he progresses to a synthesis of ethology, ecology, population genetics, evolutionary biology and sociology (to name but a few), in which the evolution of social behaviour in animals and man is explained in terms of genetics. Thus responsibility for altruism, aggression and other types of behaviour may reside in specific genes within the organism.

Sociobiology was a controversial book, not least because it seemed to extend reductionism to the very fringes of man's experience, his social activity. It was assailed because much of it was admittedly hypothetical. The analogy between man and animals, still more between man and insects, was not obviously valid. Moreover there was great danger of cyclic argument and of turning 'what should be an empirical investigation into a dance around tautologies'[18]: genes determine man's physical structure; society depends on human physical structures; therefore society is genetically determined. But the theory is devoid of explanatory power when it comes to questions about individuals (why one is more courageous, another more aggressive, and so on). As with Morris, Wilson seems to incline to biological determinism. If human behaviour is entirely under genetic control there is not a lot one can do about it. As Steven Rose complained, it is by 'fixing certain types of human society or patterns of relationship within the framework of immutable, iron biological laws by the technique of claiming they are "in the genes" that sociobiology ceases to become silly and instead becomes obnoxious'. It denies the possibility of social change and thus justifies present arrangements 'just as surely as did Social Darwinism in Victorian England'.[19]

For this last reason, and for others, sociobiology has been trenchantly criticized by Marxist writers. On this matter they are in full accord with Christians who would agree that science is an activity pursued in the light of certain transcendent values, so cannot itself determine what these values might be. Moreover Christians, like Marxists but for different reasons, can have no truck with a determinism that condemns the human race to the consequences of its genetic inheritance. They would take issue with all forms of biological determinism on the biblical grounds that man has been given responsibility for his actions by his Creator. Like the 'naked apes' at Laodicea (Revelation 3:14–21) an individual need suffer the embarrassment and indignity of moral nakedness no longer. By an act of obedience, trust and welcome to Christ, 'the Ruler of God's creation', he or she can experience joyful communion with him and a conquest over evil. That is one liberation over which one's genes have no control at all.

The bizarre notion that the ultimate purpose of man is solely to replicate his kind received powerful advocacy in Richard Dawkins' *The Selfish Gene* (1976). Genes are 'selfish' because they persist in organisms which are 'survival machines', but whose own survival is less important than that of the genes they carry. The party must go on. Replication must continue. From genes Dawkins goes on to speak of 'memes', their analogues in the evolution of culture. They are the things that can be imitated, like fashions in dress and speech, tunes and so on, which will outlive their temporary hosts. Thus cultural evolution, unlike its biological counterpart, will proceed in a Lamarckian manner with environmental factors causing the pace and direction of change. These reified 'memes' gain stability by their 'great psychological appeal' and so continue to permeate the culture. When the meaning of 'great psychological appeal' is questioned, it is at once obvious that we are dealing with several different levels of discourse all at once: social, biological, perhaps physicochemical. Such a conflation of hierarchies can only breed certain confusion. 'At this point', Arthur Peacocke observes, 'the flood-gates burst.'[20]

The enduring Word

From time to time the Anglican Church is rocked by the appearance of a collection of essays which appear to negate much of what it has hitherto been imagined to believe. Such was the case with *Essays and Reviews* in 1860. Just over a century later, in 1962, another collection was published with the title *Soundings*.[21] Like its famous predecessor it caused a considerable stir. It was edited by Alec Vidler, then Dean of King's College, Cambridge, who declared its task was rather to ask questions than to produce answers, for, in truth, the distinguished academic authors found themselves considerably at sea. To be sure the willingness to take 'soundings' implied a belief that there *is* a bottom to the ocean, but the overall impression was quite intentionally one of doubt and perplexity, coupled with a refreshing candour to face range after range of questions that troubled certain theologians in the 1960s. Many of their difficulties were, on almost any criterion, internal to theology itself; some give the impression of self-inflicted wounds. But underlying much of the debate, and surfacing explicitly in one chapter, is the view that, somehow, theology is under an irresistible compulsion to react to the new situation created by the advances of science. In that chapter John Habgood (who had previously trained in science) writes of 'The uneasy truce between science and theology', and appears to take us right back to the 'conflict' metaphor so carefully engineered by Victorian positivists. However, he makes the telling point that theology is often rejected not for any logical reason stemming from specific scientific advances, but rather on account of 'the psychological impact of science'. Ordinary religious symbolism is felt to be trivial in comparison with the immensities of space and time as we now understand them, while theology seems impotent alongside the immense achievements of modern science. Hence, although science and theology are not actually in open conflict, their relation is that of an 'uneasy truce'; he might have said a 'cold war'. Understandably 'theologians want to find a position which is secure against any possible advances in scientific knowledge'. He argues for a 'clearing of the ground' and a wider view of the nature of science than many of its practitioners allow themselves. Indeed one of the remarkable things about this essay is its insistence that science (more than theology) be considered in a new light.[22]

Habgood's chapter was one of the least contentious in the book which, on the whole, 'produced a rather muffled explosion'.[23] The reverberations had scarcely died down when a much more spectacular eruption occurred *fortissimo*, the appearance of John Robinson's *Honest to God*.[24] It was, he said, a questioning of the entire 'religious frame' in which Christianity had hitherto been presented and, as he correctly foretold, 'may seem to be radical, and doubtless to many heretical'.[25] While fully meriting those coveted adjectives, and commendable for its frankness, in many respects it was a confused, even muddled, exposure of Robinson's personal doubts, and few of the ideas it sought to popularize were new to theological discourse. The subsequent furore stemmed at least in part from the status of the author as an Anglican bishop who seemed to many of his flock and others to be busily sawing off the branch on which he was precariously seated. This fact, together with a carefully orchestrated publicity campaign, guaranteed for the book a successful run, though even the publishers could hardly have dared to expect the sale of nearly a million copies in several languages over the next few years.

Once again it is clear that deeply ingrained in the author's questioning is the science of the twentieth century. At the very outset he takes issue with the traditional three-decker universe of heaven-earth-hell, and the concept of a God 'up there'. That the Copernican Revolution had taken place centuries ago he does not deny, but he feels that errors of the old cosmology may have survived in the belief in a God who was truly transcendent, actually 'out there', beyond space and time. This traditional notion, he thinks, is increasingly hard to swallow by man who has now 'come of age':

> The final psychological, if not logical, blow delivered by modern science and technology to the idea that there might *literally* be a God 'out there' has *coincided* with an awareness that the *mental* picture of such a God may be more of a stumbling-block than an aid to belief in the Gospel.[26]

Theology, this suggests, must therefore be trimmed to make it credible. Greatly influenced by Bultmann, Tillich and Bonhoeffer, Robinson also replaces the traditional experience of God in nature by one in human relationships. *Honest to God*, it has been said, is thus an existentialist natural theology.

It appears to be a penchant of Anglican bishops of radical persuasion to attract adverse publicity to themselves. In 1984 an even greater row was generated when David Jenkins, having been nominated as Bishop of Durham, went to some lengths to make public his doubts about the virgin birth and resurrection of Christ, and miracles in general. It was not the doubts themselves (which were anything but original) so much as the circumstances of their utterance which aroused a storm of outraged protest and a petition by 12,000 members of the Church of England to have his appointment quashed. It was unsuccessful. Less spectacular examples could be multiplied almost indefinitely of cases where biblical doctrines of a transcendent God, the virgin birth, resurrection, miracles, *etc.* are set aside for reasons that are, however vaguely, associated with the state of science in the late twentieth century. And it has to be added that many of these ecclesiastical doubts are reflections of the general folk-culture of the day; in ordinary conversation a decline in religion is more often attributed to science than to any other single cause. Whether justified or not, such opinions would indicate a cataclysmic change in our views of reality beside which the Copernican and Darwinian Revolutions are tremors of relatively minor importance.

There are cogent reasons for doubting the logical inevitability of such a major assault by science on the historic beliefs in a God-who-is. Writing of post-war developments in theological thinking as, at least to some degree, a reaction against a theology that has been shaped by insights from science, J. W. Dillenberger has written:

> It is an ironic note that the revolution in theology occurred when major scientists had already abandoned the more doctrinaire position which had contributed to the problem.[27]

In similar vein the Edinburgh theologian T. F. Torrance writes:

> Since the new scientific view of the universe is not hostile to the Christian faith, theology has no need to be on the defensive as it felt it had to be when confronted with the dualist and determinist conception of the universe as a closed continuum of cauŗe and effect, which axiomatically ruled out of consideration any real notion of God's providential interaction with the world or therefore of prayer, let alone notions of incarnation and redemption.[28]

Endemic in much theological revisionism was a fear of 'miracle'. The Jenkins case rested – or appeared to rest – on a conviction that in an age of science miracles were an anachronistic survival. A letter to *The Times* from fourteen scientists (including six Fellows of the Royal Society) observed with some asperity that 'it is not logically valid to use science as an argument against miracles. To believe that miracles cannot happen is as much an act of faith as to believe that they can happen'.[29] The strategy of taking the stories in the Gospels only in a mythical, 'religious' sense was given great stimulus by the programme of 'demythologization' proposed by the German theologian R. Bultmann. Yet this was, as H. P. Nebelick suggested, a 'speculative device' imposed on 'unsuspecting persons' and based 'on false presuppositions about both science and the scientific world-view'.[30] Many other examples could be cited of miracle-rejection on supposed 'scientific' grounds. The historian Arnold Toynbee confessed that towards the end of his life his knowledge of science was 'still rudimentary', yet tells of his rejection at an early age of the virgin birth 'because I could not reconcile it with an already established belief of mine in "the uniformity of nature"'. He simply found it incomprehensible that God would break his own laws, and that, rather than any specific philosophy of science, was the difficulty.[31]

However, great caution in such matters is indicated not merely by events in science itself but also from modern insights in the history and philosophy of science. Commenting on a collection of papers on the sciences and theology in the twentieth century, Mary Hesse asks why theologians find it so necessary to come to terms with scientific detail:

> Would not a slightly less deferential view of science, such as is implied by recent epistemological and sociological critiques, suggest that such theological effort is a wrestling with shadows?[32]

In a similar way she offers a lengthy critique of the important book *Chance and Necessity* by the Nobel Prize-winning molecular biologist Jacques Monod. Monod seeks to demonstrate from modern biology the absence of purpose in the universe. He holds that our modern knowledge of genetics actually confirms that living organisms have developed by chance. His case rests upon a 'principle of objectivity', *i.e.* objective science is the only true form of knowledge. Yet as he admits, and Hesse emphasizes, this is an assumption which cannot itself be grounded in science. One could equally well argue for a theistic view of creation. Mary Hesse rightly insists 'there are extra-scientific assumptions at every crucial point in the argument'.[33] Essentially the same point is made by Stanley Jaki.[34] No-one at all aware of work in the history of science in the last twenty years could easily concede the principle of totally objective science. As Hesse further remarks:

> There is no need to go all the way with Marxists who reduce ideologies to mere epiphenomena of social and economic relations, in order to accept the insight of Marxism that man's reason is less free than was once believed to choose in the abstract among different intellectual systems.[35]

So, as the twentieth century draws to a close, dominated by science as never before, the absolutist claims advanced on its behalf can still be challenged effectively. There never has been a time when Christianity, rightly understood, has had anything to fear at the bar of rational enquiry, whether conducted in the name of science or anything else. Conflict there has certainly been, but always for reasons that are peripheral to the real issues with which science and Christianity are concerned. Only in that limited, even localized, sense has there been anything like even an 'uneasy truce'. Desperate attempts to evacuate the Christian faith of its essential content, so as not to offend the susceptibilities of 'scientific man', are not merely misguided but leave most scientists profoundly unimpressed. In the light of scientific progress this century such theological acrobatics are quaintly anachronistic. Moreover, the dependence of science on the propositions of Christian theism has been historically demonstrated time and time again. For that reason alone (and there are many others) science cannot be perceived as a threat to the gospel of Christ.

That being so, it cannot be confidently said that science itself is not under threat. Again the danger is not a new one. From the early opposition to the Royal Society, through the high noon of Romanticism to the swing from science of the 1960s, there have always been those who deplore a meddling with nature's secrets. Today, in one sense, they have more reason than ever. Yet clipping the wings of science to suit the political creed of the day is a hazardous business, as the Lysenko affair in Russia and many other episodes under totalitarianism have amply shown. What science has always required is *freedom*, even though it will always operate within a given cultural framework. In a penetrating historical analysis Professor Hooykaas has argued that 'the inner freedom necessary to scientific work is fully *guaranteed* by a biblical religion'. For the Puritans, he argues, 'it was not *freedom* which led to Truth, but it was Truth which led to freedom', and that Truth is not a mere abstraction but personalized in Christ. He adds, 'We cannot be radically free until, tired and exhausted from the vain search after truth, we have stretched our arms to the Liberator.' Only in this way can we know the true freedom of science which is 'liberation from worldly and pious traditions and from the dictatorship of Reason'.[36]

In our pluralistic world we may have to wait a long time before that kind of liberation comes our way. Meanwhile it is not Christianity or even science which is under immediate threat, but civilization itself. Whether atmospheric pollution or nuclear disaster is in view, the implication of science and technology is distressingly clear. In that connection the opinions of two distinguished historians of science and technology are extremely relevant. Professor Donald Cardwell (of

U.M.I.S.T.) denies that it is technology which threatens our society, 'for technology is itself a distinctive and dependent offspring of the philosophy, cosmology and religion of that society'. He further writes:

> It was not technology that instituted Auschwitz and Terezin, or for that matter destroyed Dresden. In all cases it was a series of military and political decisions based on certain philosophies that resulted in the crimes in question. In this matter we need look no further than original sin, for the religious explanation is not only adequate, it is obviously correct.[37]

The words on the doors of the Cavendish Laboratory epitomize the religious approach to science of many late Victorian physical scientists: 'MAGNA OPERA DOMINI EXQUISITA IN OMNES VOLUPTATES EIUS', 'Great are the works of the LORD; they are pondered by all who delight in them' (Psalm 111:2).

This may well be right, and provide an adequate explanation of much that happened in the past. But does it offer hope for the future? Indeed it does. This is the view of the Dutch historian of ancient and more recent technology, Professor R. J. Forbes, writing in 1968:

> The question is whether we, who have dominion over the earth, shall act like Sisyphus and trust to our cunning only, becoming more and more self-reliant and self-involved, self-imprisoned and self-centred. Sisyphus became his own God and his own Satan, at war with heaven, embittered with earth, and contemptuous of hell. But this author, after contemplating three-quarters of a century of technology's marvels and horrors, has no doubt that Sisyphus has already been saved from himself. This happened at Easter.[38]

This Easter faith has been the historic faith by which men and women lived and died through all the 'Christian centuries'. A personal encounter with the risen Christ has been the experience not only of saints and mystics, but of people like Robert Boyle, Michael Faraday, James Clerk Maxwell and countless other men of science down the years. They would surely have agreed that it offers the only hope for civilization, just as it gave to them a rationale and guiding light for science and for life itself.

Notes for chapter twelve

[1] As for example the publications in the inter-war years of the Royal Institute of Chemistry (founded in 1877 and the first professional institute for science in any country). On this see C. A. Russell, G. K. Roberts and N. G. Coley, *Chemists by Profession* (Open University Press, Milton Keynes, 1977).

[2] B. Feld, *New Scientist*, 1975, 67, 208.

[3] On the increasing role of the state in science see, *e.g.*, H. and S. Rose, *Science and Society* (Pelican, 1969); and C. A. Russell, *Science and Social Change* (Macmillan, 1983).

[4] A. Marwick, *The Deluge* (Penguin, 1967), p.230.

[5] S. and H. Rose, 'The myth of the neutrality of science', in W. Fuller (ed.), *The Social Impact of Modern Biology* (Routledge and Kegan Paul, 1971), p.220.

[6] *Proc. Inst. Chem.*, 1936, 60, 200.

[7] The trend has even spread to Soviet scientists: S. and H. Rose, (ref. 5), p.218.

[8] P. Biquard, *Frédéric Joliot-Curie*, trans. by G. Strachan (Souvenir Press, 1965), p.127.

[9] *Ibid.*, p.128.

[10] N. P. Davis, *Lawrence and Oppenheimer* (Cape, 1969), p.96.

[11] E. Segré in R. Jungk, *Brighter than a Thousand Suns*, trans. J. Cleugh (Gollancz, 1958), p.60. Cf. *Faith and Thought*, 1982, 109, 97–98.

[12] See D. M. MacKay, *Human Science and Human Dignity* (Hodder and Stoughton, 1979).

[13] *E.g.* R. Smith, 'Alfred Russel Wallace: philosophy of nature and man', *Brit. J. Hist. Sci.*, 1972, 6, 177–199.

[14] L. R. Graham, *Between Science and Values* (Columbia University Press, N.Y., 1981), pp.159ff.

[15] D. Morris, *The Naked Ape* (Corgi, 1969).

[16] See L. R. Graham, (ref. 14).

[17] S. Jaki, *Angels, Apes and Men* (Sugden, La Salle, Illinois, 1983), p.69.

[18] L. R. Graham, (ref. 14), p.205.

[19] S. Rose, *New Scientist*, 1976, 70, 433. On sociobiology see also N. Isbister, *Third Way*, 23 February 1978, vol. 2, no. 4, pp.3–6.

[20] A. R. Peacocke, *Creation and the World of Science* (Clarendon Press, 1979), p.178.

[21] A. R. Vidler, (ed.), *Soundings: Essays concerning Christian Understanding* (Cambridge University Press, 1962). The nautical metaphor was echoed by two replies to the book: A. Richardson (ed.), *Four Anchors from the Stern* (SCM Press, 1963), and E. Mascall, *Up and Down in Adria* (Faith Press, 1963).

[22] J. S. Habgood, 'The uneasy truce between science and theology' in

A. R. Vidler, (ref. 21), pp.21–41. The phrase 'uneasy truce' was earlier used by Malcolm Dixon in his *Science and Irreligion* (Falcon Booklets, 1960), p.19 (an address given at the British Association Meeting in Belfast, 1952).

[23] R. Lloyd, *The Church of England 1900–1965* (SCM Press, 1966), p.599.

[24] J. A. T. Robinson, *Honest to God* (SCM Press, 1963). It is only fair to add that in the next twenty years until his death in 1983 Robinson changed his position considerably.

[25] *Ibid.*, p.10.

[26] *Ibid.*, p.16.

[27] J. W. Dillenberger, *Protestant Thought and Natural Science* (Collins, 1961), p.265.

[28] T. F. Torrance, 'Divine and contingent order' in A. R. Peacocke (ed.), *The Sciences and Theology in the Twentieth Century* (Oriel Press, 1981), p.96.

[29] *The Times*, 13 July 1984.

[30] H. R. Nebelick (review of I. Paul, *Science, theology and Einstein*), *Scot. J. Theol.*, 1984, *37*, 239.

[31] A. Toynbee, *Experiences* (Oxford University Press, 1969), pp.132–133.

[32] M. Hesse, 'Retrospect', in A. R. Peacocke, (ref. 28), p.286.

[33] M. Hesse, 'On the alleged incompatibility between Christianity and science' in H. Montefiore (ed.), *Man and Nature* (Collins, 1975), p.126.

[34] S. L. Jaki, *The Road to Science and the Ways to God* (Scottish Academic Press, Edinburgh, 1975), p.279.

[35] Hesse in H. Montefiore, (ref. 33), p.130.

[36] R. Hooykaas, *Philosophia Libera. Christian Faith and the Freedom of Science* (Tyndale Press, 1957), p.23.

[37] D. S. L. Cardwell, *Technology, Science and History* (Heinemann, 1972), pp.222–223.

[38] R. J. Forbes, *The Conquest of Nature* (Pall Mall Press, 1968), p.93.

13 Epilogue

How sweet the moonlight sleeps upon this bank!
Here will we sit, and let the sounds of music
Creep in our ears: soft stillness and the night
Become the touches of sweet harmony.
...Look how the floor of heaven
Is thick inlaid with patines of bright gold:
There's not the smallest orb which thou behold'st
But in his motion like an angel sings,
Still quiring to the young-eyed cherubins;
Such harmony is in immortal souls;
But, whilst this muddy vesture of decay
Doth grossly close it in, we cannot hear it.

Lorenzo in *The Merchant of Venice*, Act V, Scene 1.

For you make me glad by your deeds, O LORD;
   I sing for joy at the work of your hands.
How great are your works, O LORD,
   how profound your thoughts!

Psalm 92:4–5

Four centuries and more have now elapsed since something recognizably like modern science emerged out of the convulsive upheavals of the Renaissance and Reformation. The world is indeed a different place because of it. Yet it is not so different that the Christian world-view has lost its relevance. Quite the contrary if church growth statistics mean anything at all, and so, whether in the post-Christian West or the burgeoning cultures of the Third World, currents of scientific and biblical ideas continue to mingle even though many are quite unaware of their origins. The relationship between science and faith, though constantly changing in its manifestations, retains certain elements that are not time-variable and may be detected in a multiplicity of diverse cultures. Occasionally a considerable number of these elements occurs in the life and thought of one man. Less frequently, the historical data from which they must be reconstructed are readily available. More rarely still have such data been subjected to competent historical analysis. Only in the most exceptional circumstances is all this true of a person who could justly be placed in the first rank of world scientists. Such a man was Michael Faraday.[1] Bestriding the period of modern science, though somewhat nearer our own end of it, Faraday displayed important attitudes to the issues of science and faith which make a brief glance in his direction an appropriate conclusion to this book.

Faraday (1791–1867) was according to almost any criterion a giant amongst scientific men. Possibly the greatest experimentalist in the history of science, and also one of its most successful popularizers, he worked and lived at the Royal Institution in London for half a century.[2] Inventor of the dynamo, discoverer of that most important chemical compound benzene, pioneer in electrochemistry and electromagnetism, he was, above all, chief architect of the classical field theory of physics. Yet Faraday was also a devoted member of (as he put it) 'a small despised set of Christians known, if known at all, as Sandemanians.' Founded in the eighteenth century by Robert Sandeman, as a union of earlier and similar movements, they stood for separation of Church and State and for a church order derived directly from the New Testament. Their nonconformist piety marked them from other evangelicals by a weekly repetition of the New Testament practice of feet-washing. Against this background of simple but intense devotion must be set Faraday's titanic achievements in a world of which most of his fellow-believers knew nothing: the world of science.

The first point that needs to be made seems, at first sight, to have little to do with Faraday's science. It is that his faith was a very private thing, though shared with the tightly-knit fellowship of his church. He even declined to discuss with his wife, a month after their marriage, his profession of faith before the church: 'That is between me and my God.' Soon he became an Elder, and more closely involved with the meeting than ever. He loved the singing (he had a good baritone voice), the fellowship and the ministry in which he often participated. One who enjoyed his friendship but did not share his faith was the physicist John Tyndall, and he connected the two parts of Faraday's life like this:

> I think that a good deal of Faraday's week-day strength and persistency might be referred to his Sunday exercises. He drinks from a fount on Sunday which refreshes his soul for the week.[3]

Whatever might be the disappointments in work or personal trials ahead Faraday was fortified. If he lacked immediate recognition, what did it matter? As a recent biographer has pertinently noted, 'When one basks every week in the glow of eternity, years, decades, even centuries seem trivial.'[4]

This private faith was manifest in many observable ways. Even his sternest critics admitted his real nobility of character which mirrored exactly the faith he professed. When scurrilously treated by Sir Humphry Davy (whose assistant he became) he refused to countenance any criticism of his master and turned on his heel when any was expressed. He never quarrelled with Tyndall, exponent of a materialistic creed, in 14 years together at the Royal Institution. As for the uncertain future he observed that the Christian 'finds his guide in the Word of God, and commits the keeping of his soul into the hands of God. He looks for no assurance beyond what the Word can give him, and if his mind is troubled by the cares and fears which assail him he can go nowhere but in prayer to the throne of grace and to Scripture'.[5] That was in 1859, the year of *The Origin of Species*. Two years later, with failing powers and 'no science to talk to you about', he wrote to the Geneva physicist A. A. de lâ Rive (who shared his Christian faith) of a serene confidence: 'Such peace is alone in the gift of God; and as it is He who gives it, why should we be afraid? His unspeakable gift in His beloved Son is the ground of no doubtful hope...'[6] Pearce Williams has well written:

> He never stooped to petty quarrels or sought revenge for any real or imagined slight...When Faraday spoke of the work of others he was attended to for everyone knew that he was guided only by the love of truth. Secure in his faith and beloved by his wife and relatives he was able to devote his entire energy for forty years to the task of uncovering one corner of it.[7]

Faraday's unsanctimonious religion was clearly far removed from conventional Victorian piety. So also was his attitude to natural theology. He echoed the book of Job (one of his favourites) in exclaiming, 'as if a man by reasoning could find out God!' His stress on the primacy of biblical revelation seems to have virtually excluded the possibility of natural theology. Whether he even accorded it the limited role suggested by St Paul seems rather doubtful though he frequently quoted Romans 1:20. His theology of the fallenness of man encompassed not only the general limitations of sense experience but also human fallibility in matters of scientific interpretation.

Michael Faraday (1791–1867).

For Faraday, faith had to come first. It was *then* possible for the eye of faith to perceive in the universe signs of God's greatness and power. Writing to de la Rive in 1859 he confessed that when he spoke of God's 'material works' in a 'common lecture' he did not like 'to deal irreverently with religion by drawing it in at second-hand'. Nevertheless 'it is impossible to forget who hath ordered them'.[8] Thus Faraday, unlike Sandeman himself, reversed the direction of logical inference associated with Paley and other natural theologians. He did not believe in a progress 'from nature up to nature's

God', but a pilgrimage in the opposite sense. More clearly than most of his contemporaries he could see the limitations of an apologetic derived from nature, either alone or as the dominant source. In his lectures and discourses the usual silence about a Divine Creator springs, therefore, not from disbelief but its opposite: a highly articulated theology based on revelation. Only then would a study of ozone disclose something more of 'the one Great Cause' (1859), or the facts of putrefaction provide 'evidences of a wisdom which the more a man knows the more freely will he acknowledge he cannot understand' (1840).[9] That perhaps is why he responded so warmly to Lorenzo's speech (above), with its intimations of harmony to be perceived by 'immortal souls'.

If Faraday was reluctant to draw conclusions about God from nature rather than the Bible he was equally reticent about 'reconciling' science and Scripture. John Glas, one of Sandeman's predecessors, had declared 'the Bible was never designed to teach mankind philosophy [science]', a position closely similar to that of Galileo. From the very few comments that Faraday permitted himself on this topic it seems that he felt the same. While it is true that his powers were failing when Darwin's *Origin of Species* was published there is little evidence that he was in the least troubled by earlier specula-tions about the age of the earth, the universality of the flood, or even pre-Darwinian ideas on evolution. It is not enough to say that these were matters of natural history as opposed to his own tradition of natural philosophy. He himself made his position plain. He once claimed 'an absolute distinction between religious and ordinary belief'.[10] In a much-quoted letter in 1844 he went even further:

> There is no philosophy in my religion... Though the natural works of God can never by any possibility come in contra-diction with the higher things that belong to our future existence, and must with everything concerning Him ever glorify Him, still I do not think it at all necessary to tie the study of the natural sciences and religion together, and, in my intercourse with my fellow-creatures, that which is religious, and that which is philosophical, have ever been two distinct things.[11]

All this is entirely in accord with his views on the limitations of natural theology. It does not, however, justify a now popular view once enunciated by Gillispie: Michael Faraday thought 'there was no connection at all between physical science and religious truth.'[12] Recent work has shown that, if there was no philosophy in his religion, there was certainly religion in his philosophy.[13] If he did not have a natural theology he certainly did have a theology of nature. As his biographer remarks, 'his deepest intuitions about the physical world sprang from this religious faith in the Divine origin of nature.'[14] Williams goes on to show that Faraday came to propose a conservation of 'force' in the universe for reasons that were derived from his understanding of God and his world. It is noteworthy that Joule and Kelvin later codified their understanding of the First Law of Thermodynamics on closely similar grounds. But that is not all.

From about 1835 Faraday had been given to dark sayings about electric induction, with force transmitted by particles which yet remained far apart. The hard 'billiard-ball' atoms of Dalton held as little appeal to Faraday as they did for Davy (and he was also inclined to associate such concepts with atheism). So he reverted to earlier notions of the eighteenth-century Jesuit priest R. J. Boscovich: atoms which were really *point-centres of force*. Atheistic association apart, why should he have done this? A clue to this strange reversion has been discovered in a private Memorandum, written to himself in 1844, to clarify his ideas. It resides in the Library of the Institution of Electrical Engineers in London. According to T. H. Levere, who first drew attention to the document, it demonstrates the main reason for Faraday's adoption of the point-atom hypothesis: 'it fitted in with the world picture imposed by his religion.'[15] Unlike Faraday's papers intended for public consumption, this short memorandum contains no less than three references to God, including the following:

> Is the lingering notion which remains in the minds of some really a thought, that God could not just as easily by his word speak power into existence around centres, as he could first create nuclei and then clothe them with power?[16]

From this it was a comparatively short journey to the supreme achievement of his life: a unified field theory in which the universe was filled with electric and magnetic fields associated with point-atoms. As one commentator put it, 'Faraday was, quite literally, at play in the fields of the Lord.'[17]

It is scarcely necessary to add that a point-atom theory was not a *necessary* deduction from Faraday's theology. It was rather *suggested* by it, much in the same way that Joule, Maxwell and Kelvin came to certain tentative conclusions in thermodynamics. The fact that the conclusions have, in these cases, turned out to be so extraordinarily fruitful is, at least in part, fortuitous. What is not in doubt is the high degree of congruity between Judaeo-Christian and scientific world-views espoused by these men. In this respect they represent a continuing tradition that stretches from Bacon to Einstein and beyond. Exploring that congruity and identifying its relevance to contemporary problems is an unending quest that cannot be avoided if humanity is to survive.

Faraday's science has transformed life and civilization today. It remains to ask how Faraday himself viewed the application of science and how, if at all, his Christian faith determined the outcome. He was, of course, required by the Managers of the Royal Institution to undertake applied research, and it is impossible to understate the magnitude of that task alone. In addition he was in constant demand as a consultant, as an expert witness at court cases involving scientific testimony, and in public enquiries into mine disasters and the like. As we have seen he was concerned with matters of pollution and its cure. All these and other innumerable calls upon his time he accepted as a matter of duty, but there is evidence that he resented many of them as unwelcome distractions from his 'real' work, research. In the rich financial pickings available for such scientific expertise he was totally uninterested, often declining a fee. Science for Faraday was chiefly to be explored for its own sake.

It has been suggested that Faraday was, at heart, a Tory, and as such not concerned in changing the status quo whether by science or by uprisings like the 1848 revolutions. When reporting on colliery explosions, for example, he suggested a technological 'fix' instead of condemning the avarice of the mine-owners. In fact, however, he was commissioned to report in scientific, not political, terms, and the evidence available suggests he was not so much a Tory by conviction as a person to whom all politics was either distasteful or just irrelevant. Thus he was not only disinterested in party politics but also in the internal politics of the British Association and the Royal Society. A committed Tory (or Whig) would surely have welcomed such a power base. Such a detachment may not be possible – or desirable – today. In Faraday's case it is eminently understandable. First, there was no obvious way in which society at large was under threat from science.

Secondly, Faraday's own limited circumstances meant minimal exposure to the political inequities of the day. But chiefly he had inherited an other-worldliness from his Sandemanian forebears who frequently reiterated the text 'My kingdom is not of this world' (John 18:36). To seek first that kingdom and the glory of the King was his overriding objective. On weekdays that was to be accomplished by science. Social benefits were a by-product, welcome though they sometimes were. On the question of social involvement – and perhaps only then – we in the late twentieth century part company from Michael Faraday, so different are our cultures from his. Nothing about the essential nature of science, the consolations of Christian belief or even the authority of Scripture has *necessarily* changed since his day. But other things have.

Faraday's laboratory at the Royal Institution.

To an almost unimaginable extent *the world* has altered. It is smaller, for one thing. Research workers in Albemarle Street no longer spend their years in cloistered seclusion, sallying forth only under strong pressure and then not too often. They are no longer unaware of the dimension of human need around them. They cannot escape the thoughts of universal disaster attributable to science. When Michael Faraday first travelled from London to Plymouth he marvelled at the 'mountains' on the way! Many a post-doctoral student today has explored substantial parts of America and Asia before he or she reaches thirty. Another changed parameter is *science itself,* not in its essential nature but in its effects. Even the most arcane and 'pure' research must now be seen to have immense potential for good or evil. When Faraday was asked by an elderly lady the value of his research, he is reported to have replied, 'Madam, what is the use of a baby?' If he, over a century ago, could perceive potential utility in science, how much more can we. It is therefore impossible for any scientist to live in a world of his own, unconcerned for the social consequences of his actions and unprepared to do anything about them. Finally, there has come about a significant change in the *Christian perception of mission.* When Faraday was born the modern missionary movement was in its infancy. Today the church, for all its trials, has a world vision unique to our own age (possibly excepting the first centuries of our era). Recovering an essential element of New Testament doctrine it seeks not earthly conquest but liberation of others in the name of Christ. Its emphasis is now not simply 'My kingdom is not of this world' but also 'Thy kingdom come'. With such a vision it depends on science and its products as never before: food technology to feed the hungry, medicine to heal the sick, engineering and chemistry to provide pure water, radio and even television to proclaim to all mankind the unchanging, liberating joyful news of the gospel. It can do so in the confidence that, as the rivers of science and faith flow ever more powerfully, they will accomplish far more together than either could do alone. And so it should be, for each is a response to the Lord of creation.

Notes for chapter thirteen

[1] Of the many biographies of Faraday one is specially noteworthy and really constitutes a definitive work: L. Pearce Williams, *Michael Faraday* (Chapman & Hall, 1965).

[2] Vast amounts of information about Faraday exist in the archives of the Royal Institution and other libraries. Much has been collected together in L. Pearce Williams (ed.) *The Selected Correspondence of Michael Faraday,* 2 vols. (Cambridge University Press, 1971).

[3] Cited in L. P. Williams, (ref. 1), p.6.

[4] *Ibid.,* p.104.

[5] Cited in H. Bence Jones, *The Life and Letters of Michael Faraday,* (1870), vol. ii, p.431.

[6] Cited in L. P. Williams, (ref. 2), vol. ii, p.1001.

[7] L. P. Williams, (ref. 1), p.106.

[8] Cited in L. P. Williams, (ref. 2), vol. ii, p.943.

[9] Cited in H. Bence Jones, (ref. 5), vol. ii, p.104.

[10] Cited in *ibid.,* vol. i, p.337.

[11] Cited in *ibid.*, vol. ii, pp.195–196.

[12] C. C. Gillispie, *Genesis and Geology* (Harper & Row, New York, 1959), p.208.

[13] R. E. D. Clark, *Hibbert Journal*, 1967, 144–147; *Christian Graduate*, 1967 (Sept.), 26–27.

[14] L. P. Williams, (ref. 1), p.4.

[15] T. H. Levere, 'Faraday, matter, and natural theology', *Brit. J. Hist. Sci.*, 1968, *4*, 95–107 (101).

[16] Cited in T. H. Levere, *ibid.*

[17] M. Berman, *Social Change and Scientific Organization, the Royal Institution, 1799–1844*, (Heinemann, 1978), p.162.

Name index

General index